THE GOTHA SUMMER

The Gotha G.II in action

Howard Leigh

The Gotha Summer

The German daytime air raids
on England, May to August 1917

C. M. WHITE

ROBERT HALE · LONDON

© *C. M. White 1986*
First published in Great Britain 1986

Robert Hale Limited
Clerkenwell House
Clerkenwell Green
London, EC1R 0HT

British Library Cataloguing in Publication Data

White, C.M.
 The Gotha Summer : the German daytime
 raids on England, May to August 1917.
 1. World War, 1914-1918—Aerial operations
 German 2. World War, 1914-1918—Campaigns
 —England
 I. Title
 940.4′42′0942   D604

 ISBN 0-7090-2791-5

Set in Times Roman by
Derek Doyle & Associates, Mold, Clwyd
Printed in Great Britain by
St Edmundsbury Press Ltd, Bury St Edmunds, Suffolk
and bound by Hunter & Foulis Ltd.

Contents

Preface

There was a dull sound like the popping of the corks of flat soda-water bottles. There was a humming, too, from very far up in the skies. People in the street were either staring up at the heavens or running wildly for shelter. A motor-bus in front of me emptied its contents in a twinkling; a taxi pulled up with a jar and the driver and fare dived into a second-hand bookshop. It took me a moment or two to realize the meaning of it all, and I had scarcely done this when I got a very practical proof. A hundred yards away a bomb fell on a street-island, shivering every window-pane in a wide radius, and sending splinters of stone flying about my head. I did what I had done a hundred times before at the Front, and dropped flat on my face ...

The drone grew louder, and, looking up, I could see the enemy planes flying in a beautiful formation, very leisurely as it seemed, with all London at their mercy. Another bomb fell to the right, and presently bits of our own shrapnel were clattering viciously around me.

From *Mr Standfast* by John Buchan
(Hodder & Stoughton, 1919)

Illustrations

Maps

The maps and the illustration of the Gotha G.IV on p.45 were
drawn by Mr Ernest F. Kirby.

Acknowledgements

My sincere thanks must go to the courteous staff of the following organizations for their unfailingly prompt and detailed attention to my requests for information:

The Imperial War Museum
The Public Record Office, Kew
The County Libraries/Archive Departments of Dover, Folkestone, Ipswich, Maidstone, Margate, Sheerness and Southend-on-Sea
The National Meteorological Library, Bracknell

I am, of course, deeply indebted to all those authors, listed under Sources, from whose works I have quoted, sometimes extensively. However, it would, I think, be somewhat remiss of me if I failed to make particular acknowledgement to Major F. H. von Bülow, Mr H. A. Jones and Lieutenant-Colonel H. G. de Watteville, without whose authoritative publications this book could not have been written.

Regrettably, I could find no successors to the defunct publishers John Hamilton Limited and Ivor Nicholson & Watson Limited. Consequently, I can but acknowledge my obligation to Mr Howard Leigh for the frontispiece, to Mr R. Dallas Brett for the quotation from *The History of British Aviation, 1908–1914,* and to Mr David Lloyd George for the quotations from his *War Memoirs.*

Who art thou that judgest another man's servant? To his own master he standeth or falleth.

Inscription by the Royal Flying Corps on the grave of the crew of the Zeppelin L.48 – shot down on the night of 16/17 June 1917.

Preface

By October 1916 the German Navy's Zeppelin campaign against London had been decisively defeated, and the citizens of the metropolis slept undisturbed in their beds for about eight months thereafter. In the following May, however, the calm was rudely shattered when the German Army, taking over the strategic role from the Navy, sent, in broad daylight, a squadron of Gotha heavy bombing aeroplanes against south-eastern England. The intended primary target for most of the eight daytime raids carried out between May and August was, of course, the capital itself, but coastal towns also received attention. Although relatively few Gothas took part in these missions, twenty-eight being the highest figure ever achieved, this shoe-string project had, none the less, very grandiose aims; the German High Command expected it to yield substantial strategic and propagandistic benefits whereby the British nation would be intimidated into demanding peace negotiations.

The insolent day-raiders caught the Lloyd George Government completely off guard – the air defences, built up at great cost during the Zeppelin campaign, had been allowed to run down to a dangerous extent because of urgent demands for replacements for overseas commands, and supply difficulties caused by the Admiralty's intransigence over service aviation. Indeed, all that the Home Defence Group of the Royal Flying Corps (RFC) had to send up against the well-defended bombing formations were some obsolete night-fighting aeroplanes which, although ideal against the conventional Zeppelins at modest altitudes, were virtually useless against the higher-flying Gothas – a fact that must have been known to the German air intelligence service prior to the raids. Furthermore, in the absence of effective unity of command, the responses from home-based RFC and Royal Naval Air Service (RNAS) units were unco-ordinated, desultory affairs, the direct result of feeble air policy decisions taken by the Asquith Government in earlier years.

This is the story of those four crucial months in the summer of 1917 – an all but forgotten period in the history of British air defence – when a few day-bombers compelled the War Cabinet not only to authorize a massive reinforcement of air defence, including the detachment of day-fighter squadrons from the Western Front at a time when they were desperately needed in France and Flanders, but also to initiate a review of the entire air organization – a review that would lead on to the formation of the Royal Air Force, a third and totally independent service, created from the amalgamation of the RFC and the RNAS.

PROLOGUE

1912 to April 1917

1

'The Almost Hopeless Task'

The development of service aviation before and during the Great War was beset, *inter alia,* by pressing problems of inter-service rivalry. Nowhere were such problems more acutely felt than in the fairly limited sphere of home defence against air raids. There can be little doubt that many of the difficulties encountered were the direct result of unpractical or naïve executive decisions taken by the Asquith Administration prior to 1914.

In April 1912 a Government White Paper unveiled an ambitious and far-sighted project for service aeronautics. This was the proposed Royal Flying Corps, an organization intended to combine military and naval air interests into a single air service. The envisaged structure for the new body provided for a Central Flying School on Salisbury Plain, a Military Wing, a Naval Wing, a Reserve and the Royal Aircraft Factory (RAF) at Farnborough, Hampshire. The whole scheme had been evolved under the personal supervision of Colonel J. E. Seely, the then Under-Secretary of State for War.

Unfortunately, this praiseworthy plan, admirable in all other respects, was ill-fated from the outset because of a fundamental deficiency: Colonel Seely had omitted, intentionally or otherwise, the vital constituent for an inter-service organization of this kind – a unified command structure. When the RFC came into being, its Military Wing remained wholly an Army unit subject to the discipline of the War Office, whilst the Naval Wing was entirely an Admiralty charge in all respects. Thus the infant RFC was effectively lumbered with a two-headed executive – the beginning of service bipartisanship in aeronautics that was to last for many tedious years to come.

Dallas Brett commented pungently on the matter, thus: 'It

seems almost incredible that anyone, even a politician, could have been so obtuse as to fail to realize that a scheme which involved the joint command and administration of a force by the War Office and the Admiralty was doomed to failure ...'[1]

Colonel Seely's failure to insist on effective unity of command probably stemmed from his reluctance or inability to challenge the obdurate Admiralty, particularly with the formidable Winston Churchill in its chair as First Lord. The Admiralty had no intention of relinquishing any of its authority over the Naval Wing, and perhaps rightly so, *at that time*. The Army and the Navy could not even agree on the types of aircraft the RFC would require, and the purposes to which they should be put. The War Office, for instance, intended that nearly all of the Military Wing's machines should be employed as aerial scouts reconnoitring ahead of the Army's expeditionary forces, and for this function the stable BE two-seater aeroplanes designed and supplied by the Royal Aircraft Factory were ideal. But that was not all: in the pre-war period the War Office had also claimed sole responsibility for the air defence of the United Kingdom, and thus should have had some interest in the production of offensive aircraft. Churchill later wrote: 'When asked how they [the War Office] proposed to discharge this duty [air defence], they admitted sorrowfully that they had not got the machines and could not get the money.'[2]

Churchill and the First Sea Lord, Lord Fisher, alarmed at the looming prospect of air raids by Zeppelins and the possibility of little in the way of air defence, set about forming flights of naval aeroplanes and seaplanes for the protection of naval harbours, oil tanks and other vulnerable points. Churchill managed this because he was 'able to procure funds by various shifts and devices'[3] and could thereby begin to let commercial contracts for the bombing and fighting aircraft that the Naval Wing would need, such machines not being available from the Royal Aircraft Factory. Churchill's independent policy effectively stimulated and nurtured Britain's infant aircraft industry – a fortunate circumstance in the long term.

The two wings of the RFC were thus separate in practically every respect: the discipline and training of each remained the responsibility of its supervising service and, without central authority, therefore, little in the way of amalgamation or co-operation resulted. Indeed, it is probable that even the friendly rivalry that always has existed between naval and military staffs contributed to the fact that the two wings drifted further and further apart until the end of the RFC as a combined air service was inevitable and predictable.

On 28 June 1914 the Archduke Franz Ferdinand of Austria was assassinated at Sarajevo, an act that was to lead to the opening of that collective madness, the Great War – 'the greatest of human catastrophes since the decline and fall of ancient Rome'. In the UK the resulting crisis stirred up a flurry of activity in the armed services whereby the Admiralty, seizing its opportunity, was able to bring about the final division of the RFC by announcing that the Royal Naval Air Service had been formed, thus effectively abolishing the Naval Wing of the RFC. Sadly, then, the concept of a single co-operative air force foundered, principally because the diverging requirements and duties of the two wings could not then be reconciled. Later in the war, however, the techniques of air fighting and bombing were to become the major activities of both naval and military aviation, i.e. activities which required no special naval or military training, and thus co-operation between the two air forces would become much easier to effect.

Asquith probably did not yet appreciate the ramifications of 'the aerial dichotomy' that he had passively allowed to come about. Not only was the country, in time of war, to be saddled with two separate air forces, but each parent service would engage in independent research, design and production of aircraft without any co-ordination between the two authorities at all. The limited resources of the country were to be divided between two competitive programmes that would lead inevitably to wasteful duplication of effort with very serious repercussions on both manpower and materials.

To be fair to the Prime Minister, however, mention should be made of the Air Committee, an advisory organization set up in July 1912 under the chairmanship of the long-suffering Colonel Seely. This committee, composed of many military, naval and civil dignitaries, was intended to co-ordinate the requirements of the two wings of the RFC. However, in the face of Admiralty inflexibility, it achieved very little and so became virtually dormant, its meetings being held less and less frequently. After the formation of the RNAS and the end of the Naval Wing of the RFC, nothing further was ever heard of the Air Committee –

it simply faded away.

The failure of the Air Committee in no way deterred Mr Asquith from two subsequent attempts to achieve air co-ordination by means of committees, as will be seen. Unfortunately, and rather pusillanimously, he was not prepared to give his committees proper executive power, and thus all would turn out to be as ineffectual, in practice, as Colonel Seely's had been.

When war was declared in August 1914, practically the entire RFC, four squadrons, was immediately prepared for service in France with the British Expeditionary Force, whilst a few elderly aeroplanes were to be left in Britain for training and home defence purposes. Such pitiful resources for the UK air defence requirement contrasted somewhat sharply with the fifty or so seaplanes and landplanes that, as Churchill later rather picturesquely put it, 'the Admiralty had been able to scrape and smuggle together.'[4]

As the First Lord had foreseen, the RFC could not possibly provide an effective contribution to the air defence of Great Britain and carry out its vital scouting role for the BEF at one and the same time; the Admiralty would have to share the burden of defence. On 3 September, then, the War Minister, Lord Kitchener, asked the First Lord, in Cabinet, whether he would accept, on behalf of the Admiralty, the responsibility for the aerial defence of the country. Churchill, in reply, 'undertook to do what was possible with the wholly inadequate resources which were available'.[5] With this somewhat cautious statement, which related to the employment of AA guns as well as aircraft, the Government was apparently content, and 'The Admiralty undertook, very reluctantly for the most part, the thankless – and as it seemed then – the almost hopeless task ...'[6]

This rather makeshift arrangement between the War Office and the Admiralty illustrated perfectly the Government's short-sighted approach to the problems of the air. Lloyd George was later to write thus: 'Concentration on the use of aeroplanes as handmaids to the operations of fleets and armies meant a failure to develop their possibilities as an independent arm, and even left it uncertain which of the two branches should properly undertake such tasks as the defence of London against attacks by Zeppelins and German aeroplanes.'[7]

Churchill, no believer in passive defence, on 5 September

produced a departmental memo in which he stated that attack would assuredly be the best means of defence against the Zeppelin menace. He saw, quite clearly, that the Germans would seek to establish Zeppelin forward bases in overrun Belgium, as indeed they were planning to do. His memo underlined the necessity for an RNAS base to be established at Dunkirk from which attacks on the Zeppelin sheds could be launched.

As far as air defence of the capital was concerned, Churchill ordered that flights of naval aeroplanes be stationed at Eastchurch, Calshot and Hendon. He was far-sighted enough to direct that landing-grounds be prepared in the London parks, complete with good lighting systems, so that the aerial defenders of the city could operate at night. The few RFC aeroplanes available for defence purposes were to be stationed at Hounslow and Joyce Green, near Dartford, and these military aviators were to operate in conjunction with the RNAS units in the defence of London. Naval aeroplanes were to defend ports and naval facilities on the coast but would operate inland when hostile aircraft had crossed the coastline, the RFC machines helping out whenever possible.

Churchill was not over-enthusiastic about AA gunnery but he accepted that the Navy must provide some guns for London and large cities, and the naval crews to operate them. Strangely enough, the AA guns for the ports were to be supplied and manned by the Army – a rather curious anomaly in the circumstances. To meet its AA artillery commitments, the Admiralty, short of trained personnel, formed, in October 1914, the RNVR AA Corps in London. This force, commanded by Captain L. Stansfeld RN was staffed by part-time gunners recruited from City and University men on a purely voluntary basis.

In May 1915, however, a profound change occurred in the Admiralty hierarchy: Winston Churchill stepped down as First Lord after the failure at Gallipoli and was succeeded by Arthur J. Balfour, a politician whose outlook closely accorded with the more traditional naval viewpoints. The RNAS, which had been run by Churchill himself 'on vigorous but unorthodox lines', now became a subordinate branch of the Admiralty and was, accordingly, reorganized as such. High officers with little or no aeronautical experience were placed in its command structure.

Churchill's sensible policy of RNAS air strikes against the

Zeppelins in their sheds was abandoned and, even stranger, the Naval Staff considered that rigid airships should be constructed because it was thought that they could serve the Fleet better in the reconnaissance role than aeroplanes. A huge programme was financed by the Admiralty to build British rigid airships of the Zeppelin type, Churchill later averring that forty millions were spent on this project. Regrettably, however, none of these airships (the R series) was ever to render any effective war service at all.[8] Such vast sums of money and the tying up of many aeronautical firms in the production of airships must have had a very serious effect on the provision of aeroplanes for the RFC as well as the RNAS itself.

Although the Zeppelin incursions had begun to increase from the beginning of 1915, they were not the most worrying problem for the RNAS. More and more naval seaplanes and aeroplanes had to be employed on anti-submarine duties as the U-boat armada, growing steadily larger, began to take an increasing toll of Allied shipping. Little wonder, then, that the Admiralty considered the submarine threat far graver than that posed by a few Zeppelins.

Lord Kitchener, on the other hand, was most alarmed about the Zeppelin raids and spoke of them to Major-General Sir David Henderson, Director-General of Military Aeronautics (DGMA) and General Officer Commanding the RFC, demanding to know just what was being done about such raids. Henderson rather nettled, replied that the aerial defence of the UK was the prerogative of the RNAS, not the RFC. He pointed out that the RFC's chief job was in France, but aerodromes and communications were, in fact, being set up in UK so that the RFC could take over some of the home defence burden. Kitchener, somewhat mollified, grunted that he would hold Henderson responsible if the RFC did not interfere with the Zeppelin raiders in the future.

By the mid-summer of 1915 the RNAS really had its hands full. The majority of its aircraft were by then engaged on anti-submarine duties, searching for U-boats around the British Isles. With the naval air arm so overloaded, it was hardly surprising that the Admiralty should seek to opt out of the air defence commitment undertaken by Churchill in September 1914. In any event, the Navy was not at all happy about its involvement in air defence activity overland: the Admiralty traditionalists saw that as entirely an Army duty, although Churchill had, of course, thought otherwise. Whilst the RNAS was as fully prepared to continue its anti-Zeppelin patrols over the sea, it insisted that once the hostile aircraft had crossed the coast they should become an Army responsibility.

The War Office, after much discussion at a joint conference, finally agreed to take back the home defence chore, AA guns as well as aeroplanes, but stated, quite firmly, that it could not do so until early in the coming year, 1916. This decision must have been rather a facer for the Admiralty because there could be little doubt that something drastic would soon have to be done about the increasing number of Zeppelin raids on the country. That of 31 May 1915 on the London area had been followed by a series of others over the eastern counties during the summer, with the population growing more and more restive and vociferous about the lack of organized air defence.

What steps should be taken in the interim period until the War Office would again don the home defence mantle? With aeroplanes in short supply, it was hardly surprising that the Admiralty, which had always preferred the AA gun to the aeroplane for air defence, should decide to reinforce its RNVR AA Corps in London to meet the threat. Admiral Sir Percy Scott (an artillery expert from the Retired List, then sixty-four) was appointed to take charge of the AA gun defences of London, with full authority to build up a substantial force as soon as possible.

The Admiral certainly had his work cut out. The RNVR AA Corps possessed, in that summer, just ten guns – hardly an impressive array of artillery. However, he set to work at once, and by February the following year, when the War Office resumed the responsibility for the air defence of London, the number of AA guns ready for action had risen to fifty, whilst another ninety-eight were in preparation,[9] a most creditable achievement in such a short time. In addition, the Admiral formed the RN AA Mobile Brigade, a force equipped with some fourteen lorry-mounted guns for rapid deployment as required. This unit was commanded by Lieutenant-Commander A. Rawlinson RNVR, an officer who was later to transfer to the Army's Royal Garrison Artillery for home defence AA duties under the War Office.

On 10 February 1916 Mr Asquith's War Committee formally

recorded the decision ultimately to transfer the responsibility for the air defence of the whole of the United Kingdom from the Admiralty to the War Office. The statement produced by the Committee was a significant if somewhat confusing document:

1. The War Committee approve the following recommendations in regard to the allocation of responsibility for the Anti-Aircraft Defence of the whole of the United Kingdom outside London which have been made by a Joint Admiralty and War Office Conference, and have for some time been in practical operation, namely:

   (a) The Navy to undertake to deal with all hostile aircraft attempting to reach this country, whilst the Army undertake to deal with all such aircraft which reach these shores.

   (b) All defence arrangements on land to be undertaken by the Army which will also provide the aeroplanes required to work with the Home Defence troops and to protect garrisons and vulnerable areas, and the Flying Stations required to enable their aircraft to undertake these duties.

   (c) The Navy to provide the aircraft required to co-operate with and assist their Fleets and Coast Patrol Flotillas and to watch the Coast, and to organise and maintain such Flying Stations as are required to enable their aircraft to undertake these duties.

   The two Services to co-operate so as to prevent unnecessary duplication.

2. The responsibility for the Anti-Aircraft Defence of London, details of the transfer of which from the Admiralty to the War Office are being worked out, to rest with the War Office from Wednesday the 16th February 1916 inclusive.

3. Having regard to the great importance of the munitions work concentrated in the Woolwich district, the Anti-Aircraft Defence of this area should take precedence over the rest of London, and the existing defences should be strengthened as soon as possible.[10]

So once again the Asquith Government had kowtowed to the Lords of Admiralty: the air defence task, crying out for co-ordination, was to be effectively divided, geographically, between the naval and army air forces. Of operational co-operation there was none, except for the feeble exhortation to the two services to 'co-operate so as to prevent unnecessary duplication' – whatever that might mean. Nowhere in the paper was there any hint that the Government had even considered the appointment of a central director who could co-ordinate the efforts of all units involved in the air defence of Great Britain. The division between the Admiralty and War Office remained, possibly wider than ever before. It could not be imagined that the Admiralty would allow any of its home fighter aircraft to be directed by the C.-in-C., Home Forces, Field Marshal Viscount French, then setting up his headquarters at the Horse Guards in London, following his appointment on 19 December 1915.

It was, of course, becoming quite obvious that the policy that had established two separate air forces was proving extremely detrimental to the country's vital interests. The division of the money available for aeronautics – the lion's share of which usually went to the Admiralty – meant that the RFC, already saddled with the stodgy Royal Aircraft Factory as design authority, could not yet be supplied with the required numbers of up-to-date machines for offence in overseas theatres, let alone defence at home.

Consequently, therefore, many voices were being raised in Parliament insisting that aeronautical reforms should be instituted as a matter of urgent national policy. Some MPs went so far as to demand that the RFC and RNAS be re-amalgamated into a single air force subject to neither Army nor Navy control. Others, however, thought it would suffice to control the production of aircraft for the existing services by means of an independent authority empowered by the Government to veto extravagant demands from either side. A further lobby considered that the two services should remain in being but a system of operational co-ordination should be devised leading on to proper unity of control in such fields as air defence, etc.

So what did Mr Asquith do? On 15 February 1916 he plumped for what was seemingly the easiest option of all: to attempt to control the design and production of aircraft for the two services. To achieve this laudable aim he decided to form another Air Committee, this one to be called the Joint War Air Committee, to distinguish it from the earlier one. Its terms of reference differed slightly from those of the old Committee but essentially it was still to be only advisory in concept; it had no executive power whatsoever.

On the face of it, the terms of reference were quite reasonable and, given goodwill on both sides, were within the bounds of possibility. The terms ran as follows:

(1) To prevent overlapping demands by the two services on the manufacturing resources available;
(2) To prevent the two services bidding against one another for contractors;
(3) To co-ordinate designs;
(4) To endeavour, by all means, to extend the output of aircraft.[11]

The chairmanship of this Committee was offered to Lord Derby, who readily agreed to fulfil the office, considering the duties of the Committee to be 'of a very minor character'. The Admiralty members were Rear-Admiral C. L. Vaughan-Lee, the Director of Naval Air Services; Commodore Murray F. Sueter, the Superintendent of Naval Aircraft Construction; and Squadron-Commander W. Briggs RNAS. The War Office was represented by Major-General Sir David Henderson and Lieutenant-Colonel E. L. Ellington, General Staff.

The Chairman soon found that only on minor matters could the Committee come to any agreement at all – on matters of policy, reference had always to be made back to either the Board of Admiralty or the Army Council, as the case might be. 'On no point, therefore,' he wrote, 'can a decision on any large question be arrived at without reference to these bodies, and the Committee simply becomes the fifth wheel to the coach.'[12] He was dismayed to learn that no official allotment of the various duties to be performed by the RFC and the RNAS had been laid down, and as the views of the two air forces conflicted at almost every point, the questions of aircraft design and production could not even be considered. In his letter of resignation of 27 March, Lord Derby told the Prime Minister that it was 'quite impossible to bring the two wings closer together than they are at the present moment unless and until the whole system of the Air Service is changed, and they are amalgamated into one service'[13] – a solution quite beyond the powers of the Asquith Administration to bring about.

Thus the Joint War Air Committee, having lasted just six weeks, had gone the way of its 1912 predecessor. Its failure was the signal for a renewed outburst against the Government's air policy, culminating in an assertion in the House of Commons, by Mr N. Pemberton Billing, the newly elected and volatile MP for East Hertfordshire, that RFC pilots in France were being 'murdered' because their outdated aeroplanes, designed by the Royal Aircraft Factory, were no match for the modern fighters then being flown by German pilots. Billing was well qualified to speak on such matters; he was an aircraft designer (the founder of Supermarine Limited) who had, as a lieutenant in the RNAS, helped to organize the naval air raid on the Zeppelin sheds at Friedrichshafen in November 1914.

It was pointed out, in no uncertain terms, how scandalous it was that the RFC had to depend upon the Royal Aircraft Factory for its designs, whilst the RNAS was being supplied with aircraft of higher calibre through private industry. The RFC must, said the protesters, be given aircraft of similar performance as soon as possible, particularly as the RFC was by then having to do more fighting than the RNAS.

Mr Asquith finally bowed to the pressure, and a Judicial Committee was appointed on 10 May 1916 to enquire into Billing's 'murder' charges. The final report of this Committee, in December 1916, would dismiss that charge as 'unjustifiable', but it would make the following observations on the thorny problems of aeronautical supply: 'Whether there should some day be a united air service combining the Royal Flying Corps and the Royal Naval Air Service we are not in a position to say. However that may be, we see no reason against having one Equipment Department charged with the equipment of both the Army and Navy Flying Services. There would, no doubt, be inter-Service jealousy to contend with, but that should not be allowed to stop a much-needed reform.'[14]

Whilst these political moves were in train, the RFC was building up its strength around London for night operations against marauding Zeppelins. By April 1916, nine airfields were in use at Chingford, Croydon, Farningham, Hainault Farm, Hendon, Hounslow, Northolt, Sutton's Farm (Hornchurch) and Wimbledon Common. Two BE2s were stationed at each aerodrome with two attendant pilots, instructors from various training establishments. This wide dispersal was, however, soon considered to be operationally inefficient, and on 25 April 1916 all personnel were grouped together under Major T. C. R. Higgins in one unit, No. 39 (Home Defence) Squadron, to operate from Hainault Farm, Hounslow and Sutton's Farm, with six aircraft at each airfield. The pilots were, however, to continue their flying training activities during the day, although still on call for night-time defence duties.

Within two months, however, the War Office was forced to abandon this unworkable scheme; the training instructors could not possibly cope with night flying duties in addition to their daytime routines. An independent Home Defence Wing was set up under Lieutenant-Colonel F. V. Holt, all connections with training being severed. The new Wing then comprised the following home defence squadrons: Nos. 33, 36, 38 (forming), 39, 50 and 51, with Wing Headquarters at Adastral House (formerly de Keyser's Hotel) on the Victoria Embankment in London.

The AA gun defences of the capital were, however, rather less satisfactory. Following the Army takeover, the Home Forces Command established no fewer than seven AA Sub-Commands, as they were called, in London, viz. Central (the fixed guns of the RNVR AA Corps), Dartford, North-West, South, South-West, Waltham and Woolwich, but, strangely enough, no overall AA command structure was evolved. In fact, Lord French was responsible only for operational control; training came under the aegis of the GOC, London District. The seven units tended, therefore, to be rather parochial in their outlooks, with wide differences in methods and procedures. To be fair, of course, their military efficiency was not enhanced by the variety of gun types bequeathed to them by the Admiralty: 4.7-inch, 6pdr, French 75mm, 15pdr and even some Russian 75mm weapons! Lieutenant-Colonel M. St L. Simon of the Royal Engineers, who had been brought home from France at this time to supervise the construction of AA gun and searchlight sites in the sub-commands, was impressed neither by the diversity of the weapons nor by their distribution throughout the London districts.

In June 1916, therefore, he came up with a scheme that entailed a ring of gun stations, each to comprise two of the admirable 3-inch 20cwt guns, to be installed around the highly populated regions of London, with single 3-inch 20cwt guns dotted about within the enclosed circle.[15] The idea was to put up heavy bursts of shell fire in the path of oncoming raiders, i.e. the first time an AA barrage had been proposed. Searchlights were to be positioned further out than the guns, and friendly aircraft were intended to operate only up to the line of lights. This scheme was approved by the War Committee, and the miscellaneous collection of guns was to be removed as soon as the 3-inch 20cwt ones became available. For the UK air defence, generally, the War Office had ordered 403 fixed AA guns, nearly all of the 3-inch type, of which eighty-four were intended for the London barrage.

In the political arena, meanwhile, the Government was not to be allowed to sit back and await the Judicial Committee's report; things had been stirred up again by a paper, *Air Services in the War*, written in April 1916 by Lord Curzon of Kedleston – the Lord Privy Seal, no less. This document proposed that an Air Board should be set up with high-ranking members from the Government, the Admiralty and the War Office, in order to attempt to accomplish all those duties 'of a very minor character' that the Derby Committee had been prevented from doing, and, furthermore, to make recommendations on matters such as air policy and the types of aircraft required by the two air services. One could, perhaps, be excused for thinking that such a task would demand executive powers but Mr Asquith, once again, would not, or could not, grant the new Board such powers – the panel was to be purely advisory.

On 17 May 1916 Harold Tennant, the Under-Secretary of State for War, made an announcement in the House of Commons concerning the formation of the Air Board. Lord Curzon himself was to preside over the meetings, and two other parliamentarians were to be co-opted: Lord Sydenham and Major J. L. Baird. The Navy was to be represented by Rear-Admiral F. C. T. Tudor (the Third Sea Lord) with, as before, Rear-Admiral Vaughan-Lee (the Director of Air Services). The Army would again field Sir David Henderson, now Lieutenant-General, supported by Brigadier-General W. S. Brancker (the Director of Air Organization, War Office). The chosen venue for Air Board meetings was No. 19 Carlton House Terrace, just off the Mall. The terms of reference for this committee were, of course, much wider than those of the previous one and were listed in the proceedings of the War Committee on 11 May 1916, viz:

(a)   The Board shall be free to discuss matters of general policy in relation to the air, and, in particular, combined operations of the Naval and Military Air Services, and to make recommendations to the Admiralty and War Office thereon.

(b)   The Board shall be free to discuss and make recommendations upon the types of machine required for the Naval and Military Air Services.

(c)   If either the Admiralty or War Office decline to act upon the recommendations of the Board, the President shall be free to refer the question to the War Committee.

(d)   The Board shall be charged with the task of organizing and co-ordinating the supply of material and of preventing competition between the two Departments.

(e)   The Board shall organize a complete system for the inter-change of ideas upon air problems between the two Services and such related bodies as the Naval Board of Invention and Research, the Inventions Branch of the Ministry of Munitions, the Advisory Committee on Aeronautics, the National Physical Laboratory, etc.[16]

Winston Churchill, after Tennant had sat down, was acidulous in his comments: 'Lord Curzon, without adequate powers, will not succeed in altering the present state of affairs, and in the choice of a policy ... the Government has followed no principle whatever, except the familiar principle of postponing until the last possible moment and then following the line of least resistance.' He considered the Asquith plans for an Air Board to be 'a feeble subterfuge', parrying the demand for a full Air Ministry by setting up another advisory committee with Lord Curzon, instead of Lord Derby, at its head. In Churchill's opinion, 'The members of the Board may advise the President but he need not take their advice, and the President may advise the Admiralty and the War Office, but they need not take his advice.'[17]

Lord Curzon was soon confronted with the major stumbling-block in Air Board matters: in Lieutenant-General Henderson the Army had someone who could make executive decisions for the entire RFC, whereas the RNAS had no such authoritative figurehead. A number of separate departments of the Admiralty controlled the RNAS, and design and production plans, etc had to be approved by some or all of them. Rear-Admiral Tudor, although Third Sea Lord, could speak only for his own department – Design and Construction – and not for the entire Board of Admiralty. In any case, Tudor attended only about half of the Air Board's meetings and thus was not always available to speak even for his own department.

As Churchill had indicated, an advisory body without executive control could not influence the financial mandarins of the Admiralty in any way. In August 1916 the Secretary of the Air Board was writing a coldly disapproving letter to the Admiralty:

> I am directed by the President of the Air Board to inform you that his attention has been drawn by the Treasury to the fact that the Admiralty have recently without any previous communication with the Air Board, obtained authority to purchase aircraft and aero-engines to the value of about £2,750,000 to meet future requirements.
>
> As the Lords Commissioners of the Admiralty are aware, the Air Board upon their creation were charged by the decision of the Government with the task of organizing and co-ordinating the supply of material and of preventing competition between the Naval and Military Air Services in this respect. The action of the Admiralty above referred to would appear to be inconsistent with the performance by the Board of this duty and to be calculated to defeat the very object for which the Board were set up, namely to secure that the supply of aircraft shall be distributed between the Services in accordance with the requirements of the country and not merely with the policy of one of the two Departments.
>
> If the Board are to be deprived of the opportunity of forming an opinion upon the financial programme which is in contemplation by the Board of Admiralty, it is not clear how they can give any useful advice in the manner prescribed to them by their terms of reference. No such difficulty has arisen in the case of the War Office, where no reluctance has been shown to submit to the Air Board their proposals for examination and approval.[18]

Obviously, Lord Curzon was quite well aware that such a vast sum could not have been allocated without Asquith's tacit approval, even though it made nonsense of the PM's public utterances about the necessity for co-ordination in aeronautical matters.

The reply from the First Sea Lord sounded the death knell for the Air Board, highlighting as it did the Admiralty's main objection to the consitution of this Air Board and the earlier Joint War Air Committee: 'If we admit that they [the Air Board members] are qualified to criticise and act as a Commission of Enquiry on the doings of the Executive Services in the war, we hand over our powers and perogatives to a body containing Admiralty representatives who are individually subordinate to the Board of Admiralty and yet can criticise and amend the Board of Admiralty decisions.'[19]

By October 1916 Lord Curzon could see that his Air Board was doomed. He produced a report at that time which underlined the two factors bedevilling the constitution of the Air Board. Firstly, the President of any future Air Board must have ministerial status in order to exercise proper control over the design and supply of aircraft for the two services. Secondly, the RNAS must be given a Chief Executive, a member of the Board of Admiralty, who would be authorized to make binding decisions at Air Board meetings.

Not surprisingly, the Admiralty, led by Mr Balfour, stubbornly resisted the idea of an Air Board Minister who would be able to interfere with naval air policies. The First Lord, finally conceding that some measure of reform was overdue, insisted that the Minister of Munitions would be the right and proper authority to undertake the design and supply of aircraft, and to provide the finance therefor. He felt that the Air Board should confine itself to vetting the air programmes of both air services, and allocating priorities in accordance with production possibilities.

Such, then, was the situation on 5 December 1916 when David Lloyd George resigned as War Minister, thus precipitating a crisis which led to the resignation of Mr Asquith on the same day. Shortly afterwards, Lloyd George was offered the premiership, and the resulting new Government included Lord Derby as War Minister and Lord Curzon as Lord President of the Council. The first Air Board was thus abruptly terminated but Lloyd George, completely out of patience with the inter-service wrangling and competitiveness over the air forces, lost no time in seeking the necessary statutory powers that the President of a new Air Board would need, as Lord Curzon had demanded. A Bill, *New Ministeries and Secretaries Act, 1916* was rushed through Parliament and became law on 22 December. The way was then open to establish the second Air

Board, whose composition and duties were laid down in *The Air Board Order, 1917* made on 6 February 1917.

Briefly, the Government accepted that the Ministry of Munitions should be responsible for contracting out the design and production of aircraft for both services, but that the Air Board's approval would be required before any contractual action could be taken. The Board would vet the proposed production programmes for naval and military aircraft, and to facilitate liaison work it was decided to move the Air Board from Carlton House Terrace to a requisitioned hotel in the Strand, the Hotel Cecil, together with certain administrative and technical staffs from the RNAS and the RFC.

It was fervently hoped that this Air Board would, in consultation with the Admiralty and the War Office, be able to make recommendations on air offensive and defensive policy, even though the Curzon Board had signally failed to so. In addition, the Board would continue to act as a forum for the interchange of ideas between the two services and other interested departments.

The industrialist Viscount Cowdray of Midhurst, the former Sir Weetman Dickinson Pearson, was invited to become the President of the new Air Board, ably supported by Major Baird, the Parliamentary Secretary, as before. The Admiralty member was now to be Commodore Godfrey Paine, who had taken over the mantle of Director of Naval Air Services from Rear-Admiral Vaughan-Lee. In response to Government insistence, Commodore Paine was given a seat on the Admiralty Board as Fifth Sea Lord and was empowered to accept complete responsibility for naval air matters at the Air Board meetings. Once again the RFC was to be represented by Lieutenant-General Henderson whilst the Ministry of Munitions' members were William Weir, the Controller of Aeronautical Supplies, and Percy Martin, the Controller of the Petrol Engine Department.

As far as the production of aircraft for the two services was concerned, this last Air Board was a complete success. The live-wire William Weir very soon had the large number of aeroplane types then in production for the Army and Navy whittled down to a few efficient and proven ones.

The Air Board was tasked, in February 1917, to organize air production so that the RFC's strength could be expanded to 106 service and 97 reserve (or training) squadrons as soon as possible. In the event, the improvement in the rate of production was so rapid that Lord Cowdray, by the following July, would be able to inform the Government that the needs of both air services were being met.

In the field of air operational policy recommendations, however, the performance of this Air Board was little better than any of its predecessors'. Although the representatives of the Admiralty and the War Office on the Board were at the top of their respective trees, they still owed allegiance to their own services, and thus their loyalty was divided. The lack of co-operation between the two air services in the operational sphere was to be the most cogent factor in the ultimate creation of a full Air Ministry, and the minor battleground of home air defence would provide the stimulus that would lead eventually to the demand for complete amalgamation of the two air services.

We may now turn from the major political and military events that impinged on the development of UK air defence between the years 1912 to 1917 and consider, briefly, the evolution of the German Army's heavy bombing aeroplane squadrons from the beginning of the war to the end of 1916.

The rapid advance of the German Army towards the Channel coast in the autumn of 1914 prompted *Major* Wilhelm Siegert – a former balloon pilot destined to be a leading light in the development of the army air service – to propose a strategic air bombardment of London using aeroplanes in an assault that would, he suggested, shorten the war. There was, however, one big snag to the Siegert Plan: the aircraft available at the time were rickety B-type two-seater machines of about 100hp, having extremely limited range and very small bombloads. If such machines were to reach London and return safely, they would have to take off from an airfield in the Pas de Calais region. However, as the Kaiser's troops would apparently soon occupy that area, the German High Command – OHL (*Obersten Heeresleitung*) – agreed to the proposal and placed Siegert in charge of the new bombing unit, the *Fliegerkorps der OHL* (the Air Corps of OHL) as it was to be known.

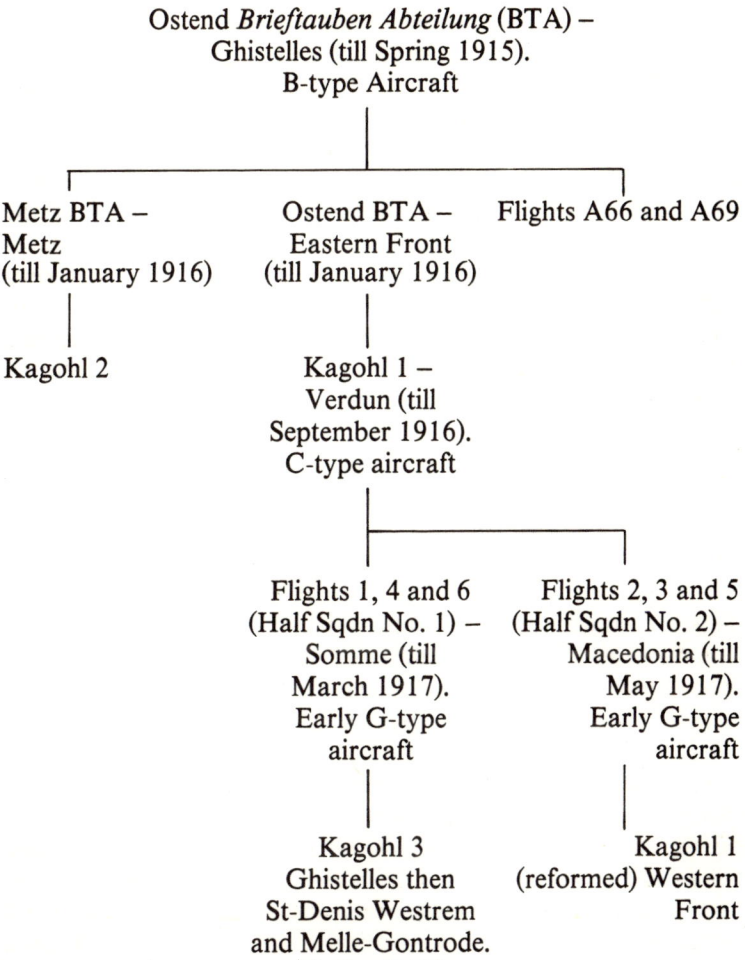

Ostend *Brieftauben Abteilung* (BTA) –
Ghistelles (till Spring 1915).
B-type Aircraft

Metz BTA –
Metz
(till January 1916)

Ostend BTA –
Eastern Front
(till January 1916)

Flights A66 and A69

Kagohl 2

Kagohl 1 –
Verdun (till
September 1916).
C-type aircraft

Flights 1, 4 and 6
(Half Sqdn No. 1) –
Somme (till
March 1917).
Early G-type
aircraft

Flights 2, 3 and 5
(Half Sqdn No. 2) –
Macedonia (till
May 1917).
Early G-type
aircraft

Kagohl 3
Ghistelles then
St-Denis Westrem
and Melle-Gontrode.
Gotha G.IV

Kagohl 1
(reformed) Western
Front

THE DEVELOPMENT OF KAGOHL 3

Whilst awaiting the signal to move to Calais, the Air Corps was stationed, temporarily, at an airfield near the village of Ghistelles, not far from Ostend in occupied Belgium. The unit was code-named, for security reasons, the Ostend *Brieftauben Abteilung* (Carrier Pigeon Squadron) but whether this extraordinarily inept cloak-and-dagger title ever deceived anybody is, of course, a matter of conjecture – it seems most unlikely.

The *Fliegerkorps* had two wings, staffed by the most experienced pilots from all branches of the army air service. Thirty-six aeroplanes were allocated to the enterprise, and arrangements were pushed ahead to equip them with the requisite number of bombs, maps, etc. The B-type aircraft had no defensive armament as such, but the crews could take along rifles and pistols if they so wished.

In the event, however, all the preparations came to nought. In November 1914 the advancing German Fourth Army was held by the British at Ypres, and thus no further move towards Calais was possible. In consequence, therefore, the Ostend Carrier Pigeon Squadron was left virtually high and dry at Ghistelles, and Siegert's plan had, perforce, to be filed away to await the day when bombing aircraft having adequate range would become available. To this end a specification for a *Grossekampfflugzeug* (large bomber aircraft) or G-type machine was then issued, and several aircraft companies, viz. Allegemeine Elektrizitäts Gesellschaft (AEG), Flugzeugbau Friedrichshafen Gmbh (Friedrichshafen) and Gothaer Waggonfabrik AG (Gotha) began preliminary design work.

In the anti-climactic days that followed the cancellation of the project, Siegert and his men made many bombing attacks on Dunkirk, Furnes, La Panne, Nieuport and other bases behind the establishing Western Front. Such duties continued until the spring of 1915, when the *Fliegerkorps* was split up into four separate units: the Metz Carrier Pigeon Squadron, detached to Metz near Nancy; a reduced Ostend Carrier Pigeon Squadron that proceeded to the Eastern Front in Galicia; and two reconnaissance units known as A66 and A69.[20]

In early 1916 the Ostend Carrier Pigeon Squadron, which had returned to Ghistelles from the Russian Front in July 1915, was again reorganized and became *Kampfgeschwader 1 der OHL* (Battle Squadron No. 1), this somewhat unwieldy title being rapidly abbreviated to Kagohl 1. The unit, which now had six *Staffeln* (flights) each, with six two-seater aeroplanes of the more powerful and armed C-type, soon began bombing operations in the Verdun area. About this time, also, the first G-planes had taken to the air, the promising Gotha G.I (two 160hp Mercedes engines) going into limited production by the company although the aircraft was actually a German Army design.

In September 1916 Kagohl 1 was reorganized yet again: *Staffeln* 1, 4 and 6 (Half-Squadron No. 1) operated on the Somme under their commander *Hauptmann* Gaede, whilst *Staffeln* 2, 3 and 5 (Half-Squadron No. 2) were sent off to the Balkans in support of the Bulgarians. Both *Halbgeschwaders* (half-squadrons) received some early G-type bombers in addition to their normal C-types. The first true Gotha design to be supplied (the G.II) gave some problems mainly because of the unsatisfactory nature of its 220-hp Mercedes engines, and these aircraft were soon withdrawn from service.

2

Operation *Türkencreuz*

In November 1916 bad weather brought that titanic struggle the Battle of Somme to an end after some four months of bloody but largely indecisive combat. During the battle, the British and French armies had reoccupied a strip of land approximately thirty miles long by some seven miles deep at its widest point, and for this tiny acquisition they had suffered stupendous losses – 600,000 killed, wounded or captured. The German Army on the Somme was in little better shape; according to General von Ludendorf, the Chief of Staff, it was 'absolutely exhausted' after the battle, its casualties being conservatively estimated at about half a million. Morale had slumped during this terrible time, a key factor, on the German side, being the introduction by the British of the monstrous Mark 1 tank in September.

OHL had lost the well-fortified positions along the Somme that it had occupied since 1914, and it now held an improvised and much longer line than hitherto. Time was urgently needed for the Army to regroup and build a shorter in-depth defensive system many miles to the rear – the so-called Hindenburg Line.

The German High Command began immediate planning to reduce the pressure on its land forces by means of two counter-strokes, one by sea and the other by air. It was considered that such actions, coupled with the Allies' depression over the Somme blood-letting, could point the way to a successful conclusion of the war. The two assaults, intended to be launched simultaneously in February 1917, were to be aimed at the arch-enemy, Britain, in a desperate attempt to drive a wedge between the Allied Powers. As Ludendorf later wrote: 'The plan was to ensure final victory by sowing dissension among the Allies, and taking from them their faith in ultimate victory. The main object was the moral intimidation of the British nation and the crippling of the will to fight, thus preparing the ground for peace.'[1]

In short, it was hoped to disable the UK to such an extent that the new Government of Lloyd George would be brought down, and peace overtures put out to the German Government.

What, then, were these two counterstrokes that engendered such high hopes? The first, and major one, was the decision to declare unrestricted submarine warfare against Allied shipping, regardless of the effect that this would certainly have on the US Government, still seething over the sinking of the *Lusitania*. Although the U-boats had been attacking ships since the earliest days of the war, they had operated, up to then, with some semblance of humanity. From February 1917, however, all that was swept aside, and the 140 U-boats began torpedoing merchantmen, including passenger liners, without any warnings at all. The effects on the British economy were immediate and horrifying; shipping losses doubled in February and almost trebled in the following month.

The other counterstroke was to be an updated version of the Siegert Plan of 1914 – the strategic bombing, by Army long-range aeroplanes, of the City and environs of London, the very bastion of imperialist power and the centre of the Allied war effort. Such attacks, carried out brazenly by day, would have a tremendous propaganda effect throughout the world – and the British Empire in particular – even though the actual material damage might be relatively minor in extent.

Of course, the German naval Zeppelins had bombed London on many occasions, by night, since the middle of 1915, but they had not dared to approach the capital since that night in October 1916 when Heinrich Mathy, the premier airship commander, had died in the flaming L.31 over Potters Bar. That victory, by Second Lieutenant W. Tempest of No. 39 (Home Defence) Squadron, had signalled the end of the conventional Zeppelin attacks on London – the defences had grown too strong for them. Now it was to be the turn of the Army to resume the attack on the metropolis; the Zeppelins could be assigned to less well-defended targets in the British Isles.

As we have seen, the lack of a suitable long-range bombing aeroplane had caused the abandonment of the German Army's plans to raid London in the early days of the war. However, the

Siegert Plan could now be dusted off and reactivated because of the rapid strides made by the German aircraft industry in producing the G-type aircraft. The ultimate requirement for the Siegert Plan was a model that possessed the necessary endurance, speed, rate of climb, manoeuvrability and load-carrying capacity to be able to attack London across the North Sea, by day if need be, and return safely to base.

After many difficulties and delays, the Gothaer Waggonfabrik AG, in September 1916, seemed to be within sight of its goal; its G.IV prototype, a development of the earlier G.II and G.III types, had been officially approved and production was about to begin at the Gotha, LVG and Siemens-Schuckert manufacturing plants. This machine would, it was confidently expected, at long last match up to the stringent specification laid down for the long-range bomber.

On the 25 November 1916 a German Army order established the Air Forces as a separate branch under the command of the *Kommandierender General der Luftstreitkräfte* (abbreviated to Kogenluft), the General Officer Commanding the Air Forces. General Ernst von Hoeppner was the first holder of this post, although, surprisingly, he was not an airman. One of his first tasks, after taking office, was to write a policy memorandum, for the benefit of OHL and his own service, on the subject of the proposed strategic air raids on the UK:

Since an airship raid on London has become impossible, the Air Service is required to carry out a raid with aeroplanes as soon as possible. The undertaking will be carried out in accordance with two entirely separate schemes:

1. Bombing squadrons equipped with G (large) aeroplanes.
2. Giant flights equipped with R (giant) aeroplanes.

The G (large) aeroplane for this task is now ready, and the R (giant) so far developed that its use will be practicable in the near future. It is therefore possible to consider carrying Scheme 1 into effect.

Scheme 1 will be carried out by Half-Squadron No. 1 using Gotha G.IV aeroplanes. The requisite number of thirty aeroplanes will be ready by 1st February 1917.

By despatching eighteen aeroplanes, each carrying a load of 300kg of bombs, 5,400kg could be dropped on London, the same amount as would be carried by three airships, and so far three airships have never reached London simultaneously.

Scheme 1 can only succeed provided every detail is carefully prepared, the crews are practised in long-distance overseas flight and the squadron is made up of specially good aeroplane crews. Any negligence and undue haste will only entail heavy losses for us, and defeat our ends.'[2]

The document continued with details of the organization required, the constitution of the new squadron, questions of training, co-operation with naval forces, and so on. The memorandum makes it quite clear that the intention was to begin operations against England in February as a parallel activity with the renewed U-boat campaign.

OHL speedily endorsed Kogenluft's proposals and came up with a somewhat curious code name for the operation – *Türkencreuz* (Turk's Cross). All details of the operation were to be classified as secret – the element of surprise being all-important to the success of the *Englandgeschwader,* as the new bombing squadron was soon to be called.

The main object of the air attacks on England, by day, was to be an extensive propaganda exercise that would, they hoped, shake the resolve of the British Government and people. However, the OHL directive indicated that secondary objects were to be attacks on munition factories, lines of communication between London and the coast, the military depots actually on or near the seashore, and transport across the English Channel. In addition, and most importantly, it was hoped that British AA defence units, i.e. guns and aircraft, would have to be withdrawn from France and retained in Great Britain for some considerable time, thus assisting the hard-pressed land forces along the Western Front. In this particular connection, it should be appreciated that Kogenluft did not need to deploy a very large force, nor indeed conduct a particularly intensive campaign. A few sporadic and relatively cheap raids would suffice to keep defence forces in the UK at constant readiness.

The principal target area was to be central London, particularly the Government buildings around Downing Street, the Admiralty, the Bank of England and the Press buildings in Fleet Street. In the event of failure to reach London, because of bad weather, lack of petrol, etc. secondary targets were to be the coastal towns between Harwich and Folkestone, and important

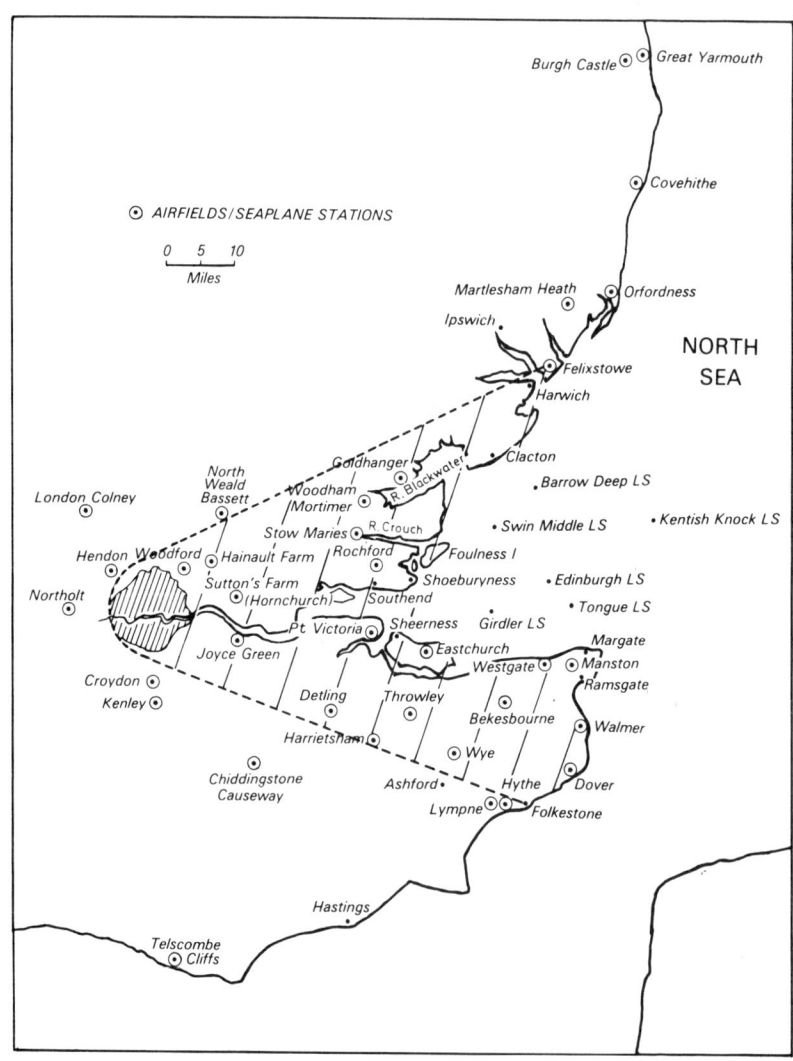

1. Kagohl 3's expected target area

places on the way to London such as Woolwich, Tilbury, etc. (Map 1).

It was planned to operate the squadron's Gotha G.IV bombers from four new aerodromes to be laid out near Ghent at Mariakerke, Melle-Gontrode (the former Zeppelin base), Oostacker and St-Denis Westrem (Map 2). These airfields, some forty miles behind the lines, were to be specially levelled because the new bomber's undercarriage was rather weak, particularly when carrying the full payload of 1,200kg, and bumpy takes-off and landings could prove expensive. This had already been demonstrated with the earlier G.II and G.III machines – the same type of undercarriage being used in all.

Of the four airfields, only two were nearing completion – those at Melle-Gontrode and St-Denis Westrem. However, they would not, in fact, be ready to accept the Gothas until April, whilst the other two aerodromes would not be completed until July. Kogenluft had, therefore, little alternative but to arrange for the new augmented bomber squadron eventually to form at Ghistelles – the base of the existing Half-Squadron No. 1. This

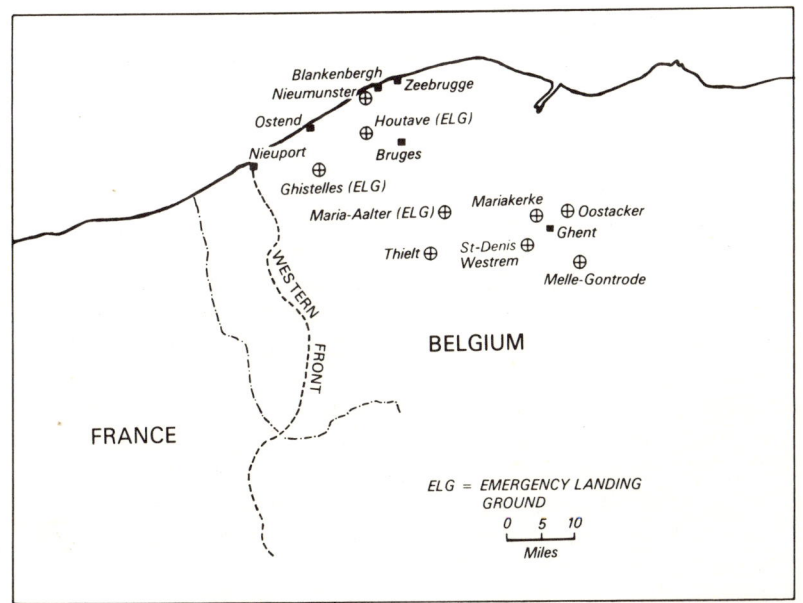

2. German air bases in Belgium, 1917

was hardly a wise move – Ghistelles was only about ten miles from the Front, and nosy RNAS and RFC reconnaissance aircraft were often about. However, few G-planes were to be seen at Ghistelles yet; Half-Squadron No. 1, in fact, continued to use its C-type machines whilst awaiting the arrival of the first G.IVs from the factories. Unfortunately for the overall plans, however, production and supply difficulties during the winter, together with failures to reach the acceptance standards required, were to delay the delivery of the new bomber until March, and, even then, in nothing like the quantity that Kogenluft had so confidently forecast would be available by 1 February.

In consequence, therefore, Half-Squadron No. 1 remained in being until the G.IVs began to arrive at Ghistelles, when the new squadron was formed under a new Commanding Officer, *Hauptmann* Ernst Brandenburg, who replaced the former CO of the Half-Squadron, *Hauptmann* Gaede. Brandenburg was an extremely capable and efficient officer, who had been personally selected by Hoeppner to organize and lead the very first strategic bombing offensive by aeroplanes.

The squadron, now to be known as Kagohl 3, came under the German Fourth Army in Flanders for administrative purposes, but its operational control remained the direct responsibility of OHL. The planned strength of the squadron (as before) was to be six *Staffeln* with, eventually, six bombers in each, i.e. a total of thirty-six in all. The original *Staffeln* 1, 4 and 6 of Half-Squadron No. 1 now became 13 (commanded by *Oberleutnant* Viebeg), 14 (*Oberleutnant* Weese) and 15 (*Oberleutnant* Walter) respectively. Further draftings-in from the entire *Luftstreitkräfte* enabled Brandenburg to form *Staffel* 16 (*Oberleutnant* von Seydlitz) immediately, but the other two, 17 and 18, would not be fully up to strength until the following July.

Each Gotha G.IV would require a crew of three: the commander of the aircraft, a non-piloting officer/observer, who was also the navigator/bomb aimer/front gunner; the pilot, who could be an officer or senior NCO; and the rear gunner, usually an *Unteroffizier* (corporal). It has been suggested that there was some friction between officers and NCOs of Kagohl 3, principally because the latter resented the class-distinction of the well-educated officers. Nor was this all: the posting of Bavarian aircrews to Prussian air units, and vice versa, as was sometimes necessary, could, and did, lead to problems. There was little love lost between the two provincial groups, even though both Bavaria and Prussia were part of the Kaiser's German Empire. However, it is interesting to note that Bavaria, in the German Constitution of 1871, had retained some elements of sovereignty, military administration being one of them. Such a curious situation can scarcely have been conducive towards general discipline in air units in which both Prussians and Bavarians were serving.

The squadron's headquarters staff amounted to seven; Brandenburg himself, *Adjutant* Gerlicht, and five officers responsible for intelligence, meteorology, photography, motor-transport and technical matters, respectively. Three Gothas were to be allocated for the HQ staff who would be flying – the after fuselage of Brandenburg's plane being painted red so that it would be instantly recognizable.

When the first G.IVs flew into Ghistelles from the Gotha factory, in March, Kahohl 3's personnel, both air and ground, must have been very interested to find out how the new machine differed from the earlier G.II and G.III types. The G.II had seen service, on the Balkan front, for only a short-time because its two 220hp Mercedes D.IV engines had proved unreliable, the aircraft structure was weak and, furthermore, the machine had poor control characteristics because ailerons were fitted to the top wing only, and thus flying demanded constant attention from the pilot. Its replacement, the G.III, had gone into limited quantity production in October 1916, and a few were in service in December. This machine was altogether a much stronger affair than its predecessor; it boasted a reinforced fuselage constructed from plywood. In addition, it had new 260hp Mercedes D.IVa engines, and ailerons were used on both upper and lower planes, the former being balanced to prevent yawing. The G.III was really a test prototype for the main production model, the G.IV, although the latter possessed a developed innovation that only a few of the later G.IIIs had. This feature was an open tunnel arrangement in the fuselage aft of the rear gunner's position, whereby the gunner could fire out under the tail of the bomber, thus eliminating a potentially dangerous blind spot. This 'sting in the tail' was to cause consternation to many defending British pilots attacking from below, until the existence of the device became well known.

The Gotha G.IV was a large, angular, three-seater and rather ugly biplane having a span of some seventy-seven feet and a length of forty-one feet, making it, at that time, the largest machine in service with the *Luftstreitkräfte*. The two 260hp, six-cylinder, water-cooled Mercedes engines, mounted on the lower wings, were each coupled to a twin-bladed pusher airscrew about ten feet in diameter.

The large, open cockpit, approximately fifteen feet long, was very roomy and consisted of three interconnected positions for the crew, with walkways between them. The commander was ensconced at the very front of the aircraft, his 'pulpit' being complete with the Goerz bomb-sight and a machine-gun ring, a part of which would be lifted to allow egress. The pilot's position, immediately behind the commander, was dominated by the large wheeled control column and the brass instruments typical of the period. The rear gunner was stationed at the rear of the cockpit, just aft of the trailing edge of the main plane.

Three 7.92mm Parabellum machine-guns were fitted: one at the front command point, one for the rear gunner to fire above the fuselage, and another mounted to enable him to fire out through the ventral gun tunnel. Each of the guns was electrically heated from a dynamo driven by the right-hand engine, in order to prevent the oil in the gun-lock mechanism from freezing at high altitudes. The ammunition in use consisted of armour-piercing Mauser bullets with a tracer bullet every fourth round as a guide to shooting accuracy. Each ammunition drum for the Parabellum machine-guns contained 200 rounds, fresh drums being stored in the compartment between the pilot's and rear gunner's positions.

The bombs to be carried by the bomber on the daytime raids were the 50kg and 12½kg PuW*types, although racks would be provided at a later date so that 100kg and 300kg ones could be accommodated for night raiding. For daylight missions, however, a maximum of seven 50kg bombs could be loaded in three racks beneath the centre of gravity of the machine, i.e. under the nose and immediately below the pilot and commander. Bomb-release levers for these bombs were fitted in the 'pulpit'

---

* PuW is *Prüfanstalt und Werft der Fliegertruppen* (Test Establishment and Works for the Air Service).

The Gotha G.IV

E.F.K.

close beside the Goerz bomb-sight. The $12\frac{1}{2}$kg bombs, on the
other hand, were stored 'in a small wooden funnel-shaped
magazine with a sliding door, which enabled the pilot to release
them by a small lever marked *Magazin*. Pulling the lever back
once through its full movement released a bomb'.[3] Both the 50kg
and the $12\frac{1}{2}$kg bombs were charged with explosives consisting of
about forty per cent hexanitrodiphenylamine and sixty per cent
TNT. Germany was, in fact, the first country to use
hexanitrodiphenylamine in bombs, the material being very
poisonous, intensely yellow in colour and insoluble in water,
alcohol or ether. People who handled fragments of these bombs
were to find their hands turning bright yellow a few days later,
with attendant irritation and swelling.

The 50kg bomb, about five feet long by some seven inches in
diameter, was fitted with a sharp steel point for penetrative action,
and a three-vaned tail that imparted rotation to the missile for
arming purposes. Two alternative nose fuzes were available, one
to give a short delay of one-fiftieth of a second, and the other
about ten seconds. The bomb, when fitted with the latter fuze, had
great penetrating power and was considered capable of
destroying a three-storey house of the period. Unfortunately for
Kagohl 3, however, the fuzing arrangements for the 50kg bombs
were not always very reliable, as was to be graphically
demonstrated during the raids on England. An incredible one
third of all the 50kg bombs to be dropped would be complete
duds, whilst another ten per cent would explode prematurely in
the air. Such defects in weaponry would, of course, seriously
weaken the overall effect of the Ludendorf propaganda plan.

The $12\frac{1}{2}$kg bomb, in contrast to the 50kg, was a purely
anti-personnel device, its fuze being of the percussion type
intended to detonate the bomb on impact. In fact, the fuze was
so sensitive that the bomb normally exploded instantaneously,
even when falling on soft earth. This missile, about thirty inches
long by $3\frac{1}{2}$ inches in diameter, was a smaller version of the 50kg,
but it did possess one unique feature. In its tail was fitted a
capsule containing a mixture of phosphorus and TNT, which,
on detonation, produced a cloud of white smoke as a marker for
the bomb-aimer. The $12\frac{1}{2}$kg bomb would prove to be much
more reliable than the bigger one, in that there would be no
known cases of premature detonation, and the proportion of

duds would be about ten per cent or less.

The Goerz bomb-sight fitted to the G.IV was probably the first scientific attempt at bomb-aiming during the Great War. The device consisted, basically, of a Zeiss vertical telescope some three feet in length, pivoted at one end on a prism. The bomb-aimer viewed the passing landscape through an eye-piece at the top of the tube and, using a fitted stopwatch, was able to record the time that a landmark took to cross a part of the sighting scale. He was then able to set on the correct aim by correlating his height against a calibration chart supplied. The act of setting the bomb-sight provided an indication of the course to fly on a meter before the pilot. At the appropriate time, the observer released the 50kg bombs by means of the bomb-release levers in his compartment.

The bombload of 300kg mentioned by Kogenluft in his memorandum had been arrived at after detailed investigation into fuel consumption for the 350-mile round trip to London, and the operational height at which to fly. The bombers, operating over UK in broad daylight, would need to fly as high and as fast as possible if they were to avoid the attentions of defending aeroplanes and AA guns. The acceptance speci-fication for the G.IV actually demanded that the machine should be capable of climbing to an altitude of 18,000 feet in one hour whilst carrying its full load of 1,200kg. There seems little doubt that the machines manufactured by Gotha were able to meet this requirement, at least initially, but later models, particularly those produced by sub-contractors, were not in the same class, technically speaking.

Calculations and tests had shown that the bomber's two aero-engines would require at least 175 gallons of petrol plus fifteen gallons of oil for even the most direct journey to and from London, a deadweight of approximately 600kg, i.e. half the available payload. Three crewmen, their machine-guns, ammunition and other equipment, would probably account for another 300kg, so it was not surprising that the bombload had to be restricted to 300kg. However, the capacity of the fitted petrol tank was inadequate for such a long journey, and the squadron had, perforce, to organize the installation of a seventy-gallon gravity tank to each G.IV that arrived at Ghistelles, in order to give an extra two hours endurance. Whilst this reserve tank would allow a small margin for detours and headwinds, the additional weight meant that the Gothas would be forced to operate with an overload of about 150kg,[4] although, of course, this limitation would be largely offset by a reduction in the weight of fuel by the time the bombers reached England.

In fact, the maximum altitude to be reached over England during the early day raids would be about 16,000 feet when fully loaded, but this figure would fall progressively to 12,500 feet for subsequent raids, because of the poorer flying capabilities of replacement machines produced by Siemens-Schuckert and LVG, the continuing 150kg overload and the onset of problems connected with the new engines.

As far as speed was concerned, the Gotha G.IV was decidedly slow; its maximum was about 80 mph with zero wind, and as low as 50 mph with a strong headwind. Apart from that, the aeroplane was quite manoeuvrable for its size and deceptively ungainly appearance; it was to prove quite capable of out-performing the slow BE and FE aircraft possessed by the RFC's home defence squadrons.

The make-up of the 300kg bombload was to vary considerably from raid to raid, but probably four 50kg and eight 12½kg bombs represented a typical bomb-up. It is true, however, that some G.IVs were to be sent over England very lightly loaded indeed, in order to operate as photo-reconnaissance units or to act as high-speed decoys to lure defending aircraft away from the main bombing force.

Aircrews were kitted out with heavy fur-lined flying-suits and gloves, against the freezing cold at high altitudes, and were also provided with primitive oxygen equipment. This apparatus utilized liquid oxygen in a portable tank for each crew member, the gas feeding into a bladder to which a breathing tube was attached. However, it seems doubtful if this equipment was used to any great extent – the aviators seem to have preferred nips of cognac when necessary!

Perhaps the most important factor in the success or failure of the Gotha missions over the sea to England would be, of course, the weather to be expected in the late spring and summer of that year. The relatively frail Gothas were getting ready to set out on overseas bombing flights that would be longer than any attempted up to that time, and thus accurate forecasts of the approach of calm, anticyclonic periods would be vital to the whole enterprise. Luckily for Londoners, perhaps, 1917 would not be a particularly good year for Kagohl 3, meteorologically speaking; suitable periods of fine weather during the summer were very few and far between.

It was essential, therefore, to set up a meteorological station on the squadron, and a former airship officer, *Leutnant* Cloessner, was appointed to take charge of its organization and direction. Cloessner, a meteorologist by profession, arranged for daily weather reports to be sent from the main weather bureau near Frankfurt in the Taunus Mountains and the observatories at Hamburg, Ostend and Bruges. The 'tree frog', as met. officers were somewhat unkindly termed, also began to conduct weather observations locally, including the release of small balloons from the roof of the University in Ghent, in order to check the velocity of the wind in the upper air.

The big problem facing the German forecasters concerned with operations against England was, and always had been, the lack of information from the west relating to the approach of deep depressions sweeping in from the Atlantic in a north-easterly direction, bringing south-westerly gales and rain. These depressions could arrive over England quite suddenly and unexpectedly, from the German point-of-view, and then move rapidly across the North Sea to the Continent. If the Gothas were to meet a south-west gale on their way to England, their fuel consumption would be accelerated and they might not have sufficient to return home, quite apart from the inevitable northerly drift that they would experience. Not that the problem was new; many Zeppelin flights towards France and England had been interrupted by unforeseen storms from the west. One answer might have been to use Atlantic U-boats as weather-reporting stations; but this was never done, as far as is known, probably because of the danger of detection whilst transmitting the weather data.

Bülow points out that visibility and orientation could be 'badly hampered by cloud banks over the English Channel and the South of England. The difference in the weather over the Continent and the Island [*sic*] made calculation of the possibility of carrying out the raids difficult.'[5]

The dearth of reliable weather data from the Atlantic was to hamper Kagohl 3 throughout its daytime operations against England and on at least one occasion would lead to near disaster. The G and R-bomber squadrons were to continue venturing out on their expeditions across the North Sea with incomplete forecasts until December 1917, when Rumpler long-range weather-surveillance aircraft would be brought into service.

Raids on London would entail a journey of up to five hours, nearly all of it over the sea. If a bomber came down in the North Sea, what chance would the crew have? Very little, even with their inflatable life-jackets. A large, heavy landplane with wheels would inevitably nose over, even in a calm sea, and if the weather was rough, the aircraft would rapidly break up and sink.

The Gothaer AG had given much consideration to these problems and had come up with two so-called safety measures: air bags to be inflated whilst actually gliding down to the surface of the ocean, and the use of water brakes fitted under the elevator allegedly to prevent the aircraft turning turtle. These incredible ideas would, so the manufacturer claimed, enable the bomber to stay afloat for up to eight hours. Bülow dismisses these 'safety measures' as impracticable and states that they were at once rejected as such by the squadron: 'The Gotha G-aeroplanes could perhaps, under the most favourable circumstances, have kept afloat for half an hour.'[6] Nevertheless, each Gotha was obliged to take along some carrier pigeons on each trip in the hope that there would be time to write the messages, release the birds and still remain afloat until naval torpedo boats had reached the area. Such a scheme was, of course, quite nugatory if half an hour was the best that could be achieved, but perhaps Brandenburg felt that the presence of the pigeons on board would help to maintain morale during the long flights over the sea.

Whilst awaiting the full delivery of G.IVs, Brandenburg began organizing the intensive training programme that was necessary if the bombers were to be able to fly long distances over the North Sea and then to operate successfully over enemy territory for extended periods, all in broad daylight.

Probably the most important part of the training scheme involved the squadron's aircraft observers in a number of exercises to accustom them to dead-reckoning navigation over wide expanses of open sea. For this purpose the officers were detached to the naval establishments at Sylt and Heligoland where they were sent off in seaplanes to find their way across the sea, with only occasional glimpses of lightships to confirm or confound their reckonings.

On their return to the squadron the navigators were issued with General Staff maps of the North Sea and the Dover Strait, in preparation for the long and arduous flights ahead. Four alternative departure points on the Belgian coast were chosen, Nieuport, Ostend, Blankenbergh and the Belgo-Dutch frontier, whilst selected landfalls on the English side were to be the North Foreland, the Tongue lightship, Foulness Island, the Swin or Clacton.

The usual flight plan for the attacks on London, by day, would involve flying out over Ostend and then setting course for Foulness, an easily identifiable landmark. After that, the squadron would attempt to approach the capital from the north or north-east, using the Epping Forest as a guide, and, after bombing, depart along the north side of the Thames to the estuary.

Kagohl 3's ability to defend itself, whilst operating in the daytime over England, was entirely dependent upon the bombers flying in a fairly tight formation, their 'hedgehog' defensive system consisting of multiple crossfire from the large number of machine-guns that the formation could bring to bear upon attacking fighters, particularly those brave or possibly foolhardy enough to make lone sorties.

The bomber formation, usually in the shape of a diamond, with three headquarter machines in the van, was led and directed by Brandenburg using elementary flare signals to indicate turns etc. No wireless equipment was carried as this would have reduced the bombload still further.

Flying the somewhat ungainly Gothas in formation was practised at the *Geschwaderschule* at Paderborn in Prussia, about 200 miles east of Ghent. Formation keeping was not, in fact, very rigidly enforced but it was emphasized that the Gothas must keep together if they were to be able properly to defend themselves. There was, of course, a serious snag concerning formation flying over hostile country by day; the squadron would present a much larger target for AA guns to fire at, assuming that the artillery could actually reach the required height. Brandenburg did not overlook this point, however, and on several occasions whilst flying over England, the squadron would open out its formation into two separate wings, sometimes at different altitudes, when AA fire became too intense, or if it was expected to be so.

In-flight messages were, passed by pyrotechnic flares, consisting usually of red, green or white lights, the latter normally used to instruct the squadron to make for a particular preselected target area. This was arranged by giving the target a number, which would subsequently be identified by firing the appropriate number of white flares from the 'pulpit' of the leading Gotha. If any of these indicator flares were not observed, for any reason, the resulting misunderstandings could jeopardize the whole assault, as was to happen on at least one occasion during the daylight attacks.

In addition to formation flying, Gotha pilots had to perform ten landings by day and another ten by night, these exercises also being carried out at Paderborn. Such training was very necesssary, because the G.IV tended to be rather difficult to land when lightly loaded, as, of course, it would be at the end of a mission. In crosswinds the stability of the aircraft was even worse, and crashes were not uncommon when landing under such conditions. In mitigation, however, it should be stated that the G.IV was quite stable with medium or high loading and was, indeed, capable of gliding, with engines dead, for very long distances.

In April, at long last, Kagohl 3 was able to move away from the prying eyes of the RNAS and RFC aircraft over Ghistelles and take up residence at Melle-Gontrode (*Staffeln* 13 and 14, together with the headquarters staff) and St-Denis Westrem (*Staffeln* 15 and 16). However, all was very far from being ready to begin the first *Luftangriffe* (air raid) against England. The principal reason for this frustrating delay was the number of engine failures that were now being experienced. The cause of these breakdowns was soon pinpointed to the metal used in the bearings of the engines fitted to the first production machines supplied. In addition, the petrol pipework installed in these aircraft left much to be desired and required considerable modification.[7] In the circumstanes, then, the final acceptance flights with full loading had to be postponed until replacement engines, with improved bearings, could be obtained and the changes to the pipework completed. These engineering tasks were to occupy the whole of April, and the delay did, at least, permit the crew training in gunnery and navigation to be perfected. Furthermore, the installation of the seventy-gallon reserve petrol tanks was also pushed along as rapidly as possible.

3

'The Diminished Risk'

At the end of 1916 the defenders of London, both in the air and on the ground, could look back with satisfaction on a year of successes against the conventional Zeppelins – 'the monsters of the purple twilight' as E. Dudley has called them. In fact, no Zeppelin had challenged the defences of the capital since the death of Mathy over Potters Bar on the night of the 1/2 October.

As time passed and the airships did not return, public confidence grew and a feeling of complacency became evident, even in Government circles. The general opinion, at quite high levels, was that the Zeppelins were finished and would never come back, and, furthermore, that the German Air Force did not then have the wherewithal to attempt long-range aeroplane raids on England. Although both ideas were fallacious (the German Navy had by no means abandoned the Zeppelin concept,* and in Belgium Kagohl 3 would soon be preparing its first assault on London), it was not really surprising to find, at the turn of the year, the Army Council, in its constant searching for replacements for the Western Front, requesting more and more men from the Home Forces Command. The military establishment at home in that autumn had no fewer than 17,000

---

* The surviving conventional Zeppelins were being modified to enable them to operate at 20,000 feet, a height that would be quite impossible for the existing types of defence aircraft to attain. These high-altitude airships were, in fact, sent on a raid to London (the so-called 'Silent Raid') on 19 October 1917, i.e. almost a year after the loss of Mathy. Fortunately for the city, and quite fortuitously, the raiders were dispersed, after only a few bombs had been dropped, by an unexpected gale arising. It is certain that the defences could not have prevented what might have been 'an appalling disaster'.

officers and men in its AA artillery service whilst the eleven RFC home-defence squadrons mustered 110 aircraft, 200 officers and 2,000 men. Although seemingly very large, such figures belied the true state of affairs: those given for the RFC, for example, represented only about half the official establishment levels, many pilots and observers having already been sent to France since October to help make up the tremendous losses in aircrew during the Battle of the Somme, officially estimated at about 300 per cent per annum.

The run-down of the home defence forces was, in fact, to continue well into the coming spring, although many influential and knowledgeable people in the UK, including officers high in the Home Forces Command, were becoming increasingly worried about the way in which the defences were being reduced. A typical comment was voiced by the redoubtable Mr Pemberton Billing, when he stood up in the House, at the end of March 1917, and made the following forthright prediction: 'In the next summer we shall experience raids of a much more serious character than Zeppelin raids. Aeroplanes may come over this country ... at night, and at 15,000 or 20,000 feet they may drop their bombs and get back before we know where they are.'[1]

Before proceeding further, it will perhaps be useful to consider the units, both Army and Navy, that were to contribute, however briefly, to the defence of the capital in the coming daylight campaign. The Army units involved, i.e. the RFC's home defence squadrons, the AA artillery Commands and the observation and warning organizations, were all part of the Home Forces Command under Field-Marshal Lord French, with Major-General Sir Frederick Shaw as Chief-of-Staff.

Firstly, then, we may look at the organization of the RFC's Home Defence Wing, the aeroplane being rightly regarded by the Army as the main plank in its anti-aircraft strategy, although the Admiralty, during it tenure of the defence office, had thought otherwise. The Home Defence Wing, now commanded by Lieutenant-Colonel T. C. R. Higgins, the former CO of No. 39 (Home Defence) Squadron, consisted of eleven active squadrons with one in reserve, but of these only Nos. 37, 39, 50 and 78 could have been regarded as defenders of London. The disposition of a home defence squadron was usually as follows:

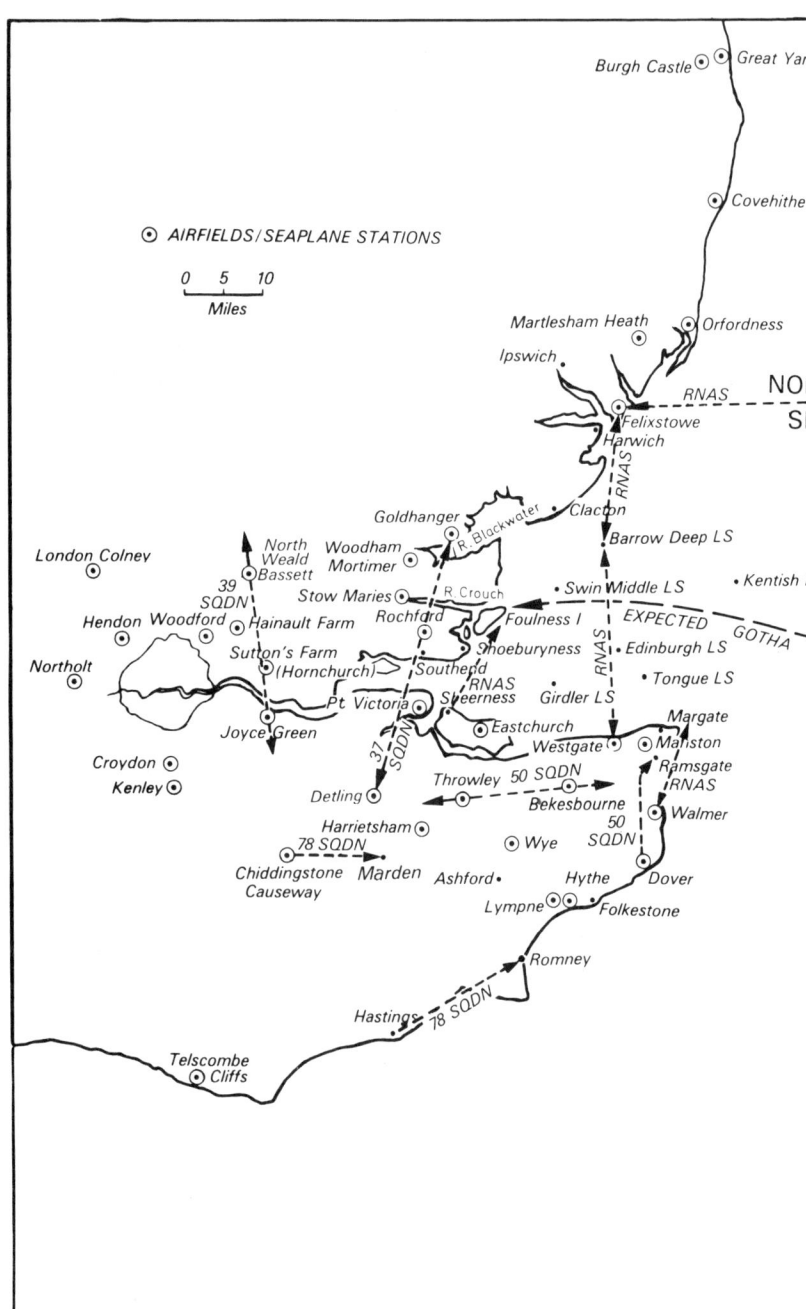

AIRFIELDS / SEAPLANE STATIONS

0   5   10
Miles

Burgh Castle ⊙   ⊙ Great Yarn

⊙ Covehithe

Martlesham Heath ⊙   ⊙ Orfordness
Ipswich •

RNAS   NOF
SE

Felixstowe
Harwich

Goldhanger ⊙   R. Blackwater   • Clacton
London Colney ⊙   Barrow Deep LS
                North   Woodham
                Weald   Mortimer ⊙   • Swin Middle LS   • Kentish K
39   ⊙ Bassett
SQDN   Stow Maries ⊙   R. Crouch   EXPECTED GOTHA
Hendon Woodford ⊙ Hainault Farm Rochford ⊙ Foulness I
⊙   ⊙   • Edinburgh LS
Sutton's Farm   Shoeburyness
Northolt   (Hornchurch) RNAS Southend   • Tongue LS
⊙   Pt Victoria ⊙ Sheerness   Girdler LS
                                          Margate
Joyce Green ⊙   37   Eastchurch ⊙   Manston
                  SQDN   Westgate ⊙ ⊙
Croydon ⊙   Throwley 50 SQDN   Ramsgate
Kenley ⊙   Detling ⊙   Bekesbourne   RNAS
                                    50   ⊙ Walmer
        Harrietsham ⊙   SQDN
        78 SQDN   ⊙ Wye   Hythe   Dover
Chiddingstone Marden Ashford •   Folkestone
Causeway   Lympne ⊙⊙

                              Romney
        Hastings   78 SQDN

Telscombe
⊙ Cliffs

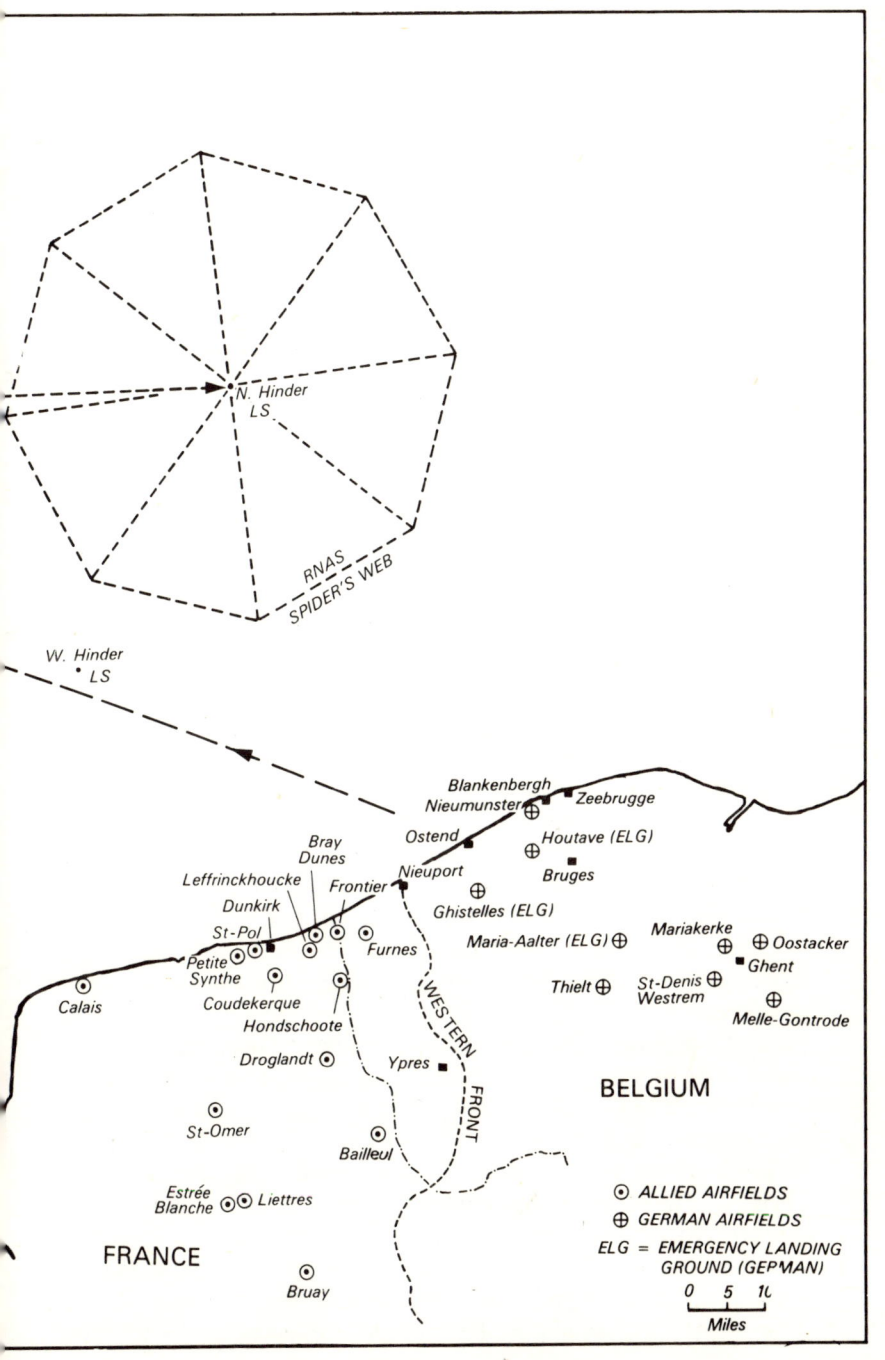

N. Hinder LS.

RNAS SPIDER'S WEB

W. Hinder · LS

Blankenbergh
Nieumunster⊕ ▪ Zeebrugge
Ostend ▪ ⊕ Houtave (ELG)
Bray Dunes
Frontier Nieuport
Leffrinckhoucke ⊕ ▪ Bruges
Dunkirk ⊕ Ghistelles (ELG)
St-Pol ⊙⊙ ⊙ Furnes Maria-Aalter (ELG) ⊕ Mariakerke
Petite ⊙⊙ ⊙ ⊕ ⊕ Oostacker
Synthe ⊙ ⊕ Thielt ⊕ St-Denis ⊕ ▪ Ghent
Calais ⊙ Coudekerque ⊙ Westrem
Hondschoote ⊕ Melle-Gontrode
Droglandt ⊙ ▪ Ypres

WESTERN FRONT

BELGIUM

⊙ St-Omer

⊙ Bailleul

Estrée ⊙⊙ Liettres
Blanche

FRANCE

⊙ Bruay

⊙ ALLIED AIRFIELDS
⊕ GERMAN AIRFIELDS
ELG = EMERGENCY LANDING
GROUND (GERMAN)

0   5   1(

Miles

3. RFC/RNAS air bases and patrol areas, April 1917

a headquarters airfield, linked by telephone to one of the seven Warning Control Centres throughout the country, and three satellite aerodromes, some miles apart, each having a flight of night-fighting aeroplanes in readiness.

No. 37 Squadron, whose task it was to defend the Essex approaches to London, had its headquarters at Woodham Mortimer, with detached flights at Goldhanger, Rochford and Stow Maries (Map 3). No. 39, nearer the city, was controlled from Woodford, its flights operating from Hainault Farm, North Weald Bassett and Sutton's Farm (Hornchurch). No. 50, covering Kent, was centred on Harrietsham, its detachments being at Bekesbourne, Detling and Throwley. Finally, No. 78, guarding the south coast, had its headquarters at Hove, with satellites at Chiddingstone Causeway (Penshurst), Telscombe Cliffs and Gosport, these airfields being the most widely separated of all – about thirty miles apart. The headquarters of Nos. 37, 39 and 50 Squadrons were, of course, connected to the London Warning Control Centre, whereas No. 78's HQ was in communication with the Portsmouth Warning Control Centre, although its airfield at Chiddingstone Causeway presumably came within the London Controller's region.

The actual patrolling by night, for about two hours at a stretch, was in an area bounded by the squadron's airfields, but this scheme was subject to some modification later. No. 37, for instance, patrolled the line Goldhanger to Detling in Kent, i.e. right across the Thames estuary. Similarly, No. 39 ranged from North Weald Bassett as far south as Farningham, in order to cover the whole of the eastern side of London. No. 50, in addition to its north Kent beat, also flew between Dover and Ramsgate, whilst No. 78 patrolled from Hastings to Romney on the coast and Chiddingstone to Marden further inland. It is interesting to note that the coastal strip from Dover to Romney, a distance of some twenty miles, was thus not covered at all, a discrepancy that was to have serious consequences during the first daylight raid.

Each of the four squadrons had complements, on paper at least, of twenty-four aeroplanes, compared with eighteen for each of the other home defence squadrons, but it is doubtful whether, in fact, any of the four had more than about twelve machines on strength with a corresponding reduction in the number of pilots available. The actual aeroplanes supplied to the squadrons were obsolescent types such as the BE2c, the BE12 and the FE2b, the best of which, the BE12, was capable of reaching a ceiling of only 13,000 feet. The BE12, although more powerful and speedier than the sedate BE2c, its predecessor, was not exactly popular with its pilots. Cecil Lewis, subsequently a fighter pilot with No. 56 Squadron, had this to say about it: 'It really was a cow ... the engine rattled like a can of old nails.'[2]

No modern fighters had been allocated to the Home Defence Wing, on a permanent basis, and this was understandable: the home defence squadrons had been fitted out and trained for one job only – to shoot down conventional Zeppelins at night. The aircraft supplied, being inherently stable in flight, were ideal as gun platforms against the slow airships, against which no great manoeuvrability was required. However, such staid machines would be quite ineffectual against fast, agile and well-defended day-bombing aeroplanes and, indeed, they would even be useless against the new, high-altitude Zeppelins because of their inability to rise to the required height. The RFC was very worried about the situation, as Ashmore relates: 'Early in 1917 the officer commanding the Home Defence Wing, realizing that raiding by aeroplanes was now inevitable, informed the Air Board that, in his opinion, the machines in use in the Home Defence units, although efficient against the airships of the time, were totally unable to deal with aeroplane attack. The only result was the issue of three Bristol monoplane fighters – which were withdrawn a few days later.'[3]

The home defence pilots, trained to operate on their own against the nocturnal Zeppelin*, had no experience of fighting and manoeuvring in formation, under a group leader, although such activities were commonplace on the Western Front. The night-fighters received no direction or help from the ground once airborne, and patrolled a lonely beat waiting for searchlights to illuminate any Zeppelin they chanced to locate. By day, however, a rather elementary ground-to-air signalling system could be used. Ashmore describes it, somewhat disparagingly, as follows: 'There was in existence a system of ground signals – the Ingram code of dots and strokes laid out in

* No. 198 (Depot) Squadron, Rochford (Major B. F. Moore), was formed as a night-fighting training school in February 1917.

white ground sheets – that could be displayed at certain aerodromes: they gave to pilots in the air points towards which they were to fly in order to meet the enemy. Our pilots had little training in the use of this system, and there was too much delay in setting the signals out to make them of any real value.'[4] The likelihood of raids by formations of enemy bombing aeroplanes, by day, must have been a disturbing prospect before Lieutenant-Colonel Higgins. He would have appreciated the dilemma that his night-fighting squadrons might soon have to face – how to expand or modify their individualistic night-time role to include the technique of in-formation day patrolling. A few of Higgins' pilots probably had had such experience in France, but it is certain that the majority had not. In any event, if the Zeppelin raids were resumed, how would it be possible to operate day and night with the limited resources available?

However, such considerations did not seem to concern the War Office overmuch. On 6 February 1917 Lieutenant-General Henderson wrote to the Chief of the Imperial General Staff (CIGS), General Sir William Robertson, stating that the RFC in France stood in urgent need of two new night-flying squadrons, and that they could be sent to France at the beginning of March if thirty-six pilots were taken from the home defence squadrons. In fact, the formation of no fewer than five such new squadrons had been approved by the War Cabinet some time before, all to be staffed from home defence units. Sir David concluded by stating that the diminished risk from Zeppelin attack amply justified the temporary reduction.[5] The War Cabinet approved this scheme on 9 February, probably to the chagrin of Higgins and Lord French, who could see the 'temporary reduction' becoming permanent.

All was not going well for the artillery defences of the capital, either. In December 1916 Lieutenant-Colonel Simon had been appointed to the newly created post of Anti-Aircraft Defence Commander (AADC), London, when all seven AA Sub-Commands in the city became subordinate to him. The intention then was to rationalize the seven local units into four larger groups, each under a sub-commander, but unfortunately this reform could not be put in hand immediately. The AADC did, however, take the first steps towards unity of command by laying down standard operating procedures etc., insofar as it was possible to do so at that time.

In February 1917, however the AADC's plans for London's new double-gun barrage foundered, oddly enough on the face of it, because of the unrestricted U-boat warfare then getting into its terrible stride. The War Cabinet, seriously alarmed at the ever-mounting losses of merchant ships, directed that approximately half of the new 3-inch 20cwt guns ordered for home defence should be diverted to the mercantile marine for shipboard use against submarines on the surface.[6] The Government, quite rightly, considered the threat to the country posed by the U-boats far more menacing than air raids could ever be. In consequence, therefore, the allocation of guns for the capital was reduced from eighty-four to sixty-five, i.e. down by twenty-five per cent. Such a reduction, although not apparently very large, was sufficient to cause the abandonment of the double-gun scheme, at least for some months, although a few twin stations were to remain at places such as Hyde Park, Bostall Heath and Norbiton. The surplus 3-inch guns released by this decision were used to reinforce the areas of London to the north and east, across the likely routes for the bombers. Under the new circumstances, the French 75s had also to be retained for the London defences, although they were to create problems later.

Great pressure was now exerted by the Army Council on FM Lord French to reduce manning in the Home Forces Command for the benefit of the overseas theatres. Whether or not the FM considered attacks by aeroplanes, in the near future, unlikely, the fact remains that he bowed to the War Office's demand and called a special meeting at the Horse Guards to discuss ways and means whereby further economies could be effected. At the meeting, held on 6 March, various proposals were put forward but it was left to the C.-in-C. himself to table the most extraordinary one of all. His plan was to forbid inland AA guns (but not coastal ones) from firing upon any hostile aircraft, at any time, in order that a dramatic cut could be made in the number of gunners and searchlight operators, etc.

Incredible as it may seem now, this proposal was endorsed, and the following remarkable order went out to the AA commands throughout the country, on the following day: 'No aeroplanes or seaplanes, even if recognized as hostile, will be fired at, either by day or night, except by those anti-aircraft guns situated near the Restricted Coast Area which are specially detailed for the purpose.'[7]

Thus, at a stroke, a large part of the country's AA artillery defences was effectively disarmed. Whilst the shutdown may have provided much-needed reinforcements in France and elsewhere, it was to have a very significant effect during the early daylight raids and would lead to bitter recriminations against Lord French and the AA Commands. Whatever the FM's real opinion was concerning the likelihood of air raids in the future, his AADC, at least, had no illusions at all. He had been working, up to the order of the 7th, on a detailed plan for AA gunfire 'to meet possible aeroplane attacks'. Notwithstanding the ban on AA guns, Simon completed his plan and then pigeon-holed it so that it would be ready as soon as the prohibition should be lifted.[8]

As March progressed, however, a significant change in official GHQ thinking became apparent. It seems quite likely that reports from agents in Belgium and reconnaissance aircraft were increasingly indicative of the build-up of bombing aircraft in the Ghent area. Commander Rawlinson, by then stationed with the RNVR Mobile AA Brigade (five guns) between the Blackwater and Crouch rivers, at Stansgate Abbey, made no bones about it:

> Reliable information was, of course, forthcoming as to the lines upon which the enemy was working in order to render his future air raids more effective. We therefore were well aware that in future we were to expect well-organised raids by formations (squadrons) of specially-constructed bombing planes, which were already ... in a very forward state of preparation. The stations from which the greatest number of these planes would take the air would, we knew, be situated in Belgium. Their direct course, therefore, to London would cross the coast somewhere about the line upon which our mobile guns were now established.[9]

On 2 March the FM dictated an angry memo to the Army Council upbraiding it for permitting the pilot strength of the Home Defence Wing to fall from 130 to seventy-one, in order to provide trained pilots for service in the new night-flying squadrons. 'I recognise', he went on, 'that the claims for trained pilots for overseas are all important, but in view of my responsibility for Home Defence it is necessary for me to say that in my opinion the Home Defence Wing, Royal Flying Corps, has been reduced to a dangerously low point, and one which does not enable the general scheme of defence on which the present disposition of the squadrons is based to be carried out effectively.'

He concluded by requesting that a minimum strength in pilots and aeroplanes should be set, and declared that the existing scheme of aeroplane defence would require a hundred trained night-fighter pilots. However, the War Office did not agree with that figure and stated that, 'The shortage at home was not disproportionate to that existing in the RFC establishments overseas'[10] – a somewhat mournful reminder of the severe losses then being inflicted on the RFC in France.

On the basis of the FM's own figure of seventy-one pilots, the strength of each of the home defence squadrons could not have been more than six – hardly a level which could have been very reassuring for Higgins, who at that time was busy with plans for the decentralization of the HD squadrons. At the end of the month the Home Defence Wing was replaced by a new Home Defence Group, commanded, as before, by Higgins, but with two separate Wings, Northern and Southern. The Southern one consisted of Nos. 37, 39, 50, 51, 75 and 78 Squadrons, the remaining five being allocated to the Northern Wing.

In April the final rationalization of the London AA artillery defences took place, as had originally been planned for the previous December. The number of Sub-Commands was reduced to four: Central (with headquarters at Whitehall Gardens, SW1), West (Putney), North (Waltham Cross) and East (Plumstead), all to be directly controlled by the AADC from the Horse Guards. West, North and East were wholly military formations whereas Central was the RNVR AA Corps, still under Captain Stansfeld, its Commanding Officer since October 1914.

The West Sub-Command, encompassing an area south and west of the capital, was equipped, in the main, with French 75s, some of which had been used by the former RNVR Mobile Brigade, by then in process of disbandment. In fact, Commander Rawlinson had been invited to transfer from the Navy to the Army in the rank of Lieutenant-Colonel, in order to take charge of this new Sub-Command.

The North Sub-Command, under Lieutenant-Colonel T. O. Lloyd, covered the north-eastern approaches to the city. The munition factories of Waltham Abbey had been a prime target for Zeppelins in the past, and a number of the North's gun stations were grouped in that district.

The guns of the East Sub-Command were distributed along both sides of the Thames from Blackwall to Ockendon. The Commanding Officer had to deploy his limited resources so as to give maximum protection to the Woolwich Arsenal and the munition plants of Erith.

The Central Sub-Command was relatively tiny, consisting of a few fixed gun stations in the middle of London, at Hyde Park, Paddington, Parliament Hill and Deptford etc., manned entirely by naval gunners.

The number of guns then possessed by the four London Sub-Commands was, as mentioned, sixty-five, namely, sixteen French 75mm, forty-eight 3-inch 20cwt and one 12pdr 12cwt. The positions of fifty-eight of the gun stations, some of which were double ones left over from the original Simon plan, are listed and located on Map 4.

Other AA Commands straddling the approaches to the capital were, of course, to be involved during the daylight campaign, the Commands being the Thames and Medway Garrison, the Dover and Thanet Command and the Harwich

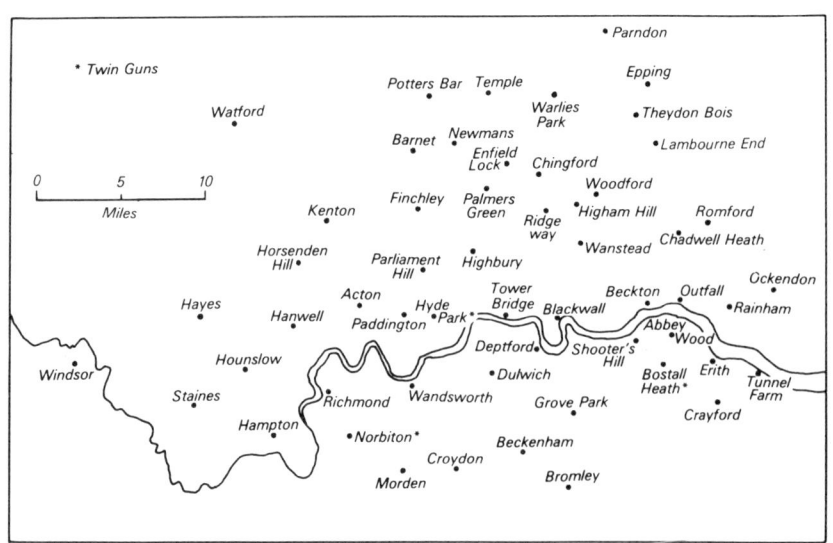

4. AA gun stations in the London area, April 1917

Command. Collectively, these Commands probably fielded about the same number of guns as the London Sub-Commands, their principal armament being, as before, the 3-inch 20cwt gun, with, initially, a few 12pdrs 12cwt scattered here and there. In addition, some 13pdr 9cwt guns, mounted on Peerless lorries, were provided by the Army Mobile AA Brigade, mainly in Essex. These mobile guns were usually operated as battery pairs at their nominated stations.

No attempt will be made here to list all the gun sites in the three AA Commands because of the many changes in deployment that occurred after May 1917; it will suffice to mention the gun stations that were actually to open fire during the daylight attacks – for whatever reasons.

Of these AA Commands, the Thames and Medway Garrison was the nearest to London and probably the smallest of all. Its gun stations were sited around the Thames estuary and, of these, eleven were to be in action on various days during the coming weeks. Their locations were as follows:

Essex	Bowers Gifford
	Canvey Island
	Hawkesbury Bush (Wickford)
	Tilbury
Kent	All Hallows
	High Halstow
	White House Farm (opposite Southend)
Isle of Grain	Port Victoria Aerodrome (RNAS)
Isle of Sheppey	Barton's Point
	Eastchurch Aerodrome (RNAS)
	Neat's Court, Queenborough

The Dover and Thanet AA Command, under Colonel W. M. Thompson, was very much larger than the Thames and Medway Garrison, its gun stations protecting the Isle of Thanet, Dover and the coastline between them. The following fifteen gun stations were to see daytime action:

Dover Area	Cauldham
	Citadel
	Frith Farm

	Langdon Bay
	River Bottom Wood
	West Hougham
East Kent Coast	Cliffsend, Pegwell Bay
	Deal
	Old Haven, Sandwich
	Richborough Castle
	Sandwich Bay
Isle of Thanet	Broadstairs
	Hengrove, Margate
	Manston Aerodrome (RNAS)
	St Peter's, Margate

The guns at Broadstairs and on the airfield at Manston were 13pdr 9cwt mobile pairs, whilst those at Margate were 12pdr 12cwt fixed installations until July 1917 when 3-inch 20cwt ones replaced them.

The Harwich AA Command was responsible for the defence of the Harwich/Felixstowe area and the Essex coast-line down to the Thames estuary, including the Army Experimental Ranges and Gunnery School at Shoeburyness. At this time it had fixed guns in the Harwich area and mobile twin batteries in Essex. The sixteen gun stations that would operate in daylight were:

Harwich Area	Dovercourt
(fixed guns)	Golf House
	Great Oakley
	Landguard
	Ramsey
	Shotley
	Trimley
Essex	Asheldam
(mobile pairs)	Barling
	Burnham-on-Crouch
	(mobile pair from July 1917 on)
	Goldsands Bridges
	Great Stambridge
	Heybridge
	Leigh-on-Sea
	Southminster
	Tillingham

In addition, the gunnery establishment at Shoeburyness would join in with a variety of 3-inch 20cwt guns plus, on occasion, a 13pdr 9cwt mobile pair.

Apart from the restrictions imposed by Lord French, the effectiveness of British AA of the period was limited by a number of technical problems whose solutions were exercising the minds of the Ordnance Committee of the day and artillery research and development teams. The problems concerned, firstly, the types of shell that were permitted to be fired; secondly, the difficulties with height-finders and fuze-setting; and thirdly, the computation of aim-off angles, i.e. the prediction of a bomber's position in flight after a given time.

The types of shell then in use consisted of the time-fuzed shrapnel shell, the time-fuzed 'common' explosive shell and the anti-Zeppelin (AZ) incendiary popularly known as the 'flaming onion'. Both shrapnel and 'common' shells were filled with a so-called low explosive such as black powder (gunpowder) or guncotton. High explosive or brisant (shattering) fillings such as Lyddite, TNT or Amatol were not yet permitted to be used because the time fuze then available was not considered safe for use with them.

The time fuze in use with the shrapnel and 'common' shell (fuze type 80) had been produced, originally, for 13pdr and 18pdr shrapnel shells in normal, i.e. terrestrial, artillery service. The time element in the type 80 fuze consisted of a gunpowder train which, ignited by the shock of discharge, would burn for a pre-set time depending on the length of train selected and the rate of burning. This type of time fuze had one very big disadvantage: on occasion the gunpowder train could break down whilst the shell was being fired from the gun, thus setting off the main charge. With a low-explosive filling, the shell usually cleared the gun before the explosion of the main charge was completed, and thus little damage was done. With an HE filling, premature detonation within the gun barrel instantly destroyed the gun – and usually the crew as well. The Ordnance Committee had thus refused to allow the existing type of time fuze to be used with HE fillings.

Commander Rawlinson, when confronted by the Ordnance Committee's edict, went ahead regardless and personally evolved a safe time fuze for use with the Melinite HE shells supplied with his French 75s. This fuze, authorized only by

Admiral Scott, was subsequently employed, quite successfully, by the RNVR AA Corps from October 1915 until the restructuring of the gun defences in April 1917. When Rawlinson was placed in charge of the West Sub-Command, he was immediately asked by his army superiors why the French 75s in his Sub-Command could fire HE shells with time fuzes whereas the British guns could not.

Having been called upon to explain the position, I related the facts exactly as they were, begging that the practice might be allowed to continue so that our defence might retain the use of high-explosive ammunition, at any rate at that most critical juncture. [But it was all in vain:] The use of high explosive for anti-aircraft work was ... forbidden in our French guns, which were, in consequence, reduced to the same state of comparative impotence as the remainder of our ordnance ... The immediate result of this decision was that our French guns were obliged to fire shrapnel projectiles in the serious raids that were then imminent, and that in consequence, as was certain to be the case, many lives were lost and such damage done by the fall of the empty and unbroken shell-cases, which were of more danger to the inhabitants of London than the shrapnel bullets which they had contained ever were to the enemy.[11]

The shrapnel shell, was, in fact, no great success in the AA role anyway – at the top of its trajectory, at extreme heights, its velocity was approaching zero, and thus its bullets, on ejection, received little impetus. In addition, the time fuze permitted with low-explosive shells proved decidedly erratic when employed in the AA mode. The rate of burning of the gunpowder train varied unpredictably, due to changes in pressure, temperature and humidity at high altitudes, and also because of the higher spin imparted to AA shells as compared with the normal field gun service. Consequently, AA shell bursts could occur some distance below their targets even though the time fuzes were set correctly for the height of operation.

The AA guns in use were, indeed, quite capable of dealing with raiders flying as high as 20,000 feet, provided the gun crews could determine, in the rather short engagement period, the height required (for fuze setting) and the required aim-off angles to set on the gun. Equipment for the former was in service; that for the latter was not, at that time, available for British guns.

The problem of height-finding during the day had been largely solved, for individual target aircraft, by means of the Bennett device, a system employing two operators along a common base line. Unfortunately, a multiple target group of aeroplanes would present an almost insuperable difficulty to the two operators – which individual target to select? By the time the operators were in agreement, the bombers would have disappeared over the horizon.

The prediction of horizontal and vertical aim-off, i.e. the computation of the deflection angles, in two planes, was by far the most complex problem then engaging the attention of the Ordnance Committee's scientific staff. Briefly, the difficulty was to ensure that the AA shell, after its flight from the gun, would arrive at the same point in the sky as the fast-moving target aircraft, and that the set fuze would detonate the shell at about the same time. In France, great strides had been made by means of the ingenious Brocq electromagnetic fire control system (Central Post Tachymeter), but few installations of this type were then operational in England.

The British air-raid warning system, devised and organized in February 1916 to allay public disquiet over increasing Zeppelin incursions, was based, essentially, upon the public telephone trunk network. By early 1917 seven Warning Control centres were in operation in Birmingham, Edinburgh, Hull, London, Manchester, Newcastle and Portsmouth, each one being directly connected to the local telephone exchange manager. The Warning Controller, usually an AA Defence or Garrison commander (Lieutenant-Colonel Simon was the Warning Controller for London, for example) could look down, in his operations room, upon a transparent map table which displayed illuminated representations of the Warning Districts (each a square thirty miles across) into which his area was subdivided.

The Controller was responsible for receiving and distributing information as to the movements of Zeppelins, and for issuing preliminary warnings, followed at a later time by imperative ones, to Warning Districts in the path of an oncoming Zeppelin so that final precautions, including the cessation of important war work, did not need to be put in hand until the enemy was in the immediate area.

The successive warning system evolved was based on the time that a Zeppelin, travelling at about 60 mph would take to overfly a particular Warning District, i.e. half an hour. It was, of course, vital that the Controller should receive reliable information on the enemy's position as rapidly as possible, and many sources of such information were available to him from the observer posts, the police, naval stations, coastguards, AA stations, RFC stations, the Admiralty and others.

Four states of alert were actually in use at this time: the green or preliminary one (*FM's Warning Only*), the red or imperative one (*FM's Order – Take Air Raid Action*), white (*FM's Order – Resume Normal Conditions*) and yellow (*FM's Notice – All Clear*). Appropriately coloured lamps glowed beneath each Warning District square in the Controller's operations room to indicate the condition obtaining in that District at any particular time.

When a Zeppelin was detected some fifty to sixty miles away from a Warning District boundary, and heading towards it, a green warning was sent out, over the telephone system, to civil and military authorities on Special Warning Lists within that District. This would give about one hour's notice, enabling preliminary actions to be taken such as the reduction in lighting, the starting up of defence aeroplanes' engines, the manning of AA guns and lights, and so forth.

Although Chief Constables were on the Special Warning Lists, and one of their tasks was to tell the local fire and ambulance services to stand by, no warnings were given to the general public. Indeed, Government policy was against public warnings, particularly by day, because of unnecessary alarm and disruption of war work, and the probability that people could be enticed onto the streets to watch instead of remaining in the comparative safety of buildings. In any event, so few hooters or buzzers were yet to be found in the entire country outside military and naval establishments that the question of public warnings was rather academic.

As soon as the approaching Zeppelin was reported to be about fifteen or twenty miles away from the District perimeter, the red order was transmitted, thus giving about twenty minutes notice. Final air-raid defensive arrangements were then initiated in order to bring the defences, both civil and military, to their highest state of readiness. This would, of course, have included the sending up of the first RFC home defence aircraft to begin their anti-Zeppelin patrols.

The Observer Corps of the day was provided by the Royal Defence Corps – a forerunner of the Home Guard of the Second World War – an organization staffed by military personnel who were unfit for active service. Fourteen companies of the RDC were deployed on observation duties throughout the country, but it seems doubtful if they had had any special training in aircraft recognition. Indeed, up to 1917 they had not really needed any – even an absolute tyro could not have failed to identify a German Zeppelin at night! The so-called aircraft recognition posters of the period were probably of little use – they referred to German aircraft as Taubes (a reference to the Etrich Taube aircraft of the 1914 period), an indication of the somewhat dated approach typical of the home establishment at that time.

Such then was the organization of the warning and tracking system in use at that period. It was obviously quite adequate for the purpose for which it had been designed – to give timely warnings of the progress of the stately Zeppelin at night. But how was it going to fare when the faster Gotha bomber was abroad? In a few weeks the system would be put to the test.

We may now turn from the Army's responsibilities in home defence and consider those still retained by the Admiralty, particularly those relating to the defence of London and the south-east of England. Obviously, the naval involvement had declined considerably since the hand-over to the Army in February 1916. In fact, it is fair to say that the Navy's primary role by April 1917 was to provide advance warning of the approach of enemy aircraft, mainly Zeppelins, to the British coast. However, RNAS fighter units, in both Kent and Dunkirk, were to play a vital part in the early daylight raids even though the Admiralty was to maintain its independent stance throughout this period.

The naval warning system, for London, depended on two principal sources of information, the lightships anchored in the Thames estuary, and the flying boats operating out of coastal air stations such as Felixstowe and Westgate, searching for U-boats in the North Sea.

The lightships were usually connected by telephone to the shore from whence their messages could rapidly be sent to the Admiralty in London. The flying boats (the Curtiss H12 (Large

America) and the Short 184, for example), although then regarded as 'of little fighting value' against aeroplanes, provided an extremely valuable reporting and tracking function by virtue of their wireless telegraphy equipment. Their crackling spark transmissions provided an effective and reliable method of communication with the Admiralty air exchange.

The anti-submarine patrols maintained by the flying boats were concerned mainly with the detection and engagement of U-boats on the surface, and the 'Spider's Web' system of aerial sea searching had been evolved for this purpose. The patrol area, centred on the North Hinder lightship, was an octagonal figure some sixty miles across, i.e. about 3,000 square miles in area (Map 3). It can be seen that the southerly perimeter of this figure was quite close to the route that Lieutenant-Colonel Rawlinson, and others, expected the bombers to use on their way to the Essex coast.

Other patrols, including anti-Zeppelin ones, were flown by Sopwith Baby seaplanes between Sheerness and the Maplin Sands, Westgate and Felixstowe (via the Barrow Deep lightship), and Walmer and the North Foreland.

Three RNAS establishments in Kent – the air war school at Manston (or Manstone as it was then known) and the two coastal air stations of Dover and Walmer – were each provided with about six modern fighter aircraft, such as the Sopwith Triplane and the Pup, for the defence of naval bases along the coast. In addition, a few Bristol Scouts were available at the flying-training school at Eastchurch, on the Isle of Sheppey, and at the aircraft repair and experimental depot at Port Victoria on the Isle of Grain.

Finally, we come to the very important concentration of RNAS fighter strength in the Dunkirk area, i.e. almost on the Gothas' doorstep. Of the eight naval fighter squadrons in being at that time (Nos. 1, 3, 4, 6, 8, 9, 10 and 11), five were normally detached on the Western Front under RFC control, whilst the other three were stationed at Dunkirk (Bray Dunes or Furnes) as part of No. 4 (Naval) Wing. Throughout the period of the day raids on England, No. 4 (Naval) Squadron was based at Bray Dunes, under naval control, whilst Nos. 3 and 9 Squadrons were present at various times in the same period. All three squadrons would be involved in anti-Gotha patrolling, with some success, as will be seen. No. 11 Squadron, although at Frontier aerodrome, under naval command, was used as a training and replacement unit for naval squadrons on the Western Front and, therefore, took no part in operations.

Not all defensive patrolling from Dunkirk was, however, to be carried out under naval control. During July 1917 the RFC's 14th Wing (4th Brigade) was to move to Flanders to participate in the great offensive to be known as the 3rd Battle of Ypres. Four of the Wing's squadrons would be transferred from the Western Front to the airfields at Frontier and Leffrinckhoucke, and some flights from there would be used on North Sea sweeps in search of the German bombers.

CAMPAIGN

May to August 1917

4

May

Hauptmann Brandenburg, surveying the amount of engineering work involved in replacing the Gothas' defective D.IVa engines, and fitting new reserve tanks and pipes, must have wondered if he would ever lead his squadron out over the North Sea towards England. However, mindful of von Hoeppner's warning that negligence and undue haste would only entail heavy losses, Brandenburg suppressed his impatience and took his time to ensure that the replacement engines, if still not ideal, were as reliable as it was possible to make them. Even so, Kagohl 3 was to be plagued with engine problems throughout its offensive against England – roughly twelve per cent of all bombers setting out for England would be forced to return home without completing their missions. As soon as he was able to do so, Brandenburg put in hand the air-trial flights with full weight loading that had had to be postponed because of the engine fiasco.

The installation of the seventy-gallon reserve petrol tanks was also not yet completed for all the available Gothas, but Brandenburg considered that events could wait no longer for the entire squadron to be modified before setting up the first raid. He arranged that the bombers should refuel at the airfield at Nieumunster, on the Belgian coast, before setting out across the North Sea. A stop at Nieumunster, some thirty miles from the bases at Ghent, would enable the unmodified aircraft to top up their tanks with an extra twenty gallons or so. This would provide just about enough fuel for the flight, assuming no detours were necessary nor headwinds encountered.

By about the middle of the month, Brandenburg was satisfied that all the aircraft were up to the acceptance criteria, and that training of the crews had reached the required standards. Accordingly, he informed Kogenluft that all was ready for the grand passing-out inspection and parade that were to be performed for the benefit of the Commander-in-Chief, *Feldmarschall* Paul von Hindenburg, no less.

Several days later, the FM descended on Melle-Gontrode, complete with the usual large jack-booted retinue, and, in bright sunshine, inspected the personnel and the white-painted Gothas drawn up in front of the former Zeppelin hangar. He was well pleased with all he saw and took his departure hoping that the first assault on Britain would not be long delayed. He was assured that only bad weather could prevent the squadron's fulfilling the requirements of the Ludendorf brief.

After the euphoria of the FM's visit, it was something of an anticlimax when the weather failed dismally to oblige – days passed with thunderstorms and high winds, although the general weather situation was anticyclonic. On the 24th, however, *Leutnant* Cloessner was quite hopeful that the following day, Friday, would be favourable for the first attack. A slow-moving anticyclone centred in France was producing fine, cloudless conditions over an area stretching from Holland to the Bay of Biscay, and, with luck, the south-eastern area of England as well. A light wind was blowing from the west, i.e. just right for the Gothas' return flight to Belgium. Cloessner was a little doubtful about the northerly extent of the anticyclone, even though the German weather stations presumably gave good reports for the day. Brandenburg, however, was not unduly perturbed – there were no thunderstorm warnings to worry about – and gave orders for the bombers to be readied for take-off that afternoon. The primary target was, of course, to be London but a list of secondary targets had been drawn up, together with the necessary pyrotechnic signal codes.

Whilst the preparations for the raid were going forward, an air attack alarm blared at St-Denis Westrem – DH4 bombers from Dunkirk had also taken advantage of the fine weather and proceeded to unload bombs on the airfield. Although 'several bombs exploded close to eight large aeroplanes',[1] damage was slight, and there was apparently little disruption of the ground crews' task of loading bombs, ammunition, oxygen etc. The RNAS strike against the aerodrome clearly demonstrated that the threat from the Gotha bombers was being taken quite seriously, at least on the other side of the Channel.

In the event, twenty-three Gothas took off, at about 14.00 (British Summer Time), from the two active airbases and set course for Nieumunster. Shortly after take-off one Gotha was forced to land at the airfield at Thielt with engine trouble, the first of many failures to occur during the coming weeks. After a short flight of some thirty minutes, the remaining twenty-two bombers landed at Nieumunster and proceeded to refuel. It was rather ironic that, having moved the squadron from Ghistelles to avoid the prying RNAS at Dunkirk, Brandenburg had had to agree to congregate his entire force at Nieumunster – even nearer the coastline!

By 15.30 the Gothas were airborne once again and heading out over the cold and uninviting ocean on a north-westerly track towards the distant coast of Essex (Map 5). For the bomber crews, oversea flying was still a risky novelty, and the prospect of descending into those rolling swells below was not one they could have regarded with equanimity.

At the usual oversea height of 10,000 feet, the bombers settled into their previously rehearsed formation, i.e. the three HQ machines in front, led by Brandenburg in his red-painted one, followed by the remainder of the squadron spread out in a diamond-shaped phalanx. This formation was shortly to be disturbed, however, as one of the bombers began to lag behind because of fuel problems. Soon it was signalling, by flare, that it could not continue its flight and must turn back to Belgium. In the end it limped back to the former airfield at Ghistelles – the nearest emergency landing ground available.

After about an hour the North Foreland was distantly in sight to port, the Tongue lightship being passed 'at a great height' at 16.45. The lightship immediately telephoned a warning to the shore, from whence it was passed at once to the Admiralty in London. Regrettably, however, tardy communication links between the Admiralty and GHQ, Home Forces, at the Horse Guards, lead to a delay of nearly fifteen minutes before the message was received by the London Warning Controller.

At 16.55 the Gothas were near the Swin Middle lightship, at which time the formation seems to have split into two separate groups for defensive purposes. These groups made independent crossings of the coastline between the Crouch and Blackwater rivers, at about 16,000 feet,[2] the best operating height that could

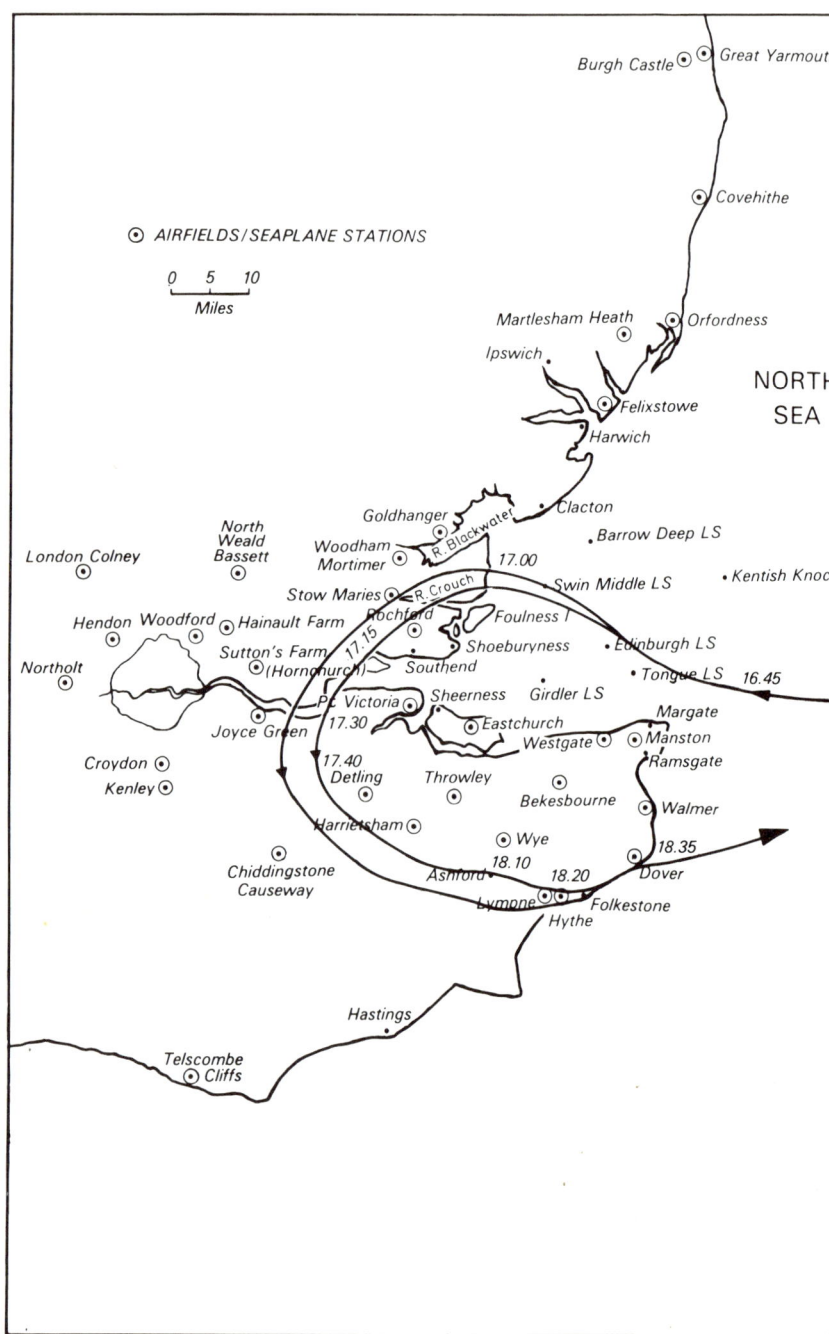

Burgh Castle ⊙ ⊙ Great Yarmouth

⊙ Covehithe

⊙ AIRFIELDS/SEAPLANE STATIONS

0   5   10
Miles

Martlesham Heath ⊙ ⊙ Orfordness
Ipswich

NORTH
SEA

⊙ Felixstowe
Harwich

Goldhanger ⊙ · Clacton
London Colney   North   Woodham   R. Blackwater   · Barrow Deep LS
⊙   Weald   Mortimer ⊙   17.00
         Bassett ⊙   Swin Middle LS   · Kentish Knock
                  Stow Maries ⊙ R. Crouch
Hendon Woodford ⊙ Hainault Farm Rochford Foulness I   · Edinburgh LS
⊙   ⊙   17.15 · Shoeburyness
         Sutton's Farm ⊙   Southend   · Tongue LS   16.45
Northolt   (Hornchurch)   Girdler LS
⊙   P. Victoria ⊙ Sheerness   Margate
         Joyce Green ⊙   17.30   · Eastchurch   Westgate ⊙ ⊙ Manston
                           17.40   · Ramsgate
Croydon ⊙   Detling   Throwley   Bekesbourne ⊙ Walmer
Kenley ⊙   ⊙   ⊙
         Harrietsham ⊙
               Chiddingstone ⊙   Wye   18.35
               Causeway   ⊙ 18.10   18.20 ⊙ Dover
                    Ashford · Lympne ⊙⊙ · Folkestone
                              Hythe

               Hastings

Telscombe
⊙ Cliffs

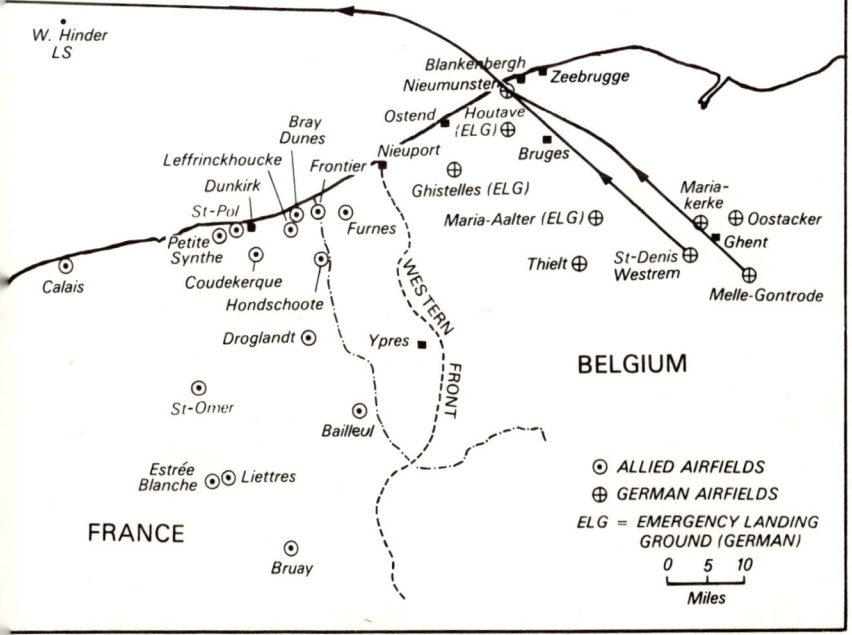

5. Friday 25 May

be achieved in order to discourage the British fighters and artillery. Lieutenant-Colonel Rawlinson's prediction was thus proved quite correct: the bombers had indeed come in along the route he had expected them to use.

The Admiralty had, by now, alerted RNAS coastal air stations and bases along the eastern seaboard from Felixstowe to Dover, seven of which were to respond with actual defensive scramblings at various times during the next hour and a half. At about 16.55, ten fighters were sent up from Manston, while Felixstowe and Westgate put up fifteen seaplanes between them.

On receipt of the alarm at GHQ Home Forces, at about 17.00, the AADC's organization would have initiated warnings to be telephoned to military/civil authorities and other persons on the Special Warning Lists for the Essex and London areas, i.e. those Warning Districts apparently in the path of the bombers.

Simon had very little to do as far as his own artillery forces were concerned: the FM's order of 6 March was in force and only coastal guns were fully manned and permitted to open fire against hostile aircraft.

The home defence squadrons, Nos. 37, 39 and 50, responded to the alert by sending up their BE and FE night-fighters, all being airborne by 17.14 and climbing to their allotted defence patrol areas. No. 37 put up eight aircraft (which may have included one or two from No. 198 (Depot) Squadron at Rochford) and patrolled the line Goldhanger to Detling; No. 39 (eleven aircraft) swung round the eastern perimeter of the city; No. 50 (thirteen aircraft) flew between Throwley, Bekesbourne and Dover.

It must have been extremely galling for the RFC pilots to witness the RNAS putting up modern agile fighters such as the Sopwith Pup and the Triplane when all they had were elderly, inherently unstable, two-seater machines with which to do the same job. This disparity in arms was, indeed, an accurate reflection, on a small scale, of the overall situation between the two services – a direct result of the division of Britain's limited air resources.

The fact that the RNAS aircraft were up some fifteen minutes before any RFC machine says much about the degree of co-operation then existing between the Admiralty and the War Office. Even though the Army had overall responsibility for home air defence, the Admiralty was evidently still initiating quite independent operations in defence of its bases, without waiting for any intimation from GHQ, Home Forces.

As Brandenburg, in his command Gotha, watched the mudflats of the Crouch estuary passing beneath him, he was probably wondering what sort of reception the defence forces were going to give him. Presumably he was, as yet, unaware of the restrictions placed upon inland AA gun batteries, and he would, no doubt, have been delighted to know that GHQ, Home Forces, had been so obliging! The embargo did not apply to the 3-inch, 20cwt gun of the 13th Mobile AA Battery at Highland Farm, Burnham-on-Crouch; it was fully manned and ready. In the event, however, it fired off just one shell because only one Gotha came briefly into range. This solitary round was, in fact, to be the only opposition offered by AA guns until the raiders passed out over the coast again on their return trip.

As far as defence aircraft were concerned, Brandenburg probably did not anticipate too much trouble from the RFC's home defence squadrons; it is difficult to believe that von Hoeppner would not have known that such squadrons were equipped only to deal with slow Zeppelins at night. The RNAS fighter aircraft both in the UK and at Dunkirk posed a much greater threat to the raiders at that time.

At about 17.15 the Gothas were actually passing close to No. 37 Squadron's airfields at Stow Maries and Rochford. Far below them the squadron's sedate BEs were beginning their laborious climb, but it would be another thirty minutes before they could even reach their inadequate ceilings between 10,000 and 13,000 feet – by which time the bombers, averaging seventy miles per hour, were going to be about thirty-five miles away! GHQ was thus confronted by the classic air defence problem: how were the defending aircraft to be got up to the Gothas' height in the very short time between the receipt of the warning and the arrival of the raiders over the city? Earlier warnings were, of course, one answer, and attempts would be made, subsequently, to speed up the passing of alerts to the home defence squadrons. Another proposal would be the setting up of constant air patrols, but these would be ruled out as too costly in terms of men and machines.[3] Major-General Trenchard was to declare later that, 'Patrolling was the least effective and most expensive way of protecting a place like London.'[4]

The obvious solution was to use fighter aircraft with much higher climbing abilities than those possessed by the existing BE and FE types of aeroplane. The Gotha, travelling at 70 mph, was able to cover the distance from the Crouch to the centre of London (fifty miles) in about forty minutes. This knowledge would have postulated a climb rate requirement for the defending fighters of at least 400 feet/minute, assuming that the bombers were approaching at 16,000 feet. Only modern fighters such as the Sopwith Camel, the Pup and the SE5 could meet such a requirement.

As the bombers steered round south-west towards the capital, it very soon became apparent that Cloessner's doubts about the weather over southern England had been well founded. A developing depression was causing the London area to disappear under a dense layer of stratocumulus cloud extending up to about 7,000 feet, and thus bombing from the Gothas' height of 16,000 feet was quite out of the question. Brandenburg, from his elevated position above the cloud bank, could see that the density of the layer declined steadily to the south, with clear, sunny conditions on the south coast some forty miles away. Over Tilbury, at 17.30, he made his decision: his flare signals told the squadron to turn south into Kent rather than west up to the Thames to London. So the attack on the capital was called off – politically desirable though it might be – and the Gothas wheeled over Gravesend, the two wings of the formation probably being about three miles apart at this point.

Brandenburg's frustration because of the weather over the metropolis would have been even sharper had he known that none of the city's AA guns would have opened fire on him even if it had been a fine sunny day, and the Gothas had flown over at tree-top height!

Secondary targets abounded in the Thames estuary but Brandenburg chose to go across Kent to strike at the South Eastern & Chatham Railway's lines, the airfield at Lympne (the RFC's aircraft park), the troop rest and embarkation centre of Folkestone and the naval base of Dover – all excellent substitutes for the London objectives, as OHL had directed.

The German's abrupt change of direction probably took GHQ, and, of course, the Warning Controller completely by surprise – it must certainly have been extremely aggravating for the defence pilots patrolling the London and Thames estuary areas. Even if the new bearing to fly was known to GHQ, and this seems doubtful, the only possible method of communicating wth the RFC pilots in air was by means of the Ingram ground signals. However, in the misty conditions obtaining, even that limited system would have been denied them. RNAS pilots, regrettably, were quite unfamiliar with the Ingram codes.

Because of the extent of the cloud bank, the Gothas were lost to sight for some twenty-five minutes until they suddenly reappeared near Wrotham, where the cloud was thinner. In the ensuing confusion the question of red and green warnings to the civil and military authorities now in the path of the raiders was evidently overlooked – an administrative bungle that was to cost Folkestone very dearly. The limitations of the warning system when attempting to deal with high-speed aeroplanes were already becoming apparent.

Although the cloud layer was reducing, it was to provide sufficient cover for the bombers in making the surprise attacks that were to follow. Strung out on a front of about five miles, the Gothas began the assault by dropping five 50kg bombs on the unsuspecting villages of Harvel and Linton, luckily causing little damage or casualties. The villagers were, however, infuriated that they had received no warning – a complaint that was to be repeated many times during the next hour.

The Gothas then aimed their missiles, without much success, at transport targets such as Marden, Smarden, Bethersden, Pluckley, Kingsnorth and Mersham – all on or adjacent to railway lines – and the waterside villages of Ruckinge and Bilsington on the Royal Military Canal linking Rye and Hythe. The noise of bomb blasts occurring quite close to the RFC airfields at Harrietsham and Detling was possibly the reason why three BE12s were sent up from No. 78 Squadron at Telscombe Cliffs at about 18.00. However, as Telscombe Cliffs were some forty miles away, there was little chance of a successful interception!

The attack continued with two 50kg and four $12\frac{1}{2}$kg bombs on Ashford, the target probably being the town's railway works. One man digging in his garden was killed and three other persons were wounded. About this time, an unarmed Bristol Fighter F2b flew, quite unwittingly, into the Ashford area on a routine ferrying flight from the factory to France. A burst of machine-gun fire from a Gotha hit the Bristol, and it was forced to land at the RFC's aircraft park and airfiring school at Lympne. The pilot, Lieutenant Baker, had no sooner touched down on the grass than the raiders hove into view and commenced an attack on the aerodrome itself. Three 50kg and nineteen 12½kg bombs whistled down here but, incredibly, there were no casualties or damage apart from some craters in the outfield. The uproar and confusion did not, however, prevent another ferry pilot, Lieutenant G. Gathergood, from dashing out to an armed DH5 fighter on the tarmac and taking off in pursuit, although it would take him some twenty minutes to climb to the raiders' height.

Hythe was the next objective; seven 50kg and nine 12½kg bombs rained down without, fortunately, doing much damage. Casualties were light: two killed and two wounded. One of the dead was the verger of the parish church whilst the two wounded were the vicar and his wife, all of whom happened to be on the church steps when a bomb fell and exploded in the churchyard.

The RFC's School of Aerial Gunnery at Hythe was, surprisingly, not attacked, although the site was quite obviously an airfield and presumably known to Kagohl 3 as such. None of the school machines was in the air at the time, probably because training activities had ended for the day. Even if they had been ready to take off, it would have been extremely unlikely for the school machines to have engaged in defensive operations because RFC policy precluded training aircraft from doing so, unless flights from home defence squadrons were stationed at the same airfield.[5] In any event, the training aircraft would have been quite incapable of reaching the Gothas' altitude even if sufficient warning had been given.

When the bombers appeared overhead, the school authorities were taken unawares and, lacking any form of ground defence, had little option but to tell the men to scatter for safety. These considerations, somewhat understandably, cut little ice with a local populace enraged at the apparent lack of militancy at Hythe, and the hapless air mechanics had to endure a period of hostility, including actual stone-throwing, immediately after the raid.

It was now about 18.20 on 'an exquisite spring evening' on the south coast, a gentle off-shore breeze rippling the calm surface of the sea. The front from Sandgate to Folkestone presented a peaceful picture, with people strolling in the sunshine along the Marine Walk, riding by in horse-drawn cabs and the occasional motor-car. Servicemen were everywhere to be seen – many recuperating from war wounds, some on leave and others on evening pass from the military rest/transit camps at Shorncliffe and Cheriton. Among the lucky civilians who had arrived in the town for this Whitsun holiday weekend was Mr A. Gathorne-Hardy, a well-known author of the day, who had strolled down from his seafront hotel after tea to smoke a pipe on the Esplanade. He was now seated 'in profound calm' under the bank below the Leas, quite close to the Victoria Pier. There was little to indicate that this perfect May evening was soon to end in 'sombre tragedy' for the town.

From the west there came the rumble of distant explosions as the Gothas bombed Hythe, but no one paid much attention because of the frequent practices by army coastal batteries and the Navy at sea. Soon, however, a hum of approaching aero-engines was heard growing steadily louder and louder until, with a roar, the bombers swept into sight far up in the cloudless azure sky. The aircraft were now back in a diamond formation spanning about one mile, its right-hand flight above the coast-line.

All over the borough people stopped and stared upwards, quite oblivious of any danger, at the 'bright silver insects' above them at about 15,000 feet. Indeed, it is doubtful if anyone on the ground yet thought that the aeroplanes were hostile – many were pleased to see 'our boys up and doing'! In any event, the townsfolk were quite used to machines from Hythe and Dover 'buzzing about' and, in the absence of any warning, would naturally have assumed that the aircraft were friendly. Unfortunately for the populace, no siren or hooter system existed here, but even if it had, it would not have been used on this occasion – the civil authorities had not been alerted in any way. The absence of any air-raid alarm gives weight to the suggestion that the London Warning Controller was unable to respond quickly enough to the Gothas' change of route. The Chief Constable of Folkestone, Harry Reeve, was to declare later that he had received no warning whatsoever, although he would normally have expected a call from the Army's Eastern Command in London, i.e. part of the Warning Control network. Consequently, therefore, no one sought shelter until galvanized

into action by the rude shock of seven bombs falling on
Sandgate. Three of the five 50kg types exploded in the air, thus
giving an effective warning over a wide area. Regrettably,
however, not everyone was able to take cover in time: a large
number of people, including many children, were to be caught
out on the open streets with tragic and terrible results.

Whilst the bombers on the right flank were attacking
Sandgate – without inflicting casualties or damage –
commanders of others were peering through their Goerz
bombsights waiting for the army camps at Shorncliffe and
Cheriton to appear beneath them. In the absence of any defence
opposition, from either AA guns or aircraft, the Gothas were
able to take their time, deliberately and insolently, to make
almost copybook bombing runs upon the camps which held, at
that time, a large number of Canadian troops resting or in
transit to France. Throughout this area six 50kg and twenty-one
$12\frac{1}{2}$kg bombs were scattered, one of them exploding among a
company of soldiers preparing for an evening route march.
Seventeen of the Canadians were killed outright and ninety-three
others were wounded, an undoubted strategic success for the
Germans.

The raiders, continuing their south-easterly course, then
began to cross the Folkestone urban area, in which an estimated
fifty-one bombs were released during the following ten minutes
or so. Twenty-one of the bombs were 50kg types and thirty
$12\frac{1}{2}$kg, of which ten were duds and two exploded in the air.
Whilst it is probably true that some, at least, of these bombs
were intended for legitimate targets of the war machine, by far
the heaviest weight of bombs crashed down on purely residential
and commercial districts. To be fair, that may have been due, in
some measure, to shortcomings in the bombsights but in any
case the Ludendorf brief had opened the way to purely
terroristic actions for propaganda purposes.

Although no AA guns were stationed in the Sandgate/
Folkestone area itself, nearby Dover had six army shore
batteries, two of which (a 12pdr at West Hougham and an
18pdr at Cauldham) were in the Capel le Ferne district,
approximately two miles to the east. As soon as the Gothas
came into range, these two guns opened fire, acting, if nothing
else, as a warning system for Dover, alerting the naval gunners
aboard the monitors and other vessels in the harbour there.

The majority of the bombs on Folkestone fell in an area of approximately one square mile north and west of the harbour. This area included a large part of the old town, a shopping quarter of narrow streets and alleyways leading down to the harbour and seafront. On this particular Friday evening, a pay-night just before the Whitsun holiday, these streets were thronged with shoppers, mainly women and children. Tontine Street, a thoroughfare about a quarter of a mile long running north from the harbour, was typical. Its entire length was crammed with shops, public houses and wine stores, all doing good business at that hour. Halfway up the street stood a large drapery store, Gosnold's, opposite a greengrocery business owned by the brothers Stokes, the latter so busy at that time that a queue had stretched out into the roadway.

The Gothas' approach from the north-west was heralded by the roar of exploding bombs and the appalling crash of innumerable shop windows breaking. Those who were able to do so took shelter in buildings but the rapidity of the attack meant that few of the many people crowding the streets had time to seek cover even if there was any immediately to hand.

Thus was the scene set for the worst incident of the entire raid: at least two, and probably more, 50kg bombs fell in the Tontine Street vicinity, one exploding among the queue gathered before Stokes' emporium, with horrific results. The roof of the greengrocery store collapsed upon the crowd below, killing many including nearly all the serving staff. The frontage of shops across the road was completely demolished, whilst a shattered gas main sent a fifty-foot flame into the air. Some sixty people were killed or seriously injured, a high proportion being very young childen waiting outside in the street.

The police, fire and ambulance services were quickly on the scene. As the fire in front of Gosnold's was being contained and the rescue teams began their work, the Chief Constable surveyed the shattered street. He had this to say at the subsequent inquest: 'I saw an appalling sight which I shall never forget to my dying day. Dead and injured persons were lying about; several horses were lying dead and a fire had broken out in front of premises which had been demolished. Several of the business premises were very seriously damaged; others had their plate-glass windows blown out.'

Other areas of the town were assailed, damage being

particularly severe in the Bouverie Road and Cheriton Road districts, although casualties were much lighter than those in Tontine Street. The Central railway station, the Pleasure Gardens Theatre, hotels, shops, cafés, schools and houses – all were included in the trail of destruction and damage spread throughout the square mile region.

The bombers roared on towards the naval base of Dover, the next and probably the most important target area. The thunder of bombs exploding in Folkestone, coupled with the barking of the two gun batteries, had by now fully aroused the garrison, and the local air-raid siren in the dockyard began to howl as the first of the Gothas reached the Western Heights. All six army gun batteries were now in action, firing some 358 rounds during the next few minutes. The naval vessels joined in with a fusillade from their 7.5-inch, 9.2-inch and even larger calibre guns, although probably to little effect. Amidst all this hubbub a single Sopwith Pup piloted by Flight-Lieutenant R. Leslie took off from RNAS Dover whilst another two arose from Walmer.

Mr Gathorne-Hardy viewed the scene from his vantage point on the sea front. He contributed the following account to the local newspaper, the *Folkestone Herald*:

I had just finished my pipe and was going to return to the hotel, when I heard the sound of distant aeroplanes and of constant gunfire, and apparently the dropping of bombs, with an occasional crash. I went up on to the parade, and, looking round, saw crowds collected at the west end, and began to see the aeroplanes, of which I counted more than eight, faint and white in the sunny sky nearly overhead, and heard the falling of bombs. I then returned to my old seat, as I thought I should be safer there sitting under the top of the cliff with cover above and only a very narrow place where a bomb could make a direct hit; they were falling too close to be pleasant, and the aeroplanes were right overhead. One of the wounded soldiers, of whom the town is full, shouted to me, 'Lie down! Lie down!' but I saw no advantage in taking his advice.

Just then the nearest bomb fell and I saw it splash into the sea just below me. As it fell I heard it hurtling through the air quite close. I could see little clouds, probably shrapnel, bursting round the aeroplanes, but they were really too high up to be in much danger. The heavy guns from Dover began to roar, and went on for some time. I watched the raiders passing in a south-easterly

The public temper was further inflamed when, after some vacillation, a Home Forces communiqué was finally issued to the Press at about 12.45 on the day after the raid. This remarkable statement ran as follows: 'A large squadron of enemy aircraft, about sixteen in number, attacked the south-east of England between 5.15 and 6.30 p.m. last night. Bombs were dropped at a number of places, but nearly all the damage occurred in one town, where some of the bombs fell into the streets, causing considerable casualties among the civilian population. Some shops and houses were also seriously damaged.'

What the Government hoped to achieve by suppressing the names of towns attacked is difficult to imagine; the Germans, in daylight, could hardly have been in any doubt as to their targets! Be that as it may, no-one (not even the King) was told, and as soon as the communiqué was published in the London evening papers, the telephone system, quite naturally, became jammed with anxious people calling their relatives all around the south-east coast.

The clamour for publicity grew more and more insistent over the weekend, but nothing was done until the following Monday, when *The Times* was permitted to carry the following report from the German official news agency: 'During the course of a successful raid one of our air squadrons dropped bombs on Dover and Folkestone, on the south coast of England.' Whilst not wholly accurate, this report prompted the Government to publish full details of the areas raided. So great was the public outcry on this matter that questions were subsequently addressed to the Prime Minister in the House concerning the rapid change of policy that must have taken place between the Saturday and the Monday. Certainly, no further attempts were made to censor daylight raid reports in this way – the Government had obviously learnt its lesson!

On the same day, Monday the 28th, the RNAS at Dunkirk hit back at St-Denis Westrem, bombs landing, once again, close to the Gothas on the tarmac.

The next day the enraged citizens of Folkestone crowded into an 'Indignation' meeting promoted and presided over by livewire Councillor R. Forsyth. A reporter from the *Folkestone Herald* scribbled busily away as the Councillor declaimed about the 'awful calamity' that had befallen the town – the worst event in it was, had been confined, by the FM's order, to the coastal regions. Brandenburg could scarcely have foreseen that the opposition overland would be as feeble as it had turned out to be. As he headed out across the Dover Straits, he must have felt jubilant. However, he would not have allowed himself to be deluded into thinking that all was now over bar the shouting: determined attacks were yet to be made by UK-based aircraft, and the Dunkirk area still had to be skirted. At this very time (18.35), a signal was being sent from Vice-Admiral Dover Patrol to the 4th (Naval) Wing HQ at La Panne, which resulted in the scrambling of a flight of five Pups from No. 4 (Naval) Squadron at Bray Dunes, and a flight of three Triplanes and a Pup from No. 9 (Naval) Squadron at Furnes.

By this time Lieutenant Gathergood, in his DH5, had reached a height of about 14,500 feet and was, at last, able to open fire on a Gotha at close range. But his valiant efforts were in vain: his Vickers gun immediately jammed (or jambed, in the parlance of the day). By the time he had cleared the stoppage, the enemy was too far ahead to catch.

Flight Lieutenant Leslie from Dover managed to overhaul a lone Gotha labouring along with engine trouble in mid-Channel at about 12,000 feet. Although the Pup's armament consisted of only one Vickers gun, the pilot got off about 150 rounds and had the satisfaction of seeing the bomber go down smoking in a dive. Flight Lieutenant Leslie was, unfortunately, unable to follow it down because he himself was then attacked by other Gothas arriving on the scene. He was subsequently awarded the Distinguished Service Cross for his part in the action, but the bomber was never confirmed as a victory.

At about 19.45, the sun now low on the western horizon, the patrolling flights from Nos. 4 and 9 (Naval) Squadrons managed to intercept groups of the returning Gothas some thirty miles out from Dunkirk, despite a gathering sea mist. The integrated attacks by pilots of No. 4 Squadron resulted in an immediate victory – one of the bombers was shot down into the sea north of Westende. The pilots of No. 9 Squadron had no immediate success but another Gotha was extensively damaged by machine-gun fire although it landed safely. A third raider crashed at Beernem, near Bruges, with the loss of the crew, but it was impossible to determine whether the crash was caused by pilot's error on landing, engine failure or damage from the air attacks. This was probably another in the sorry record of landing crashes for which the Gotha design was largely to blame. The instability when landing lightly loaded, and the flimsy construction of the undercarriage have been referred to in Chapter 2. Kagohl 3 was to suffer greater losses through take-off and landing accidents than those inflicted by all the defending forces put together.

The RNAS squadrons at Dunkirk had demonstrated two important points quite clearly: the most successful anti-Gotha engagements were to be those made on the bombers' return trip, close to their Belgian bases, when fuel was running low and little remained for evasive action; and the Gothas' formidable cross-fire defensive system could be matched only by multiple attacks, preferably launched under in-air leadership. Individual attacks, particularly by the poorly armed and inefficient aircraft possessed by the RFC home defence squadrons, were to prove almost suicidal.

Disturbed by the success of the RNAS fighters, Brandenburg immediately requested Kogenluft to provide fighter cover for the Gothas, on their return trips, as far out over the North Sea as practicable. Von Hoeppner readily agreed to the proposal even though the losses for this particular raid had been very small. Although, of course, disappointed that London had not been attacked and that the element of surprise had been lost, he was well pleased with the results achieved and proceeded to decorate some of the aircrew concerned – *Leutnant* Elsner, *Leutnant* Reulner and *Feldwebel* Helger.[7]

In battered Folkestone, meanwhile, the clearance of bomb damage continued amid a growing sense of public outrage and shock. The destruction of property and the loss of life were bad enough, but the fact that the Germans had been able to bomb the town with impunity, free from defensive intervention, was too much. The Home Forces were castigated on every street corner in the town and, indeed, throughout the land. The public was angry because the feeling of security built up following the defeat of the Zeppelins had been rudely shattered – who knew what further attacks were to be expected in the future? Retaliation in kind was the demand, but few were aware that the RFC was in no position to carry out long-range strategic bombing; this latter function had been left to the RNAS at Dunkirk with its handful of Handley Page and Short heavy bombers.

direction over the Straits, and long after I could no longer see them I observed little clouds shining in the air.

The fact that Gathorne-Hardy chose to ignore the wounded soldier's advice and continued to stand and view the raiders illustrates perfectly the public's bewilderment during the initial daylight raids. Many of those maimed or killed by blast would have escaped injury if they had had the sense to prostrate themselves on the ground.

Gathorne-Hardy also noted that the shrapnel bursts seemed to occur around the Gothas, but this was probably an illusion – he goes on to say that the aircraft were too high to be in danger. The general opinion was that the Archie bursts occurred, in fact, at too low an altitude (about 4,000 feet short) and probably some distance to the rear of the actual targets. In fairness, it must be stated that the AA gun crews had had little practice against fast aeroplanes by day; they had been accustomed to co-operating with searchlights against slow Zeppelins at night. The problems connected with height-finding have already been mentioned in Chapter 3; it was difficult for the two operators to agree on the particular target to sight upon.

The vigorous artillery barrage put up by the Dover defences, although somewhat inaccurate, was sufficient to force Brandenburg to give up the idea of attacking Dover, and to wheel away out to sea. German sources spoke later of 'several good hits at Dover including a direct hit on the Mole'[6] but British reports do not confirm such claims.

The Gothas had been over British territory for about an hour and a half, during which time they had released some sixty-five 50kg and 104 12½kg bombs (about 4.4 tons), killing ninety-five people and seriously injuring another 192. These figures were higher than those of any air raid on Britain up to that time, dwarfing those sustained in the worst-ever Zeppelin raid of 13/14 October 1915, when seventy-one were killed and 128 wounded. Folkestone itself was left with the unenviable distinction of the largest casualty figures for any British town to date: seventy-two dead and ninety-one seriously injured, of whom approximately seventy-eight per cent were women and children.

The bombers had not, as yet, been attacked by any home-based defence aircraft at all, and the AA gun fire, such as its long history. He recalled, somewhat bitterly, how, nearly forty years before, the fishermen of Folkestone had braved the elements to rescue the crew of the German battleship *Grosse Kurfürst* which foundered off the town in 1878 after a collision. 'And how', he cried, 'have the Germans repaid this act of common humanity? They have singled the town out for an abominable attack in which women and children have been the major sufferers!' This naïve belief was widely held by those who signally failed to realize the importance of Folkestone to the Allied war effort: not only was it virtually an armed camp but it was also a communications centre vital to the Western Front. The Germans could hardly have abstained from attacking such a prime military target on purely sentimental grounds.

The Councillor was warmly applauded when he declared that the air attack on defenceless Folkestone had been an outrage which must never occur again. He stated, amid further cheers, that a deputation from the town would be going to London, on the following day, to speak to Lord French and demand that the community should have proper protection from aerial attack. He insisted that the military authorities must give adequate warnings, and that a buzzer or hooter should be installed in the town without delay. The meeting passed the following resolution:

The residents of the Borough of Folkestone demand that the Government be asked immediately to hold an enquiry into the air raid of Friday last, May 25th. We ask how it was possible for a large number of hostile aircraft to attack the town in broad daylight, inflicting appalling loss of life and damage to property, and if the military authorities had knowledge of an impending attack why no warning was given, so that the people could return home and take cover. We urge that the Government should take such steps as will prevent further attacks of a similar nature and the wholesale murder of the women and children of the town.

Not everyone in Folkestone supported the cry for local defences. A retired admiral, also writing in the *Folkestone Herald,* was quite forthright in his opinions. He felt that the demand for gun and aircraft defences in the UK was simply playing the German game, and thus false strategy. 'The best defence is attack, and not one gun or one fighting aeroplane

which could be used at the front – where the real issue will be
decided – should be detained in this country for local defence.'

The Admiral ended his enlightened letter with a plea that
righteous anger and sympathy with the bereaved should not
cause the loyal community to attempt any interference – with a
view to local security – in the air strategy of Lord French and
his staff, 'who know far more about the business than we do'.
The Admiral's faith in the Field Marshal's strategy might,
however, have been somewhat undermined if he had known
about the ban on inland AA guns, the run-down of RFC home
defence squadrons and the lack of co-operation between naval
and military air units in the UK.

Mr Noel Pemberton Billing, on the other hand, bitterly
attacked Lord French in the House for the shortcomings of the
defence forces during the raid. He recalled that, only a month
previously, he had forecast the very type of disaster that had
now occurred. He demanded that the control of air defences be
given to a younger man with appropriate air experience. This
remarkably prescient outburst accurately foreshadowed what
would have to be done some two months – and many casualties
– later. Regrettably, Billing had, not for the first time, to accept
the role of Cassandra: he was quite unjustly dismissed as a
scaremonger or bogeyman.

On the morning of Wednesday 30 May a strong deputation
made up of aldermen and councillors from both Folkestone and
Hythe travelled up to town and called upon Lord French at the
Horse Guards to seek an assurance that adequate protection
would be afforded their respective districts in the future.

Lord French, in reply, stated that, whilst it was not possible
absolutely to prevent attacks by hostile aeroplanes, the existing
carefully planned scheme of defence had been reconsidered in
the light of experience gained in the recent raid. He hoped that,
even if the German aircraft could not be prevented from coming,
new measures being taken would make any future raid a very
risky operation with heavy losses to the enemy. With this
soothing syrup the deputation had to be content.

But how could the FM's statement to the deputation be
reconciled with his restrictions on AA guns and his letter to the
Army Council of 20 March in which he had declared that the
then Home Defence Wing had been reduced to a dangerously
low point? He was well aware that the thinly stretched Home

Defence Group would shortly have to find about 400 pilots and mechanics for two new night-bomber squadrons (Nos. 101 and 102) for service in France. What, then, were these 'new measures' he had mentioned to the deputation? His optimism presumably sprang from a decision of the War Cabinet, which, alarmed at the poor showing of the UK-based defence forces, tasked the CIGS to convene an urgent conference of all air defence authorities in order that recommendations be made to remedy the situation.

The meeting assembled at the War Office during the morning of the following day, Thursday the 31st,

> ... to consider and report upon the question of the defence of the United Kingdom against attack by aircraft, with special reference to:
> 1 The measures necessary to secure effective co-operation between naval and military forces.
> 2 The organisation of communications,
> 3 The distribution of information about hostile aircraft, and
> 4 The allotment of the air forces.[8]

The conference had eight members, five from the Army and three from the Admiralty. Lieutenant-General Sir David Henderson, as usual, took the chair on behalf of the War Office, whilst Major-General Shaw and Lieutenant-Colonel Higgins represented the C.-in-C., Home Forces. Naval interests were in the hands of Rear-Admiral G. Hope (the Director of Operations Division) and, of course, Commodore Paine (Director of Naval Air Services). Curiously enough, the problem of AA artillery did not figure on the agenda – discussions were to be concerned, essentially, with the RFC and RNAS interests. Consequently the technical problems of AA gunnery would not be considered, nor would the wisdom of the AA artillery ban even be mooted.

Sir David, in his opening remarks, maintained that the policy laid down by the War Committee in February 1916 (that the Navy would deal with enemy aircraft flying oversea towards the UK, while the Army undertook to deal with raiders who actually crossed the coastline) had been, in general, adhered to, although subject to some local modification. The Navy's principal task, at that time, was to give warning of the approach of hostile aircraft and to attempt to intercept them on their return journey by means of fighters sent up from the RNAS squadrons at Dunkirk.

The Admiralty came in for some censure because of the fifteen-minute delay, on the 25th, in passing the warning from the Tongue lightship to the GHQ. It was agreed that the higher speed of the raiders meant that the distribution of warnings and tracking information must be speeded up as much as possible. To reduce the dependence upon the civilian crews of lightships, it was arranged that trained aircraft-spotters (some twenty-four army NCOs and men from the Western Front) should be stationed aboard seven lightships in the Thames estuary and east coast areas.

As far as active co-operation between the RFC and RNAS was concerned, the meeting produced few practical benefits. True, the Admiralty undertook 'to instruct the RNAS at Dunkirk to keep a careful watch on the enemy aerodromes at Ghistelles and St-Denis Westrem for any unusual movement of enemy aircraft', and this presumably meant that photo-reconnaissance flights over these two airfields were to be stepped up. For some obscure reason there was no mention, at this meeting, of the airfield at Melle-Gontrode. The Admiralty agreed to look into the possibility of RNAS pilots being instructed in the use of Ingram ground signals, but it is doubtful if this proposal was ever implemented – the RFC pilots themselves disliked the signals because there was too great a delay in setting them out.

Rear-Admiral Hope was anything but co-operative when a suggestion was tabled by Henderson that fighter aircraft should be fitted with wireless equipment so that effective control from the ground could be established. The Navy, fearing that Fleet communications might be jammed, managed to have this remarkably far-sighted idea pigeon-holed for discussion at a separate meeting to be held later.

The existing regular patrols flown by RNAS seaplanes and flying boats over the North Sea were reviewed at the meeting, and it was agreed that, while such aircraft were unsuitable for attacks on Gothas, they provided a useful early warning service.

Lieutenant-Colonel Higgins underlined the seriousness of the run-down of RFC HD squadrons when he declared that, during the 25th, only twenty-two army defence aircraft had been available in the area attacked. This somewhat curious statement presumably referred to the number of aircraft collectively scrambled by Nos. 37 and 50 Squadrons; Nos. 39 and 78 were probably considered outside the area of operations on that day. Higgins, was, however, pleased to be able to announce that agreement had been reached with Brigadier-General J. M. Salmond, the officer commanding the RFC's Training Brigade, to provide *ad hoc* reinforcements to the Southern Home Defence Wing by calling upon available elements of training squadrons to assist in patrolling in the area considered to be subject to attack during the day. This area, the conference decided, was bounded by the coastline from Southwold, Suffolk, to Rottingdean, Sussex, and a line drawn through Bury St Edmunds, Suffolk, and Brentford, Middlesex. The training squadrons in this area that would be activated would include Nos. 35 (Northolt), 40 (Croydon), 56 (London Colney), 62 (Dover) and 63 (Joyce Green). Further support was to be forthcoming from a regular fighter squadron (No. 65) then converting to Sopwith Camels at Wyton, Cambridgeshire. A detachment of this squadron, probably one flight, was to be sent to Wye, Kent, to be summoned as and when required.

In addition to the above reinforcements, the RFC's experimental establishment at Orfordness and the testing one at Martlesham Heath, both in Suffolk, were directed to organize daytime defence squadrons 'for the protection of Essex north of the River Blackwater'. Finally, the RFC aircraft parks at Hendon, Lympne and (eventually) Kenley were to set up defence flights to provide assistance during daylight attacks.

After describing the system of patrolling by the four RFC home defence squadrons in the London approaches, Higgins told the meeting that the total reinforcements from all sources could be about fifty aircraft, but he probably thought that such a figure was rather optimistic.

The augmented allocation of aircraft to the various RFC patrols was, hopefully, to be: forty machines for the patrol around London (No. 39 Squadron's designated area); seventeen for the Goldhanger/Detling run across the Thames estuary (No. 37 Squadron's area); eight for the Chiddlingstone Causeway/-Marden and Hastings/Romney patrols (No. 78 Squadron's area); and sixteen for the Throwley/Bekesbourne and Dover/Sandwich patrols (No. 50 Squadron's area).

Of these allocations, the conference was most concerned

about the seventeen machines for the vital Goldhanger/Detling patrol, a distance of some thirty-five miles. Seventeen were considered to be less than adequate particularly as the aircraft involved would be mostly of the antiquated BE types. Sir David undertook to arrange for some fighting aeroplanes of better climbing ability to be provided as soon as possible.

The conference felt that further reinforcement of the defence aircraft available was not possible without detriment to the requirements of the Western Front, but the new arrangements proposed should mean that the enemy bombers would not 'be able to avoid an engagement with our own fighting machines'. Whether the members of the conference really believed this prime example of wishful thinking, it is, of course, quite impossible to say. Certainly coming events would soon show that the effectiveness of the home defence squadrons would not be greatly improved by extemporizing with makeshift daytime reinforcements from training, experimental and test establishments etc., in numbers that would obviously vary from day to day.

Another important factor would arise if regular night-fighting units, both RFC and RNAS, were to be asked to patrol by day as well. Although Higgins had insisted at the conference that 'the arrangements for dealing with Zeppelins had not been interfered with', the imposition of day patrols would represent an additional and perhaps intolerable burden which, if continued, could lead to a breakdown in operational efficiency.

In the long term, the RFC home defence squadrons would need in-formation training, re-equipment with modern machines and considerable expansion before there could be any guarantee that the Gothas, in daylight, would be unable to avoid an engagement over the UK.

May concluded with a Home Office statement published in the *Daily Express* on the 31st concerning the lack of warning for Folkestone:

> The tragedy of Folkestone will not be repeated anywhere if timely warnings can avert it ... It is certain that hereafter an entirely new and thorough system of notification will be introduced, and we shall lose no time in applying it. The details are not yet fixed, but it will ensure that the whole of the coast towns, and possibly towns as far inland as London, shall be notified as soon as hostile aircraft are sighted over the land.

Certain lights and alarms may be used at night, and other means will be adopted in the daytime. One system strongly favoured is the ringing of all telephones public and private, by an arrangement now under consideration. People with telephones in their houses would be expected to communicate with neighbours not on the telephone.

Previously to the Folkestone raid the inhabitants of towns might have complained of being unnecessarily alarmed if a warning were not succeeded by an attack. They will be less likely to complain now. The warnings will enable them to take cover. Undoubtedly the death-toll at Folkestone must have been much lower if the streets had been empty.

Whilst this statement was, no doubt, a very worthy and well-intentioned effort, its practical effect was virtually nil. The idea of ringing telephones, *en masse,* was dismissed as unworkable and undesirable because it would have produced unacceptable interference with calls of national importance, apart from the dislocation of hospital and fire services etc.

Although the statement declared that warnings would, in future, be given, the actual type of warning device to be used during the day was still in the discussion stage. Folkestone, quite naturally, had little patience with such deliberations and went ahead and installed a siren as a matter of urgency, just as Councillor Forsyth had demanded. Elsewhere, however, little was done and it would need a daylight attack on London itself before the Government was jerked out of its lethargy in this respect.

The general public, however, had already learnt two hard lessons from Tontine Street: there had to be early public warnings of the approach of hostile aircraft, and the open street was certainly no place to be during an air raid.

5

June

Lieutenant-Colonel Higgins quickly followed up the decisions of the air defence conference by writing, on Friday the 1st, to Major-General Brancker, the Deputy Director-General of Military Aeronautics (DDGMA) at the War Office, in an attempt to stem the steady flow of aircrew and mechanics from the Home Defence Group to overseas squadrons. In particular, he pointed out that the proposed formation of the new night-bomber squadrons Nos. 101 and 102, scheduled for July and August respectively, would siphon off about 420 trained men from the already thinly spread personnel available to the twelve home defence squadrons. Higgins went on to show that seventy-seven trained night-flying pilots had been withdrawn from the Home Defence Group since the previous February, leaving only 107 pilots compared with the establishment figure of 198.[1] Whilst, on paper, the figure of 107 was an improvement on that given by the FM on 20 March, it was still only about half the complement needed for both day and night patrolling. The letter urged that the formation of the two new squadrons be postponed, preferably until August for No. 101 and October for No. 102. The breathing-space thus obtained would permit the work of the home defence squadrons to be carried on without interruption, whilst ensuring adequate training for replacement personnel newly posted into the squadrons.

On the very day that Higgins was writing his letter, the RNAS at Dunkirk sent its DH4 bombers on another raid against the aerodrome at St-Denis Westrem. These raids on Gotha airfields, which were to continue throughout June and July, were presumably intended as a support operation for the imminent British offensives in Flanders, and also to comply with the Admiralty's instructions arising from the air defence conference in London.

On the following Monday, the 4th, the weather picture was being dominated by a ridge of high pressure building up over France and England, similar to that which had presaged the first daylight raid eleven days previously. GHQ, Home Forces, should have regarded the latest meteorological development as a possible pointer to a further attack but No. 27 Squadron, RFC, was certainly switched, on that day, from bombing duties on the Western Front, to join No. 5 (Naval) Squadron in another attack on St-Denis Westrem. Nine of No. 27 Squadron's Martinsyde bombers unloaded thirty-nine lightweight bombs on the aerodrome during the morning and succeeded in damaging a hangar.[2] Doubtless this raid was another in the 'softening-up' process prior to the Flanders offensives – General Plumer's attack at Messines was to take place on the 7th – but it also helped to hinder the Gotha operations against England.

The British air attack did not, however, deter Brandenburg one iota: he had already studied the weather forecast provided by Cloessner and was of the opinion that the next day, the 5th, should prove a suitable one for the next attempt on London. The air raid on St-Denis Westrem could, in fact, have made him even more determined to strike back.

Meanwhile, at the Horse Guards in London, Lord French called a special meeting on this Monday morning, attended by Major-General Shaw and Lieutenant-Colonel Higgins, to discuss the run-down of the home defence squadrons, as outlined in the letter to Brancker. Furthermore, Higgins, having by then had time to consult the Training Brigade, probably reported that the reinforcements to be expected were not going to be substantial. The FM, after studying the full implications of the two factors, decided to ask for an immediate interview with the War Minister, Lord Derby, who was able to arrange a meeting at the War Office during the morning of the next day.

One of Lord French's final actions on the 4th was to call for a practice alert for RFC air units of the Southern (Home Defence) Wing. The practice, called an 'aircraft concentration', was timed to begin at 15.00 on the 5th and was designed to test the squadrons' response to day warnings. The FM could not, of course, have appreciated that by arranging his practice session for that particular time he was setting in train a truly remarkable coincidence. How was he to know that Brandenburg was planning a raid for approximately the same time?

In Lord Derby's office suite, on the following morning, the FM tabled a copy of Higgins' letter together with a covering one he himself had written to the Army Council earlier that day. In his letter the C.-in-C. had pointed out that any further reduction of the home defence squadrons would mean that the air defence of the UK would be in a worse position than it was when he wrote to the Army Council on the subject on 20 March. He was rather acid about the help to be expected from the Training Brigade: 'The impracticability of securing adequate aeroplane home defence by relying on such machines and pilots as happen to be at any given time available at Training Squadrons was recognised by the formation of the Home Defence Wing over a year ago. Various demands have been, and are being made for the supply of machines, pilots and other personnel from the home defence squadrons for overseas, and the object with which the Home Defence Wing was originally constituted appears in danger of being lost sight of.'

Lord French ended his letter with a solemn warning that 'Continuance of the present policy may have disastrous results.'[3] Lord Derby was left in no doubt how serious the air defence situation was, and the FM and Higgins departed convinced that some help would be forthcoming. If the C.-in-C. believed that this help would include the postponement of the formation of Nos. 101 and 102 Squadrons, he was going to be disillusioned; the squadrons would, in fact, be formed in July and August just exactly as originally planned. The demands of the Western Front were still paramount; the threat to the homeland was not yet being taken very seriously.

Whilst the FM was actually speaking to the Minister, Kagohl 3 was preparing to underline and give sharp point to the sombre statements being made. *Leutnant* Cloessner, after perusing the latest weather reports, was much happier with the outlook on this occasion than he had been on 25 May. His little meteorological balloon rising in the morning sunshine, as the barometer steadied at 30.15 inches, was able to show that there would be little air movement at the lower altitudes, but a light wind from the south-west could be expected up to 20,000 feet. This was welcome news for the bomber crews – the following wind on the homeward journey would be a great asset. The possibility of local thunderstorms in England could not, however, be ruled out: such occurrences commonly develop in anticyclonic conditions.

Brandenburg was not deterred, however, and he ordered that the Gothas be bombed up and ready for take-off at about 16.00. A refuelling stop at Nieumunster would not now be necessary because every bomber in the squadron had, by this time, been fitted with an additional fuel tank.

Brandenburg had a further task on this occasion: to request an escort of fighters to meet and accompany the bombing force during the last half hour of the return flight to Belgium. The so-called *Seefront Staffel*, stationed at Houtave, near Bruges, was one of the units ordered to deploy its seven fighters on this duty, over and above its normal escort work for seaplanes over the North Sea.

At 15.00 the practice alert was initiated by GHQ, Home Forces, and sent out by Higgins to appropriate squadrons of the Southern (HD) Wing. A motley collection of aircraft, about thirty in all, took off within thirty minutes and proceeded to their designated patrol areas before and around the capital. Their instructions were to continue patrolling for about two hours, after which they could land for tea and refuelling. No one then had any notion that this possibly rather boring rehearsal was soon to be transformed into actual combat.

At a little after 16.00, twenty-one laden Gothas lumbered into the air from the two airfields and began the rather slow climb to 10,000 feet for the coming oversea flight. Thirty minutes later they passed over Blankenbergh, Brandenburg setting a much more northerly track than the one he had followed on 25 May. He intended to keep well out to sea on this occasion in order to avoid being observed by the RNAS at Dunkirk. He was aware that a telephone call on the line that ran from there to Dover would immediately alert the UK defence forces, with probably serious repercussions for the raiders. In fact, he was to be unlucky because the bomber formation was spotted, quite by chance, by a routine patrol of three Pups from No. 4 (Naval) Squadron, Bray Dunes, led by Flight Commander Newberry. This patrol endeavoured to catch up with the Gothas and then proceeded to harass the tail-enders all the way across the North Sea, but regrettably without success. In the area of the Kentish Knock lightship the Pups broke off the engagement and flew to

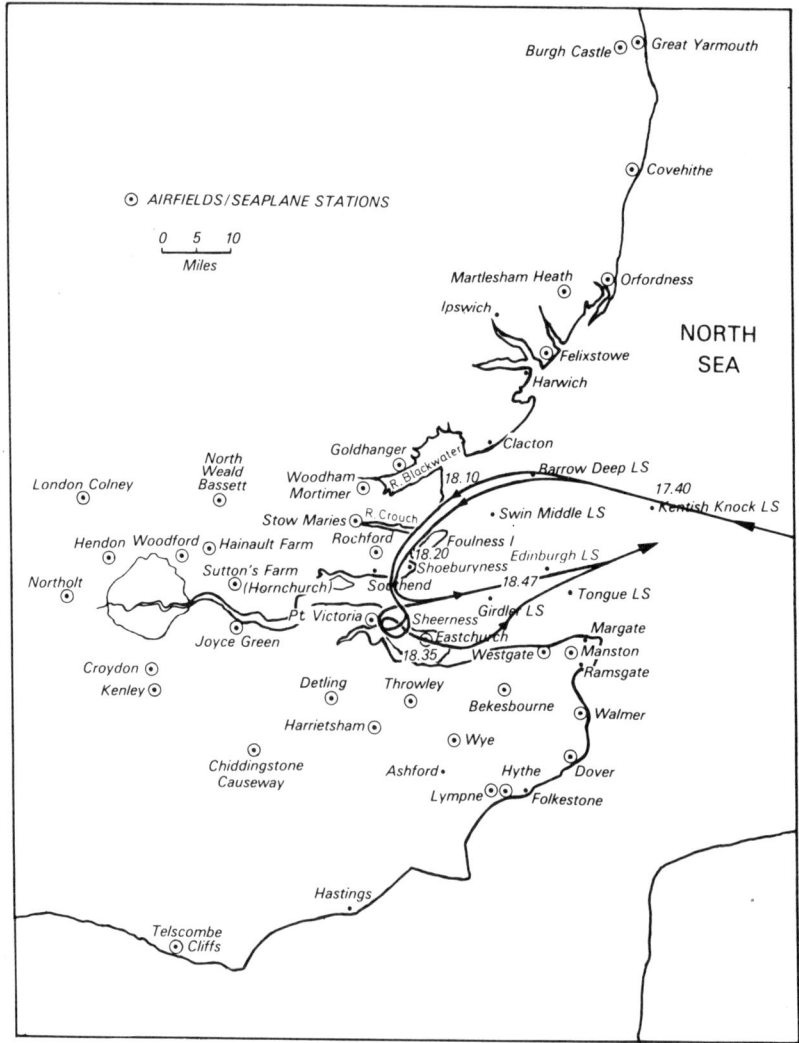

6. Tuesday 5 June

Manston to refuel and re-arm.

At about 17.40, in good visibility, the observers on the lightship watched Kagohl 3 passing quite close, heading for the Essex coast some thirty miles distant (Map 6). A hasty telephone call to the shore soon alerted the Admiralty in London, GHQ being informed a few minutes later – there was no delay on this occasion! An action warning at this time must have come as something of a shock to GHQ – its staff was presumably still collecting data concerning the FM's test. Lieutenant-Colonel Simon, did not delay, however: a real alert was sent out immediately, red to the Essex area and green for London. Higgins, aware that the RFC defence aeroplanes had landed only about thirty minutes before and were still being refuelled, was probably pleased that No. 50 Squadron managed to get its first BEs off from Bekesbourne, Throwley and Detling a few minutes after 18.00 – a creditable turnround. Machines from Nos. 37, 39 and 78 Squadrons soon followed, a total of thirty being sent up from the four home defence units. The reinforcements from the Training Brigade were certainly not numerous: five aircraft took off to assist, three Bristol Fighters from No. 35 (Training) Squadron at Northolt and two Camels from No. 65 Squadron at Wye. Nine aircraft of miscellaneous types arose from the aircraft parks at Hendon and Lympne, and thus the total reinforcement on this day amounted to just fourteen aircraft.

The Admiralty managed to fly off twenty-two assorted machines between 18.05 and 18.20, the usual seaplanes from Grain and Westgate, whilst fighters went up from Dover, Manston, Eastchurch and Walmer.

At 18.15 the raiders crossed the Crouch at about 15,000 feet and began to swing south towards the Thames estuary, possibly intending to fly up river to London. Once again, the pilots of No. 37 Squadron were to be mortified by seeing the Gothas passing almost overhead whilst they themselves were still at low altitude. The story might have been different if the Gothas had arrived in the area about an hour earlier, whilst the BEs were still patrolling.

Kagohl 3, in its usual diamond formation, was now engaged, admittedly at rather long range, by the indefatigable 13th Mobile AA Battery at Highland Farm, Burnham, but only two ineffectual rounds were fired. At 18.20 the Gothas began their attack by dropping two 50kg bombs at Great Wakering and another by the gasworks at North Shoebury. The heaviest weight of missiles in Essex was, however, reserved for the Army's gunnery establishment at Shoeburyness, where twenty-one 50kg and three 12½kg were unloaded. Most of these bombs fell on waste ground or the beach, but three 50kg exploded in the Artillery Gun Park, killing two soldiers. Fire was now opened on the raiders by two 3-inch 20cwt AA guns in the Artillery School, followed a few minutes later by another stationed out on the gun range. The gunfire proved much more accurate and concentrated than that of 25 May (probably because the gunners were more adept with their school height-finders), and the Gotha formation was forced to scatter to present less of a target. Brandenburg, somewhat rattled and mindful of possible thunderstorms in the London area, signalled to his force, by white flares, to abandon the London raid plan and go for the secondary objective of Sheerness, the garrison and dockyard town on the Isle of Sheppey, six miles across the Thames estuary. Two of the Gothas, however, signalled back at this juncture that they were returning to base, either because they had dropped all their bombs on Shoeburyness or, more likely, because they were experiencing the usual engine problems. These two bombers then wheeled away eastwards and flew down the estuary towards the sea, whilst the remaining nineteen Gothas formed up and turned, in brilliant sunshine, towards the distant Medway.

On this occasion there could be no doubt at all as to the direction the bombers were taking, and telephoned warnings were soon made to alert all the Medway towns, now squarely in the raiders' path. Sheerness, by virtue of its military importance, was provided with air-raid alarm sirens, but these would not be sounded until the bombers were in the immediate vicinity.

In Sheerness, at this time, the seafront was crowded with people taking the air on such a beautiful early summer evening. Nurses and children predominated but there were also many convalescent soldiers, some enjoying trips in small boats off the shore.

When the Gothas had approached to within about two miles of Sheerness, the guns at Barton's Point and Whitehouse Farm opened up, with ear-splitting bangs. Although, as at Folkestone, it was at first assumed that the guns were only practising, as was usual at this hour, the howl of the sirens in the town and dockyard caused everyone to stare up into the blue sky. The AA smoke puffs drifting on the wind and the advancing group of white specks were sufficient to send holidaymakers, both service and civilian, scuttling for shelter. Notices were promptly displayed in places of entertainment stating that enemy aircraft were approaching and audiences should make their way home as quickly as possible.

The Barton's Point Gun was to fire some ninety-three rounds in the next few minutes, nearly all the so-called HE AA shells, i.e. the time-fuzed, common explosive types. The shooting was so good that bursts came near to the formation, causing one of the Gothas (No. 660) apparently to detach itself and descend to 9,000 feet, perhaps to swat the offending gun emplacement. Four bombs fell close to the gun, but Gotha 660 shortly afterwards went into a spin and finally crashed into the sea about 3,000 yards from the shore, quite close to the Nore lightship. Although the Barton's Point gun claimed this bomber as a victory, subsequent examination of the recovered wreckage showed that the right-hand engine had stopped because its magneto had failed, but whether this was due to a shell burst is not known.[4] The pilot, *Vizefeldwebel* Kluck, was drowned, but the commander, *Leutnant* Franke, and the rear gunner, *Unteroffizier* Schumacher, were picked up by naval vessels, although Franke was so severely injured that he would die on the following day.

At 18.30 the Gothas began circling over the town, and thirty-two 50kg and thirteen 12½kg bombs fell in the triangle formed by Garrison Point, Barton's Point and Queenborough within the next few minutes. If the bombing of Folkestone had been rather indiscriminate, it was not so on this occasion: the missiles were aimed, in the main, at purely military targets. The Army was assailed at its Well Marsh and Botany Camps, and the coastal gun battery near the Ravelin Bridge was straddled. The dockyard received five 50kg bombs, one falling on the Grand Store which caught fire and burned for three hours afterwards. A dry dock was damaged, and a goods shed at the dockyard railway station was destroyed.

In Sheerness High Street, a 50kg bomb severely damaged the Crown, Anchor and Pier Hotel – its piano landing in the street! Gieves, an outfitter's shop close by, was destroyed by a direct hit, the manager and a Chief Warrant Officer RN, who had just entered the shop, being killed instantly. A few bombs fell upon houses in the area but civilian casualties were very light: three killed and nine injured. The Army/Navy casualties for the raid, on the other hand, reflected the German concentration on military objectives: ten killed and twenty-five injured.

The attack on Sheerness lasted only five minutes, from 18.30 to 18.35, but throughout this time the raiders were being bombarded by the four AA guns at Barton's Point, Whitehouse Farm, Port Victoria and Queenborough. Curiously, the gun at High Halstow fired just one round but the raiders were never within its range.

The Gothas now turned for home, the majority flying straight down the estuary whilst a few others went across Sheppey towards Whitstable. These latter machines were fired on by the Eastchurch AA gun as they passed, and also by the gunboat HMS *Blazer* anchored in the mouth of the Swale.

Up to this point none of the RFC or RNAS defence pilots had even seen the raiders – presumably most of them were still on their beats in the approaches to the metropolis. However, two Pups from RNAS Manston, patrolling off the coast of Sheppey, observed the group of bombers leaving the vicinity of the Isle at about 15,000 feet. One of the Pups managed to climb to 17,000 feet and launched an attack on one of the Gothas but was driven off by fire from other bombers coming to the aid of his opponent.

The only other defence pilot to intercept the raiders was Squadron Commander C. Butler from Manston. Flying a Sopwith Triplane, he spotted six Gothas over the Tongue lightship about 6,000 feet above him. Because his engine was giving trouble, he was unable to rise to the raiders' height until some distance past the Kentish Knock lightship. At that time he attacked one Gotha but it escaped by diving away in the haze. He found another raider ten miles off Ostend and fired 150 rounds at it, but it too fled inland and got away. Now running short of fuel, Butler landed at Bray Dunes at 20.15.

In the meantime, Nos. 4 and 9 (Naval) Squadrons had been alerted from Dover, and a patrol of seven (Pups and Triplanes) from No. 9 and one of three (one Camel and two Pups) from No. 4 were waiting for the bombers to return. Coming out of the sunset, they pounced on the Gothas and their escorting fighters between Nieuport and Ostend. Flight Commander A. Shook, the leader of the trio from No. 4 Squadron, flying the Camel, claimed two fighters destroyed whilst Flight Sub-Lieutenant Enstone, also from No. 4, stated that he had shot down another. The Gothas apparently suffered no loss during this encounter, which was probably the first time a Camel had been used in battle.

Although forty-four RFC and twenty-one RNAS defence aircraft had taken off from bases in south-east England, only five of them (all RNAS) had been able to make any sort of contact with the raiders. Most of the home defence pilots had seen nothing of the bombers at all – because there were no means, apart from the time-wasting Ingram signals, of informing them of the situation quickly enough. Speedy communications with ground observers via a central co-ordinating authority were to prove essential, because the fighter pilot was restricted to visual sightings only – he was not able to track by sound, as the ground observer could, because he was deafened by his engine. The lessons of 25 May had not yet been learnt – without proper directions and support from the ground, the defence aircraft (even the most modern) were quite ineffectual.

On Thursday the 7th, GHQ, Home Forces, sent out, at long last, a verbal cancellation of the ridiculous order of 7 March which had prevented inland AA batteries from firing during the two daylight raids. Lieutenant-Colonel Simon was now able to restore his AA command to full fighting strength and indeed was permitted to issue his original plans, drafted in March, which modified the original night-time techniques, with searchlights, to include daytime procedures against aeroplanes.[5]

On Saturday the 9th, the RNAS bombers from Dunkirk paid another visit to the Gotha airfield at St-Denis Westrem, following up General Plumer's victory at Messines in the Ypres salient. GHQ, Home Forces, during the day, held another practice alert or 'aircraft concentration' to test the reaction time and readiness of home defence squadrons. On this occasion thirty-two machines were up twenty minutes after the warning sounded, a decided improvement on the earlier practice session.

On Tuesday 12 June, the German weather bureaux were unanimous in predicting exceptionally favourable flying conditions for the next day, with little air movement in the Channel/North Sea area. The barometer was rising above the thirty-inch mark as the result of two large anticyclones becoming established over south-east England and northern France. *Leutnant* Cloessner, after tests with his met. balloon, confirmed the prognosis and, furthermore, was able to forecast light winds over the sea, easterly up to 14,000 feet and westerly above that altitude, i.e. just right for the Gothas' outward and return flights. The met. officer did, however, sound a note of warning: thunderstorms, with hail, were a strong possibility after 15.00.

After close study of all the available weather reports, Brandenburg took the decision to launch an attack on London on the 13th but arranged the take-off time to be much earlier on this occasion, at 09.00, for two very good reasons: one, the British capital would be assaulted at about midday, thus giving maximum terroristic effect; and, two, the bombers should be back home in Belgium before any thunderstorms could break.

Secondary and diversionary targets were selected, the list including Shoeburyness, once again, and Margate. In addition, one Gotha was detailed off to perform a purely photoreconnaissance mission over the Medway and Thames estuary. As before, Brandenburg requested that fighter cover should be provided, for the last part of the return flight, by naval landplanes and seaplanes from bases along the Belgian coast. Motor torpedo-boats had also to be alerted to await any possible distress calls concerning bombers descending into the sea.

At about 09.00, in bright sunshine, twenty-two Gothas began taking off from St-Denis Westrem and Melle-Gontrode, setting a north-westerly course once over the coastline. Soon they had taken up station in their normal grouping, but not for very long; two bombers began signalling that they were suffering from the inevitable engine troubles and must perforce return. The remaining twenty raiders closed up the formation and flew on over a sea sparkling and calm on this perfect summer morning, a complete contrast to the sombre nature of the Gothas' intent.

At 10.30 the Gothas were ten miles north of the North Foreland, and a prearranged signal flare then arced up from the leading machine. Obediently, a single bomber detached itself (Map 7) and banked away on a southerly course for the Isle of Thanet, in order to make a diversionary attack on Margate – a ploy that was to be used on three subsequent day raids to decoy away some of the home fighter aircraft, particularly those from RNAS

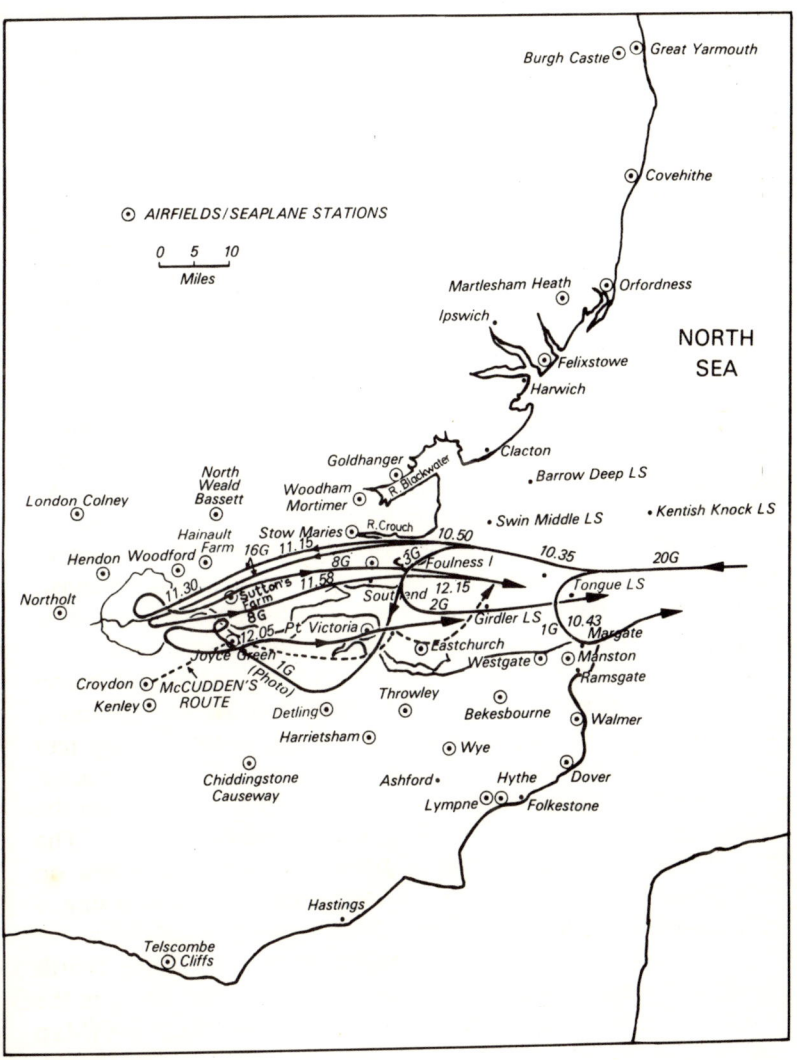

7. Wednesday 13 June

Manston. Some fifteen minutes later then, this Gotha appeared, without warning, at about 14,000 feet over Margate Station, anxious to create as much disturbance as possible by drawing the fire of the AA guns. The German airmen were not disappointed; the 12pdr 12cwt guns at Hengrove and St Peter's immediately opened up at the raider, firing off some twenty-four HE rounds in the few minutes that the bomber was over the town. Four 50kg bombs were dropped, aimed, it would seem, at the town's railway facilities, but little damage resulted, apart from broken windows in approximately 120 houses and shops. Four people were slightly injured in the raid.

Whilst GHQ was being informed, by telephone, that Margate was under attack, another message was being received from the Edinburgh lightship, via the Admiralty, that nineteen Gothas had passed in a north-westerly direction towards Foulness Island. Quite obviously GHQ would then have discounted the Margate attack as a feint – and a rather feeble one at that. However, the naval observers on the spot at Manston and Westgate, seeing at least one raider bombing Margate and hearing the guns in action, took the bait. Without further ado, defence aircraft were scrambled from both naval bases – nine fighters from Manston and four seaplanes (probably Sopwith Baby types) from Westgate. None of these machines was to return until some three hours later, having been successfully lured away from the routes to be taken by the main Gotha force. It is quite possible that the day's events could have been significantly different had the Manston aircraft patrolled the Thames estuary instead of chasing a speedy lone raider across the North Sea.

On the other hand, the principal reason for the deployment of naval fighter aircraft in the UK was to defend naval shore establishments – and this the Manston and Westgate machines had done, albeit without much consideration of the possible effects on GHQ's overall defensive strategy.

Once again, the usual red and green warnings went out from GHQ to the listed authorities in Essex and London. The AADC had more to do on this occasion: he was at last able to bring his entire AA artillery force to a state of readiness.

At 10.50, or thereabouts, observers at the mouth of the Crouch heard the roar of many aero-engines as the nineteen Gothas approached, and then watched them appearing out of the somewhat hazy conditions. At this juncture Brandenburg fired off another flare, the executive signal for three more bombers to leave the formation – two to carry out a further feint attack, this time on Shoeburyness, whilst the third was to reconnoitre and photograph military and naval establishments south of the Thames, as far west as possible. This Gotha apparently carried no bombs at all – speed and height would be vital when operating far from the protection of the rest of the *Geschwader*. Accordingly, the three machines now peeled off to port and flew across Foulness in a south-westerly direction, one dropping an ineffectual 50kg bomb on Barling as they passed. Just before Shoeburyness, however, the crew of the photo-reconnaissance machine waved farewell to their commrades and flew south across the Thames estuary towards the Medway, following the route taken on 5 June. Over Shoeburyness, at 11.00, the other two bombers were assailed by one of the 3-inch 20cwt AA guns in the Army barracks. Despite the haze this gun managed to fire off thirty-eight HE rounds during the very short time the two raiders were within range, but no hits were scored on this occasion. Five 50kg bombs fell near the village of Shoeburyness, slightly injuring two civilians although little structural damage was reported. The two Gothas thereafter disappeared into the mist and flew eastwards towards the North Sea – and home.

There seems little doubt that the Shoeburyness diversion failed, unlike the Margate one, in decoying defence aircraft away from the Thames estuary. Indeed, it may have had the opposite effect to that intended by Brandenburg; it could have resulted in a higher concentration of fighters along the very route the full Gotha squadron would be using on its return from London in about an hour's time.

The three RFC home defence squadrons Nos. 37, 39 and 50 scrambled a total of thirty-five aircraft, the first of which were airborne at 11.00, a better response time than hitherto. At least two BE12s from No. 39 Squadron had, in fact, been in the air since about 10.30, engaged on practice firing, but were alerted to the presence of hostile aircraft by means of Ingram signals laid out at Sutton's Farm.

Another twenty-one reinforcing aeroplanes went up, at various times thereafter, from RFC establishments and training squadrons at Croydon, Dover, Hendon, Lympne, Northolt,

Orfordness and Wye. No. 78 Squadron, for some obscure reason, was to send up a BE at 12.12 – about the time the All Clear was issued! A few of the RFC aircraft in use on this occasion were first-class fighting machines: a handful of newly received Sopwith 1½-Strutters from No. 37 Squadron, two Camels from No. 65 Squadron, Wye, two Bristol Fighters (piloted by Captain C. Cole-Hamilton and Second Lieutenant J. Chapman) from No. 35 (Training) Squadron, Northolt, and two Pups from No. 40 (Training) Squadron, Croydon, one of which was piloted by the veteran air fighter Captain James B. McCudden (later Major, VC), at that time an air fighting instructor with No. 63 (Training) Squadron at Joyce Green, near Dartford.

The home-based RNAS, apart from Manston and Westgate, put up a further twenty-three machines, of which thirteen were land-based fighters whilst the remainder were seaplanes, the latter mainly from Felixstowe.

At about 11.05 Kagohl 3 was visible, in whole or in part, to the personnel of No. 37 Squadron at Stow Maries and Rochford. Indeed, Second Lieutenant J. Young stated later that he saw at least six Gothas over the aerodrome at Rochford (presumably the left wing of the German squadron) before he took off as pilot of a 1½-Strutter. The aircrew of this squadron, climbing up to their patrol area across the Thames estuary, were probably not very hopeful of intercepting the raiders, after what had happened on 25 May and 5 June, but in fact they were to be luckier on this day: some of the bombers would be returning along almost the same route as their in-going one.

The Gothas, in their now familiar configuration of two flights abreast led by the three headquarters machines, then turned south-west and flew directly across Essex towards the capital, their height being about 14,000 feet. The right wing passed over Brentwood at about 11.23, the left wing then in the vicinity of Upminster. As the formation approached the Greater London area, the 3-inch 20cwt AA guns at Romford, Rainham, Abbey Wood and Shooter's Hill began barking away as their respective districts were traversed. The visibility in the environs of London was, however, now rather poor – a patchy layer of cloud had formed at about 5,000 feet in addition to the general haziness. Such conditions were ideal for the raiders on their approach, but observation from the ground was made extremely difficult. The gun crews at Chadwell Heath and Ockendon reported the noise of the bombers' engines almost overhead but no useful sightings could be made.

Bombing was begun by the left wing at Barking at about 11.30, when a 50kg type fell on North Street, followed shortly after by a stick of seven bombs on East Ham, killing four people and injuring another thirteen. This group of bombers then succeeded in striking a military target: two 50kg bombs crashed down on the Royal Albert Docks at Silvertown. Railway facilities including rolling-stock were damaged in this incident whilst eight dockers were killed and nine others wounded.

These attacks were, however, in the nature of an opening skirmish; in pursuance of their main objectives, Brandenburg now brought the two wings of the formation closer together and steered towards the glass roof of Liverpool Street station, sparkling like a beacon in the fitful sunshine. The Blackwall AA gun came into action against the left wing at this time but was unable to fire more than a few rounds because of a breech jam.

Captain Cole-Hamilton and Second Lieutenant Chapman, hurrying eastwards in their Bristol Fighters from Northolt at about 11.40, witnessed the distant Gothas wheeling over the City of London. In response to a flare fired by Brandenburg, the bombers, now assailed by the Tower gun, released seventy-two bombs within a radius of one mile of Liverpool Street station, a quite indiscriminate attack on mainly residential districts ranging from Clerkenwell in the west to Whitechapel in the east, and from Hoxton in the north to the Thames in the south. The worst-hit area was, in fact, Hoxton, which received twenty-seven bombs, closely followed by the City of London with seventeen, and Shoreditch with ten.

In the City, three of the bombs landed squarely on Liverpool Street station itself, wrecking two trains, one of which caught fire. Sixteen men died, including three trapped in the blazing coaches, whilst another fifteen were injured, many by flying glass. Although no bombs fell anywhere near the Bank of England in Threadneedle Street, a declared target for the raiders, the business quarter of Fenchurch Street/Aldgate was not so fortunate. 65 Fenchurch Street, for instance, a four-storey building, was almost completely demolished by two 50kg bombs – twenty people died here and fourteen were wounded. In

Aldgate High Street a bomb burst on the pavement, killing thirteen and injuring twenty-two people caught out on the street. Another serious incident occurred when a 50kg bomb descended on a foundry in Beech Court; eight workers lost their lives here and ten others were injured.

In Shoreditch, a factory in Charlotte Street was set on fire and completely destroyed. Oddly enough, a bomb also damaged the nearby fire station in Tabernacle Square, but whether this prevented the appliances' getting to the fire in Charlotte Street is not recorded! Children in the Cowper Street Foundation School, City Road, were extremely fortunate; a 50kg bomb passed through the roof and five floors, and then buried itself in the basement without exploding.

After the concentrated attack in and around the City of London, the Gotha formation appears to have divided; half the bombers circling in a north-easterly direction whilst the other half turned south-east and crossed the Thames near Blackfriars Bridge, the AA gun at the Tower continuing its bombardment of this latter group. Regrettably, however, as Captain Cole-Hamilton was to report later, the AA shells from this and other guns burst far below the bombers, either because of poor setting or from erratic time fuzes.

The northerly group of Gothas released three bombs over Dalston and then, turning south-east, proceeded to bomb Stepney, Limehouse and Poplar, broadly along the line of the Commercial and East India Dock Roads. Subsequently they swung north-east again and ended their attacks by further bombs in the neighbourhood of Bow and Stratford.

It was in Poplar, which received five 50kg bombs, that the most horrifying incident of the daylight raids occurred, an event which, more than any other, would serve to strengthen British resolve to prosecute the war – a reaction that was never envisaged in the Ludendorf directive. One of the 50kg bombs struck the roof of the Upper North Street Schools, passed through three floors and then burst in a room on the ground floor. In this room were gathered sixty-four children, of whom eighteen were killed outright whilst terrible injuries were inflicted on thirty others. Four adults were also hurt in this appalling disaster, the ramifications of which were to have a material effect on the Government's air defence policy.

Meanwhile, the Gotha half-squadron, south of the Thames,

delivered its last six bombs on Southwark and Bermondsey and then, continuing its easterly progress, probably recrossed the Thames near Erith. In Southwark, a 50kg bomb landed on the British & Bennington Tea Company's store and strong-room in Sumner Street, killing three girls and injuring twenty-four other persons. In Staple Street, Bermondsey, a 12½kg bomb fell on Pink's jam factory where three men working on the roof were killed.

The transpontine flight of bombers was engaged by AA guns at Abbey Wood, Beckton, Shooter's Hill, Grove Park and Dulwich, the latter admittedly at extreme range. East of Woolwich the two groups of Gothas drew together again but their formation was now much more open than previously, probably to present less of a target to the AA guns. Some southerly machines flew along the Essex bank of the Thames whilst the northerly ones returned back along almost the original track to the city. AA guns at Rainham, Romford, Chadwell Heath, Ockendon and Tilbury opened up as scattered groups of bombers droned over on their way to the east coast.

The photo-reconnaissance Gotha had flown, at about 13,000 feet, from the Medway as far south as Maidstone, but thereabouts it was attacked, probably at fairly long range, by at least three RFC defence aircraft. These included Captain T. Grant* in a BE12 from No. 39 Squadron (one of the pilots who had been aloft prior to the warning being given) and Captain Lloyd in a BE2d from No. 198 (Depot) Squadron at Rochford. This Gotha did not seem much perturbed by these attacks; it made a fairly leisurely circle over Erith while taking photographs and then rapidly outdistanced its pursuers, disappearing into cloud cover over Greenwich.

The two Bristol Fighters from No. 35 (Training) Squadron at Northolt, probably in company with Captain S. Stammers, in a BE12 from No. 39 Squadron (the other pilot up before the warning), caught up with three of the bombers 'straggling' over Ilford. All three RFC machines attacked the Gothas, one of whom was seen to be flying one wing down, but in the action Captain C. Keevil, Captain Cole-Hamilton's observer, was shot

---

* He was actually a Norwegian, Tryggve Gran, who subsequently wrote a book about his experiences with the RFC/RAF, entitled *Under British Flag, Krigen 1914–1918*.

dead, and the Bristol's front gun jammed. Captain Cole-Hamilton dived away, whilst the other two RFC machines, plagued with engine troubles, were also forced to break off the engagement shortly afterwards.

The Gothas flew on without opposition until, at about 12.00, they were approaching the Southend area, where they were fired upon by the 12pdr 12cwt guns stationed at Bowers Gifford and Hawkesbury Bush, and the five 3-inch 20cwt and two 13pdr 9cwt mobile ones attached to the Shoeburyness barracks and ranges. The bombers were now crossing the area patrolled by No. 37 Squadron, and various combats took place. Captain C. Cooke, Lieutenant G. Keddie and Second Lieutenant J. Young, all piloting 1½-Strutters, Captain W. Sowrey in an RE7, together with Captain Grant from No 39 Squadron, in his BE12, who had hurried thence after his earlier encounter near Maidstone, bravely launched determined but unco-ordinated assaults on the Gothas, hits being reported by both Captain Cooke and Second Lieutenant Young. However, no bomber was brought down, and the defenders were soon outdistanced or evaded in the cloud cover by the now much lighter German aircraft. Captain Grant had good reason to complain: his machine was hit by wild AA fire from Shoeburyness, and he was forced to land at Rochford. Such embarrassing encounters would point the way, eventually, to the necessity for separate zones for aircraft and artillery.

An RNAS pilot from Grain (Flight Lieutenant Fox) flying a Pup, attacked a Gotha at 14,000 feet over Southend, his tracer entering its fuselage. Unfortunately, his gun then jammed and he had to pull out of the fight about ten miles off the North Foreland.

Captain James McCudden managed to catch up with the German formation somewhere near the Girdler lightship (Map 7). He fired off three drums of ammunition from his wing-mounted Lewis gun and registered hits, but having no more ammunition he was forced to return to Joyce Green. His extremely graphic account of his part in the day's action is given in his book *Five Years in the Royal Flying Corps*, and as few such contemporary reports exist, no apology is offered, for repeating it here, in full.

During June I carried out a lot of instructional work on various types of machines, and on the morning of the 13th I left Joyce Green in my Pup, to fly to Croydon* to give a lecture. I arrived at Croydon after fifteen minutes flying and taxied up to the sheds, and noticed that everyone seemed rather excited. I got out of my machine just as the CO came and told me that a hostile formation of aeroplanes had crossed the coast and were making for London. I was much annoyed, for my Lewis gun and ammunition were at Joyce Green, and to get them meant wasting valuable time.

However, I got off the ground again and made an average of 105 m.p.h. from Croydon to Joyce Green. In fifteen minutes' time I landed there, and while taxying in I noticed that some German prisoners who were employed on the aerodrome seemed to be very pleased with life, and were all looking aloft. I got out of my Pup, yelled to my mechanics to bring my gun and ammunition and, while we were putting the gun on, I could plainly hear the roar of the many engines of the Hun formation which had just passed over. Towards Woolwich I could hear the occasional bang of an English Archie, but I could not see the Huns at all as there was an irregular layer of woolly clouds at about 5,000 feet which blocked one's view. The overlap of the exhausts of the many powerful engines sounded very formidable and, judging by the noise, I was certain that there were well over a dozen machines.

In a minute my machine was ready, and I took off in an easterly direction, towards the south of the Thames. At 5,000 feet I climbed into the woolly clouds, and not until I had reached 10,000 feet did I see the ground again through the small gaps between the clouds. It was an ideal day for a bombing formation to get to their objective unobserved. When I again was able to note my position I found myself over Chatham. I still flew east and arrived over Sheerness at 13,000 feet.

My mind was now divided as to exactly which way the Huns would return, and I conjectured that they would fly SE from Chatham over Kent, so I still climbed, and when I had got to 15,000 feet over Sheppey, I caught the flash of a gun from Southend,† and looking upwards saw a characteristic black and white British Archie bursting over Shoeburyness at about my own height. I increased my speed at once and flew in a direction east of the Archie and, after a few minutes, could distinguish a lot of

* No. 40 (Training) Squadron.
† Probably the Bowers Gifford gun.

machines in good formation going towards the south-east.

I caught up to them at the expense of some height, and by the time I had got under the rear machine I was 1,000 feet below. I now found that there were over twenty* machines, all with two 'pusher' engines.

To my dismay I found that I could not lessen the range to any appreciable extent. By the time I had got to 500 feet under the rear machine we were twenty miles east of the Essex coast, and visions of a very long swim entered my mind, so I decided to fire all my ammunition and then depart.

I fired my first drum, of which the Hun did not take the slightest notice. I now perceived another Sopwith Pup just behind this rear Hun at quite close range, but after a while he turned away as though he was experiencing some trouble with his gun.

How insolent these damned Boches did look, absolutely lording the sky above England! I replaced my first drum with another and had another try, after which the Huns swerved ever so slightly, and then that welcome sound of machine-guns smote my ears and I caught the smell of the Hun's incendiary bullets as they passed me. I now put on my third and last single Lewis drum (each drum held forty-seven shots) and fired again and, to my intense chagrin, the last Hun did not take the slightest notice.

I now turned west and the coast of Kent looked only a blur, for although I was over 14,000 feet, the visibility was very poor. On my way back to Joyce Green, I was absolutely furious to think that the Huns should come over and bomb London and have it practically all their own way. I simply hated the Hun more than ever. I landed at Joyce Green after having been in the air for two hours, and I was dispirited, cold and bad-tempered, but after I had had lunch and a glass of port, I thought that life wasn't so bad.[6]

As Brandenburg led the squadron out over the North Sea on the homeward run, he was, without doubt, highly delighted that his airmen had at last succeeded in bombing the imperial capital, just as Ludendorf had demanded. Furthermore, not a single Gotha had fallen to the defences, but this merely underlined how ineffectual the ill-directed fighters and AA guns had been. The bombers had cruised overland for about ninety minutes, and in

---

* Sixteen bombers at this time, but the presence of other British aircraft would have made counting difficult.

that time they had dropped some four tons of bombs (probably seventy-six 50kg and fifty-two 12½kg), the majority of which had fallen on London itself. The resulting casualty figures were, for the period, savagely impressive: 162 people killed and 432 injured, making this easily the worst air raid on Britain of the entire Great War. As had already been sombrely demonstrated in Folkestone, such heavy casualties could have been dramatically reduced if some form of public warning system had been in operation to enable people on the streets to take cover.

Approaching the Dunkirk area, the bomber crews kept a sharp look-out for the expected RNAS fighters, but in fact the deteriorating visibility, prior to the forecasted thunderstorms, was to be the best protection the Gothas could have. No. 4 (Naval) Wing had been alerted by telephone as soon as the raiders passed over the Essex coast on their return journey, and a flight was scrambled by No. 4 Squadron consisting of six Camels and one Pup, led, as before, by Flight Commander Shook, with Flight Sub-Lieutenant Enstone and five other pilot officers in support. Although they searched diligently, they were unable to locate either the returning bombers or their fighter escorts because of the worsening weather conditions over the Channel. No. 9 Squadron also sent up a patrol, again of seven Pups and Triplanes, but this flight had no better luck: it flew right across to the Thames estuary and back without success.

In the face of the gathering storm clouds, all sixteen Gothas landed at their bases at about 14.00, without mishap. They were extremely lucky not to have been delayed by aerial attack or winds, because the storm broke half an hour after touchdown, when heavy rain with 'hailstones as large as pigeons' eggs'[7] descended. Kagohl 3, whilst toasting the successful conclusion of the mission, had every reason to be grateful to *Leutnant* Cloessner; many of the Gothas would have come to grief if they had still been flying when such a tempest occurred.

In London, throughout that warm, sultry afternoon, the fire, ambulance and other services toiled on amid scenes that were a microcosm of the Blitz to be visited on the city a quarter of a century later. A widespread reaction was already building up among Londoners outraged at the spectacle of sixteen German bombers calmly and unhurriedly unloading their bombs, without warning, on the metropolis, with apparently little opposition from the RFC/RNAS defenders. Few people in London could have appreciated the dilemma then facing the RFC home defence squadrons, equipped as they were with a predominance of antiquated machines. How could the defence aircraft possibly prevent the Gothas arriving over London from the east coast if they themselves were still engaged in climbing to the raiders' altitude? Ninety-four home-based defence aeroplanes (fifty-seven RFC and thirty-seven RNAS) had been sent up – fifty more than on 5 June – but only about a quarter of these could have been regarded as first-class fighters having the required rate of climb and speed. The remainder were of little real value; they were no match for the raiders in any respect. However, some steps were being taken towards re-equipping the home defence squadrons, as forecast by Lieutenant-General Henderson on 31 May. Captain Grant, after his enforced descent at Rochford, was delighted to be ordered by Lieutenant-Colonel Higgins, during the same afternoon, to proceed immediately to the Royal Aircraft Factory, at Farnborough, in order to oversee the erection of six SE5 fighters for No. 39 Squadron.

Brandenburg had, by his astute diversionary feint at Margate, achieved a tactical advantage in decoying fifteen of the RNAS aircraft (including some modern fighters) away from his main bomber force, thereby reducing the effective air defensive strength to seventy-nine.

Because of the time needed for defence aircraft to rise to the bombers' height, all attacks by the defenders had had to take place on the return flight from London, when, perversely, the bombers, lightened of their loads, were capable of a much better performance than on the inward journey. As has been seen, only twelve defence machines were able to open fire on the bombers, but these attacks were piecemeal affairs and thus largely ineffectual against the Gothas' superior fire power. Even pilots from the same squadron (No. 37, for instance) were unable to co-operate in launching simultaneous attacks. This was not really surprising: they were essentially individualistic in their approach, as one would expect night-fighters to be. They had had, as yet, little or no training in multiple attacks by day with in-air direction from a single leader. The very size of the bombers was also an important factor: few of the pilots had seen such large aeroplanes before, and thus it was very easy to misjudge the range or fail to hit vulnerable points. In addition, pilots attacking from below were disconcerted or beaten off by machine-gun fire directed downwards through the Gothas' ventral gun tunnels. Another serious problem was the distressing frequency of gun jams caused by faulty ammunition. It is probable that many attacks by defence pilots would have been successful but for these infuriating stoppages.

The remaining sixty-seven RFC and RNAS machines, lacking any effective direction from the ground, either patrolled areas far removed from the Gothas' route or were little better than spectators of the actions high above them. Ashmore had this to say later: 'It is essential to give information from the ground, where observation is easier and aircraft can be seen at far greater distances. And, to render this information timely and effective, a great system of ground observation, communication and control is required.'[8]

The artillery, too, had achieved precious little during the raid. No Gotha had been brought down by AA shell-fire, although eleven gun stations in London and nine outside (the latter mostly at Shoeburyness) had been in action, some guns firing on both the inward and outward runs. The London ordnance discharged 174 rounds, Shoeburyness 140 and the rest forty-six, but the firing was desultory and badly directed. Whilst the intermittent gun-fire probably forced the Gothas to spread out somewhat, it was not intense enough to break up the formations and thus improve the interception chances of the RFC. In mitigation, it must be stated that the hazy conditions and poor height-finding techniques contributed to inaccuracies in ranging, as remarked by Captain Cole-Hamilton.

There could be little excuse, however, for the bombardment of friendly aircraft by AA guns, culminating in the virtual shooting down of Captain Grant over Shoeburyness. Such mistakes were to be a common feature of subsequent day raids until the establishment of separate zones for AA guns and aircraft, and adequate recognition training was given to gun crews.

Sadly, the 75mm AA gun-fire was responsible for the deaths of two people and the injuring of eighteen others by falling shrapnel shell cases, just as Lieutenant-Colonel Rawlinson had predicted would happen unless the fragmentation of the shell cases was improved.

All in all, then, the day had not gone well for the defenders, either at home or abroad. Whilst the German aviators had had remarkably good fortune, and the British forces had been

dogged with ill luck, there could be little doubt in anyone's mind
that there was something seriously amiss with the air defences of
London.

The War Cabinet met at 10 Downing Street later that same
afternoon in order to study reports of the raid and, presumably,
to enquire how it was that the large Home Forces Command
had been able to defeat the Zeppelins but could not now,
apparently, deter the Gothas from attacking the metropolis,
even with Admiralty assistance. No policy decisions were
reached at this meeting, and the War Cabinet adjourned until
the following morning.

The morning newspapers carried wide coverage of the raid,
with choleric references to the length of the casualty list, the lack
of public warnings and the apparent ineptitude of the defence
organizations headed by FM Viscount French. In Parliament
Pemberton Billing lost no time in adopting an 'I told you so'
stance, to the discomfiture of all those MPs who had howled him
down after the Folkestone raid. With commendable tenacity he
moved a resolution asking for an immediate extraordinary
debate on the state of the air defences of the United Kingdom.
The Speaker, however, refused to allow the normal business of
the House to be interrupted, and consequently turned down the
request. Mr Billing was on his feet in an instant to protest
against the decision amidst a growing uproar. When he ignored
the Speaker's call to order, he was deemed guilty of disrespect to
the Chair and was escorted from the Chamber by the
Serjeant-at-Arms. It is hard not to feel sympathetic towards
Billing – he was obviously quite right in his concern for the
people of London. Had he used the appropriate machinery for
initiating a debate, it is possible that positive remedial action by
the Government might have been taken earlier. He was not
alone in his concern, however, and anxious questions were also
levelled at the War Minister, Lord Derby, in the Lords. His
evasive reply that 'Lord French was doing all in his power to
secure the city' could have reassured no one – certainly not
Pemberton Billing and his friends!

The War Cabinet met again during that morning,[9] five
permanent members being in attendance: Lloyd George, Lord
Curzon, Lord Milner, Mr Bonar Law (Chancellor) and
Lieutenant-General Jan Smuts. Somewhat paradoxically
perhaps, the former Boer general had been asked by Lloyd

George to join the War Cabinet after attending, during April and May, the sessions of the Imperial War Cabinet as the representative of the South African Government. In addition to the permanent members of the War Cabinet, the following were also called upon: Sir Edward Carson (First Lord of the Admiralty), the CIGS, Lord Derby and Admiral Sir J. Jellicoe (First Sea Lord). The assemblage listened in stony silence to an up-to-date report on the raid, which significantly concluded with the observation that, 'Out of all the casualties caused by the raid, there was not the name of a single soldier.' With this inaccurate statement the scene was set for a renewed international *exposé* of Germany, for propaganda purposes, as a nation of vandals 'waging war against defenceless women and children'. Among the military authorities, however, the mood was quite different, as Cecil Lewis was to recall later: 'Actually that raid was a very stout effort. And nobody in his right mind would deny that the Germans were perfectly right to bomb the capital of the British Empire. Their objectives were Woolwich, Whitehall, the Houses of Parliament – the very nerve-centres of the whole organism. The Allies would have bombed Berlin without hesitation if they had happened to have machines good enough to get there. But they hadn't.'[10]

The War Cabinet, nevertheless, opted to discuss with FM Sir Douglas Haig the question of possible reprisal raids against German cities nearer than Berlin, Mannheim being mentioned as a strong possibility. As it happened, the Commander-in-Chief was due to come to London on 17 June for discussions on the forthcoming offensive in Flanders, and it was decided to add the matter of air raids on UK to the agenda. It was further agreed that Major-General Trenchard, the General Officer Commanding RFC in France, should be invited to accompany the FM to London, to give the RFC's opinion on the most effective steps to take and, in particular, whether fighter squadrons should be withdrawn from the front 'to give an exceptionally hot reception to the raiders on the occasion of their visits'.

During the debate on the shortcomings of the existing defence forces, the CIGS came to the rescue of the poorly equipped air defence squadrons by pointing out that, 'The time occupied by the enemy aeroplanes in flying from the coast to London is less than the time taken by British machines in ascending to the great heights necessary to engage them.'

General Robertson then went on to table a most far-reaching proposal when he affirmed that British air policy was not extensive enough. In his opinion the number of aeroplanes should be increased on a large scale, even at the expense of other weapons of war, the revolutionary land tank not excepted. Practically everyone at the meeting seems to have been taken aback by this, but it was enthusiastically welcomed by the Army members, although probably the Admiralty representatives had reservations about it. The War Cabinet agreed to the proposal, in principle, and decided that, 'The Air Board, in consultation with the Ministry of Munitions, the War Office, and any other Departments concerned, should be invited to draw up a scheme for the development of aircraft, stating at whose expense the development must take place.'

No decision was yet taken concerning the provision of public warnings of air raids, and it was left to the Home Secretary to sound out the opinion of the Lord Mayor and the mayors of all the London boroughs. A conference for this purpose was arranged for 21 June, but the Lord Mayor, aghast at the casualties occasioned by the lack of public warning and out of patience with the proposed long-winded procedure, announced that he had asked the Dean and Chapter of St Paul's to toll the great bell (Great Paul) of the cathedral immediately intimation was received that hostile aircraft were approaching the city. In the event, the cathedral authorities refused to do this, because they felt that the bell would be audible only to people in the immediate vicinity of St Paul's itself.

GHQ, Home Forces, although not involved in the argument for or against public warnings, announced that the issuing of successive warning to authorities across the countryside (the Zeppelin tracking system) had proved almost unworkable when dealing with the faster Gothas[11] – as the events of 25 May had demonstrated all too clearly.

In Germany, meanwhile, Kaiser Wilhelm II was immensely pleased with the results of the air operation against London, and commanded that *Hauptmann* Brandenburg be presented to him at the Supreme Headquarters at Kreuznach near Mainz in southern Germany. Not all Germans shared the opinion of the All Highest, however: the newspaper *Volkswacht* of Breslau openly deplored the death and destruction meted out to London. For this heretical outburst the newspaper was promptly suppressed.

The BE12 – the Home Defence
Squadrons' principal night-
fighting aircraft, 1916–17

A Kagohl 3 aviator inflating his
life-jacket before take-off

A Gotha in flight over the Belgian countryside

Gothas being prepared for a raid on England

Feldmarschall Hindenburg inspecting the 'pulpit' of a Gotha G.IV during the final parade at Melle-Gontrode in May. A 50-kg bomb is visible beneath the nose of the aircraft

Gothas before the huge Zeppelin hangar at Melle-Gontrode

(*Left*) London's Central Telegraph Office in St Martin's-le-Grand on fire on 7 July. (*Right*) Firefighting in Little Britain, London, 7 July

The top floor of the Central Telegraph Office after the raid of 7 July

A house in Gloucester Road, Southend, shattered by a 50-kg bomb on 12 August

Pitted walls and boarded-up windows of the Ordnance Hotel, Felixstowe, after the raid of 22 July

A typical mobile twin 13-pdr 9-cwt AA battery in action

Hauptmann Brandenburg in office at Melle-Gontrode

Leutnant Georgii (centre) about to release a meteorological balloon from the roof of the University of Ghent. His adverse forecasts were sometimes ignored by *Hauptmann* Kleine

(Left) Field Marshal Lord French, Commander-in-Chief, Home Forces. *(Right) Hauptmann* Kleine in conversation with *Adjutant* Gerlicht

The wreckage of Gotha 660 being hauled from the sea off Sheerness
on 5 June

Nevertheless, some regret for the civilian casualties, particularly the child victims, was expressed in a semi-official telegram from Berlin to Amsterdam a few days later, but the UK was held mainly responsible because it had not removed civilians from the war centres such as Sheerness, Dover and London!

Brandenburg, on the day after the London raid, took off from Melle-Gontrode in an Albatross two-seater piloted by *Oberleutnant* von Trotha. At Kreuznach, Brandenburg described the raid in detail to the attentive Kaiser and his General Staff, with particular reference to the fulfilment of the Ludendorf brief. The Kaiser congratulated the *Hauptmann* and concluded by presenting him with the *Pour le Mérite* (the 'Blue Max'), a decoration held by Richthofen, Immelmann and other air aces.

In the early morning of Tuesday the 19th, the Albatross lifted off from Kreuznach to begin the 200-mile journey back to Melle-Gontrode. Before it had achieved a safe height, however, the engine failed and the machine stalled and spun into the ground. Von Trotha was killed instantly but Brandenburg survived although severely injured in the legs. It was ironic that the Kaiser, by his command, had been directly responsible for the removal of the very man who, more than any other, had brought the *Englandgeschwader* to its peak of success.

Kagohl 3 was distraught when the news of the disaster came through, and the loss of this able leader, organizer and administrator led to a reduction in confidence, discipline and *esprit de corps* that would, in fact, never to be made up.

Kogenluft, anxious that the momentum of the bombing campaign should not be allowed to falter, began an immediate review of suitable staff in search of a replacement for Brandenburg. Following a recommendation by *Oberstleutnant* Hermann Thomsen, the Chief-of-Staff, the choice fell upon *Hauptmann* Rudolf Kleine, a thirty-year-old pilot who had had a distinguished air career, including a period as a flight commander in Kagohl 1. Although Kleine had only just recovered from wounds received in air action, arrangements were put in hand for him to join Kagohl 3 as soon as possible. Although undeniably a dedicated and respected officer, Kleine was, in fact, to prove somewhat impulsive in operational decision-making, particularly in the face of adverse weather forecasts. In consequence, therefore, he would never become as popular with the staff as his predecessor had been.

It is doubtful if Kleine was able to put in an appearance at Melle-Gontrode before Monday 25 June, and with the weather continuing unsettled over the period, no further *Luftangriffe* could be put in hand before the beginning of July.

The RNAS bombers at Dunkirk did not remain idle, however, and No. 5 (Naval) Squadron was despatched on a raid against St-Denis Westrem on 15 June. The War Cabinet's pressure on the Admiralty to hit back at the Gothas on the ground doubtless coincided, yet again, with the tactical preparations for the third Battle of Ypres.

At Adastral House, meanwhile, Higgins was gratified that the reinforcement and re-equipment of the RFC home defence squadrons were now under way. No. 37 Squadron was already receiving some Pups and 1½-Strutters. No. 39 Squadron would soon take delivery of the SE5s being erected under the eye of Captain Grant at Farnborough, plus one or two Armstrong-Whitworth FK8s; and No. 50 Squadron was to get some FK8s and Pups. Plans were already being prepared to create three new day-fighting detachments from elements of these HD Squadrons, but the night-fighting capability had still to be retained – sensibly, as was soon to be demonstrated.

On the night of 16/17 June, two Zeppelins nosed across the English coast, the L.42 and the L.48, and RFC and RNAS pilots went up in pursuit. The L.42 caused much damage at Ramsgate before making off, but L.48 was subsequently shot down, in flames, at Theberton, near Saxmundham, Norfolk, by Captain R. Saundby from Orfordness and Lieutenant L. Watkins of No. 37 Squadron. These occurrences highlighted the strain that must have been imposed upon air defence units expected to be air fighters by day as well as by night!

Higgins had a major retraining programme to organize: his BE12 pilots would require a period of familiarization in order to be able to fly and fight in their new machines. In addition, the intricacies of formation flying had to be learnt by trainee day-fighter pilots. The few experienced pilots available to the Home Defence Group would have to be employed as a training nucleus. No. 198 (Depot) Squadron at Rochford, the training squadron for the defenders, presumably now had to consider day-fighting techniques against the Gothas as well as the night-fighting ones against the Zeppelins.

The RNAS at home was also being reinforced: five Camels, originally intended for the conversion of the naval squadrons at Dunkirk, were diverted to RNAS Eastchurch on or about the 15th. It was clear, therefore, that Kagohl 3 had been successful in achieving one of OHL's principal aims – the enforced retention of modern fighters in the UK, to the detriment of the British air forces overseas.

On the 17th FM Haig and Major-General Trenchard arrived in London to begin their round of discussions with the Government. Among their papers, for presentation to the War Cabinet, was a memorandum dated 16 June that set out five important points in connection with the air defence of the UK:

1 The capture by us of the Belgian coast would be the most effective step of all, as, in addition to increasing the distance to be traversed, it would force the German machines either to cross territory occupied by us – when going and returning – a considerable advantage to us – or to cross neutral territory, where our Secret Service could doubtless establish means of giving us warning quickly.

2 The next most effective step is to inflict the utmost damage on the enemy's sheds and machines behind his Western front. Much has been done in this way. The amount which can be done is limited by the number and capacity of machines and pilots available in France. Increased activity on the Western front serves the double purpose of assisting the Armies in overcoming the enemy and at the same time reducing his power to send expeditions to England. To the Germans this reply would be most disappointing.

3 Any system of patrols would entail the use of a great number of machines and pilots. To justify any hope of such a system being effective (except by sheer luck) the number of machines and pilots required would be entirely beyond our present power of supply. The great object the enemy has in view is undoubtedly to weaken us in France, and if we adopt a patrol system we play his game.

4 As a temporary measure a modified system of patrols might be tried, working on both sides of the Channel. To give this its best chance of success an extensive system of communications, by wireless and other means, would be required; and it is essential that there should be unity of command over the whole system of

patrols and communications. A competent officer could be supplied from France for a short period, but both he and machines
and pilots sent from France will be urgently required to be back
there by the 5th July.

5 Reprisals on open towns are repugnant to British ideas, but we
may be forced to adopt them. It would be worse than useless to do
so, however, unless we are determined that, once adopted, they
will be carried through to the end. The enemy would almost
certainly reply 'in kind' and unless we are determined and
prepared to go one better than the Germans, whatever they may
do and whether their reply is in the air, or against our prisoners, or
otherwise, it will be infinitely better not to attempt reprisals at all.
At present we are not prepared to carry out reprisals effectively,
being unprovided with suitable machines. If we decide to provide
the necessary machines and to adopt the system, we might do
good by sending out machines now to drop notices in selected
German towns warning them of our intentions if the raids on our
open towns continue, and pointing out that their towns are within
our reach. We should not do this, however, unless we intend, and
are able, to keep our word. We might, however, drop notices
pointing out that they are mistaken in thinking they are not within
our reach, and although we have heretofore refrained from the
brutalities of which their Government has been guilty it is not
owing to lack of power to exact reprisals.[12]

This document, not unexpectedly perhaps, came down
heavily on the side of offensive rather than defensive action.
Primarily, the FM expected that success in the impending
offensive in Belgium would automatically solve the Gotha
problem once and for all as the flank of the German Fourth
Army in Flanders was turned and the pestilential air bases near
Ghent were overrun. Before that 'most effective step', he
advocated a policy of aerial bombardment of the Gotha airfields
– a policy that would pay better dividends than any system of
defensive air patrols could ever do. In any event, neither he nor
'Boom' Trenchard wished to see the thinly spread RFC/RNAS
fighter strength on the Western Front reduced even further by
the detachment of fighter squadrons to home defence. Finally,
however, the C.-in-C. grudgingly proposed a system of patrols,
as a temporary measure, on both sides of the Channel. It is
significant that the FM put forward the idea that a competent

officer should be sent from France in order to establish unity of command over the patrols and necessary communications. The officer and aircraft were to be returned to Haig's command on 5 July, when the air offensive in Flanders was due to commence. It would be interesting to know what GHQ, Home Forces, made of the proposal to send an officer to take charge of what would be, in fact, a part of the home defence system commanded by Lord French.

The Cabinet's War Policy Committee, chaired by the Prime Minister, met on Wednesday 20 June, with FM Haig and Major-General Trenchard in attendance, to clarify and expand the points made in the memorandum. Although Lloyd-George was in favour of a raid on Mannheim, FM Haig effectively quashed this by declaring that the RFC 'had no aeroplanes to spare for such an operation. The diversion of aeroplanes for a bombing attack of this kind would entail such risk to the army operations that I am not justified in recommending it.'[13] After much further discussion, the meeting finally plumped for Item 4 of the memorandum – a temporary system of air patrols along both sides of the Channel by two fighter squadrons to be detached from the Western Front. The problem of unity of command was ignored, and no officer, competent or otherwise, was sent over from the BEF to supervise the arrangements.

The fighter squadrons concerned were two crack units – No. 56 (SE5s) commanded by Major R. Blomfield and No. 66 (Pups) commanded by Major O. Boyd. The two squadrons flew from their airfield at Liettres (Estrée Blanche) on the morning of the 21st, No. 56 proceeding to Bekesbourne, Kent, the home of C Flight of No. 50 (Home Defence) Squadron, in order to cover the South Coast area, whilst No. 66 went to an airfield near Calais ready to patrol the French side of the Channel. Both squadrons, of course, immediately came under the authority of the C.-in-C., Home Forces. These movements were a serious setback for the RFC's Ninth Wing in France: it was left with only one fighter squadron (No. 19), a unit plagued with engine problems.[14] It is certainly true that German air activity was stepped up on the British Second Army's sector at Messines during the two weeks the two squadrons were absent in the UK.

The members of No. 56 Squadron (the late Captain Albert Ball's unit) were highly delighted that they were back in England, if only for a short period. The pilots, Lieutenants

Arthur Rhys-Davids and Cecil Lewis among them, had (as the latter subsequently wrote)

> ... arrived at Bekesbourne without incident, vastly elated. Machines were put away, and the men, who had been rushed home, took charge of them. Needless to say, all the musicians were among them. The defence of London was quite a secondary affair. The things of real importance were squadron dances. To fight Hun bombers over London would have been a picnic for us after a month of gruelling Offensive Patrols. Good old Jerry! Good old Lloyd George!
>
> A large marquee was run up as a Mess. The Major scrounged some planking, and very soon there was a regular Savoy dancing floor. Visits were paid to Canterbury to enrol the fair sex. Those lightning two or three-day acquaintanceships began to ripen.[15]

Captain James McCudden flew his Pup over from Joyce Green to Bekesbourne a few days later in order to renew old acquaintances such as Lieutenant G. Bowman and others in No. 56. He was very impressed with the spirit of the Squadron, 'which was entirely different from any Squadron with which I had yet come in contact, and everyone in the Squadron was as keen as anything to get at and strafe the Huns'.[16]

Lieutenant-Colonel Simon, worried by the paucity of guns on the eastern perimeter of the city, put forward, on the 21st, a plan which, if it had been approved, would have needed an additional forty-five guns to implement. His scheme, which was rejected because neither sufficient guns nor gunners were available at that time, would have created 'a shower of shell bursts' some distance out from the city, in order to break up the Gotha formations.[17] This was, of course, a modified scheme similar to the one he had first proposed almost exactly a year before.

The Home Secretary's conference into the question of public warnings of air raids also took place on the 21st. The Lord Mayor and the mayors of the London boroughs were unanimous in their opinion that public warnings were necessary. It was suggested that the red warning *Take Air Raid Action* might be followed by a later one when the raiders were approaching a particular district. GHQ, quite understandably, pooh-poohed this: the successive warning system had already been virtually abandoned, because of the Gothas' speed, and blanket alerts over a wide area were the best that could be provided. The mayors' feelings concerning public warnings were conveyed by the Home Secretary to the War Cabinet for a decision.

The War Cabinet deliberated on the matter on the 26th but in the end decided against the promulgation of air-raid warnings to the general public. The Home Secretary made an announcement in the House of Commons, to that effect, later in the same day. The reasons advanced by the War Cabinet[18] for not acquiescing to the public demand seem quite extraordinary now, but no doubt No. 10 was quite convinced of their validity at the time.

The first point in the statement reiterated the earlier Government opinion that an air-raid alarm would encourage people to throng the streets to view the proceedings instead of remaining in their homes or work places. The impression thus given was that a warning could, in fact, endanger the citizens rather than protect them! This incredible idea took no cognizance whatever of unfortunate people who might be caught out on the streets without any warning at all – as had happened in Folkestone and London.

Secondly, it was alleged that the public objected to a period of suspense following a warning, and furthermore, if no raid succeeded an alert, people would tend to disregard future alarms!

Thirdly, it was considered that business activities and war-factory production would be unnecessarily deranged by air-raid alarms. It was, apparently, quite usual for workers who had been withdrawn from work places because of raid alerts to take the remainder of the day off, irrespective of the length of the red warning period.

The War Cabinet's remarkable statement concluded with the observation that, as a principal aim of the German raiders was the widest possible disruption of war work, no warnings at all would confound the enemy's strategy!

On the 26th, also, a conference was held at the War Office, under the chairmanship of the War Minister, Lord Derby, to consider the subject of aerial policy, as directed by the War Cabinet on 14 June. Dr Addison (Minister of Munitions), Lord Cowdray (Air Board) and the CIGS, who had initiated the review, attended, as well as many other officials. The plans tabled by Dr Addison were intended to expand the RFC establishment from the projected 106 squadrons (in February

1917) up to 200, i.e. almost doubling the proposed stength; 'the provision of personnel, etc., to be commenced at once'.[19] The existing records do not appear to make any reference to the War Cabinet's original point concerning the departments that should be penalized financially to pay for this extra burden. The plans were passed by the meeting and then sent to the War Cabinet for final approval. The approval was forthcoming a few days later but with a proviso that the RNAS establishment should be increased in the same ratio.

Meanwhile, at Melle-Gontrode, *Hauptmann* Kleine was settling in as the new commandant of Kagohl 3 and beginning to plan for the resumption of the air bombing raids across the North Sea. One of his main concerns, like Brandenburg's before him, was to ensure that reliable weather forecasts would be available to the squadron. It is intriguing, and possibly significant, to note that *Leutnant* Cloessner, who had provided Brandenburg with excellent weather data up to that time, was immediately replaced by *Leutnant* Walter Georgii, an officer of wide meteorological experience, who had been engaged in forecasting for the Army's Zeppelin service.

6

July

During the first few days of the month the weather, which had been rather unsettled from about the middle of June, began to improve, and a period of anticyclonic conditions developed over the British Isles. The significance of this fact, whilst very welcome to the impatient *Hauptmann* Kleine, did not go unnoticed on the other side of the Channel. Lord French, on Monday the 2nd, wrote urgently to the Secretary of the War Office concerning the effect of the imminent departure of Nos. 56 and 66 Squadrons from the Home Forces Command:

It is understood that the two squadrons Royal Flying Corps which have recently been at my disposal for Home Defence will be withdrawn on the 5th instant.

Although the number of machines and pilots available for day defence have been to some extent increased during the past few weeks, the withdrawal of these squadrons will leave the means at my disposal to repel aeroplane attacks dangerously weak, and it cannot be supposed that the danger of attack can be any the less after the 5th instant than it is now or has been in the past. In fact, it is probably much greater; for, as far as is known, this new type of enemy machine is now being produced in considerable numbers. Further, there is a reasonable probability that the enemy may send fast machines to create alarm on the coast and induce us to put our machines into the air, following them with a strong attack of large Gotha aeroplanes.

If this is the case, the main attack may take place when our machines have been some time in the air and are short of petrol. The only means of meeting such tactics is to have such a force of aeroplanes available as will not necessitate the putting up of all our available forces at once.

It is understood that the monthly allotment of machines will be made tomorrow, and I trust that the claims of Home Defence may receive particular consideration in the light of what I have stated above.

Moreover, the number of machines placed at my disposal from sources other than the Home Defence squadrons is a diminishing quantity.'[1]

At that point bureaucracy took a hand in the story because the Secretary of the War Office noted that the fourth paragraph of the letter would urgently concern Lieutenant-General Henderson as Director-General of Military Aeronautics, the authority responsible for 'the monthly allotment of machines'.[2] Instead of a copy of the letter for Henderson's attention, the original letter was sent on circulation, and thus the War Minister did not see it until several days later – a crucial delay in the circumstances.

The letter is interesting on two counts: firstly, it indicated that a fairly large number of defensive aeroplanes would be needed to protect the city should Kagohl 3 resort to the decoying tactics it had already employed in a small way, quite successfully, at Margate; and secondly, the FM took the opportunity to express his disappointment with the level of reinforcement that the Training Brigade and aircraft parks etc. had been able to provide thus far to the Home Defence Group.

In Flanders, meanwhile, *Leutnant* Georgii, after studying the available weather reports and conducting his own tests, was of the opinion that Wednesday the 4th might be suitable for the Gothas to venture overseas again. Although a light easterly wind would assist the raiders on their outward journey, the 'tree frog' warned Kleine about the possibility of local thunderstorms developing *en route* – a meteorological feature that became quite familiar to Kagohl 3 during that summer.

After some consideration, Kleine decided to set up a raid on the 4th, but the somewhat uncertain weather conditions, coupled with the presence of No. 56 Squadron at Bekesbourne and Rochford (the detachment of the two squadrons could hardly have gone unnoticed by the *Luftstreitkräfte* reconnaissance and intelligence services), prompted him to limit the foray to targets on the Suffolk coast (the port of Harwich and the naval air station of Felixstowe), rather than to venture inland to London.

Furthermore, for this shorter raid he chose to depart from Belgium at dawn, in order, hopefully, to catch the defences off guard and also to avoid the thundercloud formations that might appear later in the day.

By an odd coincidence, RNAS bombers from No. 7 (Naval) Squadron at Dunkirk struck at the airfields of Ghistelles and Nieumunster during the night of the 3rd/4th – a further attack in support of the British Fifth Army's build-up at Ypres. Neither Melle-Gontrode nor St-Denis Westrem was included in the naval air attentions on this occasion, and thus the preparations for the Gothas' take-off were not impeded.

Shortly after sunrise, on a rather cold morning, the Gothas were started up, and at about 05.30 twenty-five bombers set off from their two bases and steered for the Belgian coast. However, the temperamental Mercedes engines soon began to play up, and no fewer than seven of the raiders, nearly thirty per cent of the force, had to signal, at various times, that they were unable to continue the mission and must return to the Belgian airfields.

In no way daunted by these setbacks, Kleine, in bright sunshine, steered a mainly northerly course in order to avoid both the RNAS at Dunkirk and the lightships in the Thames estuary. As he approached the Suffolk coast at about ten minutes to seven, Kleine was pleased to see a layer of patchy cloud over the land, and he hoped that this would enable him to attack the selected targets with little warning to the defenders. He was somewhat taken aback, therefore, when a DH4 aeroplane suddenly zoomed down through the formation, its guns chattering. Thinking that this could presage an attack by a squadron of British fighters, Kleine immediately signalled Kagohl 3 to turn eastwards away from the land. In fact, the DH4 was entirely alone and had stumbled on the Gothas quite by chance. Captain J. Palethorpe, the pilot, and Air Mechanic J. Jessop, the gunner/observer, had taken off from the Testing Squadron at Martlesham Heath at a very early hour in order to carry out some acceptance tests on the DH4. This machine was fully armed, and Palethorpe did not hesitate to make a determined and gallant attack as soon as he had identified the bomber squadron as hostile. Coming under the concentrated fire of the startled formation, however, Jessop was killed outright and Palethorpe had no option but to break off the fight and return to Martlesham.

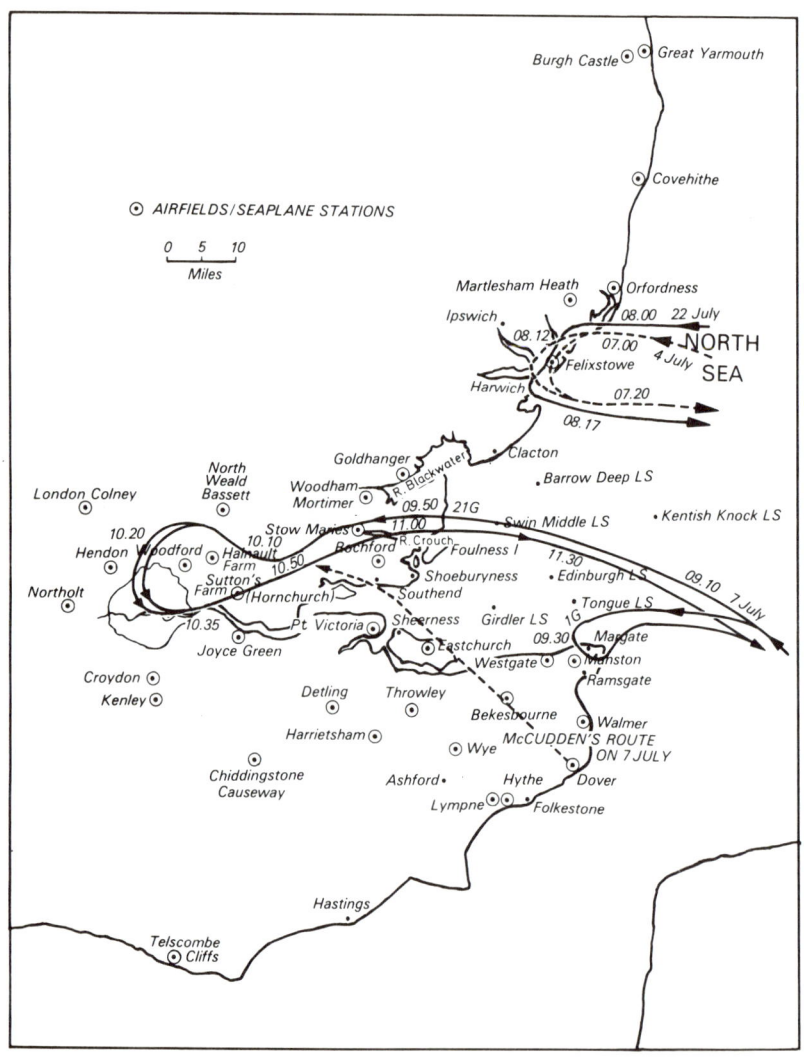

8. Operations in July

Kagohl 3, at about 14,000 feet, now turned back towards the land (Map 8) and lined up on the Martello towers between Felixstowe and Orfordness, finally crossing the coast at Shingle Street at seven o'clock or thereabouts. The roar of many engines and the fleeting glimpses of the bombers through the clouds no doubt resulted in a telephone call to the Horse Guards, whereupon the new blanket warning from Suffolk to Kent would have come into operation. In all, sixty-six RFC and seventeen RNAS home-based aircraft were to be scrambled for the London defences, but all this activity was to be in vain – Kleine did not intend to challenge the experienced day-fighters of No. 56 Squadron in their SE5s.

Leaving the coastline, the Gothas banked round to the south-west, crossed the River Deben and then divided into two wings, the right-hand one continuing down across the rivers Orwell and Stour to attack Harwich, whilst the left-hand one wheeled east again towards Felixstowe. It was now about ten minutes past seven, and the two towns were soon awakened by the explosion of bombs and the answering fire from the seven 3-inch 20cwt guns of the Harwich Command, as the sleepy crews came into action. The guns were sited at the Golf House, Landguard and Trimley on the Felixstowe side of the estuary, and Dovercourt, Great Oakley, Ramsey and Rose Farm at Shotley on the Harwich side. About 135 rounds were fired off in the few minutes the Gothas, estimated at about 14,000 feet, were in the area, but the lack of warning, the cloudy conditions and the problem of height-finding inhibited the effectiveness of the AA artillery. About sixty-five bombs, were dropped, mostly of the 12½kg type, but of these some twenty-three fell harmlessly in the sea or on the foreshore. Little damage and no casualties were sustained at Harwich, where only two bombs were reported, but the RNAS air station of Felixstowe received several direct hits. A Curtiss Large America flying boat was completely gutted, another was severely damaged, and the air station's telephone exchange was put out of action.[3] Casualties on the station were six naval ratings and three civilian workmen killed, and nineteen others injured. Three more naval men died in an incident at the Shotley balloon station, and five soldiers of the 3rd Battalion, the Suffolk Regiment, were killed at an Army camp, another ten being wounded.

By 07.15 this hit-and-run affair was over. The Gothas droned away out to sea, the crews quite elated as they looked back at the column of black smoke rising over the RNAS base. Kagohl 3 had sailed unharmed through the fairly heavy but inaccurate AA fire, and no defending aeroplane had come anywhere near the area.

As his squadron headed back across the North Sea, Kleine was, no doubt, wondering about the possibility of interception by the RFC's No. 66 Squadron at Calais, and the RNAS squadrons then at Dunkirk. It seems likely that No. 4 (Naval) Wing received a telephone warning as soon as the bombers began their return journey, and a simple calculation would have shown that the Gothas would be approaching the Belgian coast about 1½ hours later. Consequently a patrol from No. 4 (Naval) Squadron, once again led by Flight Commander Shook, took off from Bray Dunes at about 08.00 and steered north-east to try to head off the raiders. The patrol, consisting of eight Camels and two Pups, was lucky; some of the Gothas and their escorting fighters were spotted about thirty miles out from Ostend. In the ensuing engagement, Flight Sub-Lieutenant Ellis 'fired over 300 rounds at one machine which went down in an erratic manner, with smoke issuing from its back seat'.[4] German sources, however, did not report any Gotha losses on this day so the damaged bomber must have managed to limp home to its base.

No. 3 (Naval) Squadron, which had replaced No. 9 at Furnes under No. 4 (Naval) Wing, did not take part in anti-Gotha patrolling on this occasion, presumably because of other commitments.

No. 6 (Naval) Squadron, although attached to the 4th Brigade, RFC, happened to be at Bray Dunes at this time, its pilots converting from the Nieuport 17 to the Sopwith Camel. This squadron also scrambled a patrol of ten fighters but it was unable to locate the bombers, probably because the weather conditions were deteriorating somewhat.[5]

As far as No. 66 Squadron at Calais was concerned, an administrative mix-up delayed the arrival of the alert, and thus the Pups were not airborne until 08.20, by which time the Gothas were too close to Belgium to be caught. The reason for the delay in warning the squadron has never been satisfactorily explained, but it was probably due to a fault in the communications network that 'a competent officer' might have been able to sort out quite easily. Although the squadron searched assiduously for some time, it was finally forced to return to Calais because of the weather situation.[6]

Although this raid had helped to underline Lord French's argument, as set out in his letter of the 2nd, the fact that Lord Derby had not yet seen the letter meant that there was to be no reconsideration by the War Cabinet of FM Haig's provisional return date (the 5th) for Nos. 56 and 66 Squadrons.

Accordingly, on that day, the personnel of No. 56 at Bekesbourne and Rochford had, somewhat sadly, to pack up and return to Estrée Blanche, the pilots by air and the ground crews by sea. No. 66, at Calais, was, however, to remain there for one more day before its Pups would fly over to rejoin No. 56.

On the 6th, Field Marshal French, understandably annoyed because he had received no reply to his letter, produced a somewhat terse memorandum for the CIGS:

The two squadrons recently placed under my orders have now been withdrawn. Apart from the slower machines which have neither the climbing power nor speed sufficient to make them effective against such machines as the enemy may be expected to employ, the means at my disposal to repel aeroplane attacks are as follows:

Sopwith Scouts	12
SE5	3
DH4	6
	—
Total	21

... I desire to place on record my most emphatic opinion that even with the addition of twelve Sopwith Scouts, which it is hoped will be available by the 15th instant, the aeroplanes which I can dispose of are not sufficient for effective action against raids in force. Such raids may certainly be expected, and if London is again subjected to attack the results may be disastrous.[7]

The FM's list of twenty-one efficient fighters included twelve Sopwith Pups, obviously those supplied to Nos. 37 and 50 Squadrons after the London raid of 13 June. In addition, the SE5s mentioned were three of the six sent to No. 39 Squadron at Sutton's Farm, where experienced pilots, including Captains Grant, G. Murlis-Green, W. Haynes, and others, were being concentrated to fly them.[8] The six DH4s were presumably machines of the home defence flights of Hendon and Martlesham. The other twelve Pups expected to be delivered on the 15th must also have been intended as replacements for Nos. 37 and 50 Squadrons. The FM made no mention of the Sopwith $1\frac{1}{2}$-Strutters and Armstrong-Whitworth FK8 machines already in use by those two squadrons: they were evidently dismissed as being in the 'slower machine' class.

The departure of Nos. 56 and 66 Squadrons was obviously reported by the Germans' 'effective system of espionage',[9] and Kleine must have been pleased by the fact that the movements coincided with an improvement in the thundery weather conditions still affecting the North Sea area. The commander decided to take advantage of the situation and ordered an attack on London for Saturday the 7th, secure in the knowledge that the defences had been reduced and that the weather, if not really settled, at least promised a fairly fine day without much chance of electrical storms. However, secondary targets were selected just in case the weather over London was inclement, and a diversionary attack on Margate was again to be one Gotha's duty. In addition, two or three Gothas were to carry cameras in order to engage in photo-reconnaissance work over the capital.

There is some evidence to suggest that the bombload for each Gotha, was, on this occasion, reduced from the usual 300kg in order to improve the operational speed and height during the loaded run-in to the British capital. Kleine wanted an average speed of some 80mph coupled with a height requirement of about 16,000 feet or more, a move intended to offset the improving efficiency of the London defences.

Preparations for the raid proceeded during the night of the 6th/7th although disturbed by RNAS bombers dropping bombs on both airfields. The RNAS attack was probably mounted as a reply to the Gotha assault on the Felixstowe air station and, as such, could have been in no sense a pre-emptive strike; it was quite fortuitous that that particular night was chosen. As it happened, little damage was done and there was no interruption of the preparations for the impending mission against London – the second great daylight raid.

At about eight o'clock on a fine, warm but somewhat sultry and hazy summer's morning, twenty-four Gothas took off in sequence from their airfields, after which they began their laborious but steady climb to 10,000 feet. At that height they assembled into the usual narrow V formation and droned off across the Ostend area *en route* for the Crouch. Two of the bombers were, however, not destined to reach Essex on this day – they developed the inevitable engine problems and were forced to signal, bank round and return home.

The remaining Gothas sailed on with Kleine and the three headquarters machines in the lead. Unbeknown to the commander, however, his force was seen much earlier than usual – at about ten minutes past nine, in fact – but whether the sighting was by lightships, naval vessels or naval aircraft is not known. At all events, the Admiralty was alerted and a warning was relayed to the London Warning Centre shortly afterwards, resulting in a general warning for London and the eastern counties.

At approximately the same time, Kleine signalled to the single Gotha detailed for the Margate diversion, whereupon it swung away and headed for the Isle of Thanet. Just before 09.30 the raider was spotted, at 12,000 feet, by the gun crews at St Peter's and Hengrove, and a lively bombardment began. The Gotha replied with three 50kg bombs that destroyed three houses and damaged thirty-one others. Three people were killed and three others injured in this attack.

It seems likely that the bomber then proceeded to fly along the Margate/Broadstairs railway line 'trailing its coat', as it were, to the RNAS at Manston. The bomber's commander was quite unaware that a warning had been received before 9.30 and that six fighter aircraft (two Camels, one Pup and three Triplanes) had already been scrambled from Manston. The pair of 3pdr 9cwt mobile guns stationed on the airfield there came into action for about five minutes, followed by the 3-inch 20cwt one at Cliffsend (Pegwell Bay) a little later.

Ringed by shellbursts, the Gotha dodged about and then finally disappeared eastwards into the haze. The five AA guns had fired off some 115 rounds in approximately five minutes – but the bomber flew on undamaged.

It is doubtful if the naval fighter aircraft wasted much time in pursuing the bomber on this occasion; they soon turned north towards Essex in an attempt to engage the main bomber force as it approached the Foulness area. They did not succeed in finding the enemy and returned to Manston after about an hour.

Kleine's decoying tactic had, therefore, signally but not surprisingly failed. That the commander of Kagohl 3 should have supposed that the RNAS would fall for the same ruse twice in three weeks is curious, to say the least, but evidently he did think so.

The receipt of an early warning enabled the four RFC home defence squadrons to send up a total of forty-six aircraft by 09.30, i.e. before the Gothas had even crossed the Essex coastline. On this day, then, the defending pilots did have time to reach the altitude required for successful interception prior to the attack on London. However, only twenty-six of the squadron's machines, i.e. just over fifty per cent, possessed anything like the necessary rate of climb and speed at high altitudes: eleven Pups, six 1½-Strutters, five Armstrong-Whitworth FK8s, two SE5s (from the six at Sutton's Farm) and two Vickers single-seater types. The remainder consisted of a collection of BE2 and BE12 night-fighters plus, incredibly, the same old RE7 that had gone up from Goldhanger on 13 June.

Support was given by thirty-four aeroplanes from RFC training squadrons and depots, the majority of which, in contrast to the home defence squadrons, were modern fighters such as the Pup, Camel, DH4, DH5 and the Bristol Fighter.

The RFC aircraft proceeded to their allotted patrol areas, mostly independently or in pairs, although the 1½-Strutters from No. 37 Squadron, Rochford, flew together along their Joyce Green – Goldhanger beat. Few pilots from units south of the Thames, such as Nos. 50 and 78 Squadrons and the AEP at Lympne, would see anything of the Gothas at all – Kleine had no intention of going south of the Thames.

The RNAS contribution, at home, totalled eleven fighters, six of which had already been scrambled earlier from Manston plus another three that would take off later. Two of Eastchurch's Camels roared off at about 09.30 and headed towards London.

The list of home-based RFC and RNAS pilots taking part on this day contained several names of interest. First and foremost, there was Captain James McCudden, who happened to be on a visit to No. 62 (Training) Squadron at Dover when the warning came through. He at once set off in his 'whitish-blue' Pup 'and climbed away towards the south of the Thames'.[10] Then there was Captain J. Palethorpe, who had so gallantly attacked the raiders off Harwich on 4 July, aloft on this day in a DH4 with

Second Air Mechanic F. James as gunner. From Rochford came Major B. Moore, the commanding officer of No. 198 (Depot) Squadron, and possibly the most senior officer airborne, in a Vickers FB12c single-seater pusher fighter – a machine probably little better in performance than the BE12. In a BE12 from No 37 Squadron at Goldhanger was Lieutenant L. Watkins, who had been responsible for shooting down the Zeppelin L.48 at Theberton on the night of 17 June. He was one of a number of night-fighters who had, perforce, to perform daytime duties in addition to nocturnal ones. Squadron Commander C. Butler from RNAS Manston, another quite senior officer who had seen action on 5 June, led the fighter patrols being scrambled from the air station.

At ten minutes to ten, in hazy sunshine, the twenty-one Gothas appeared over the mouth of the Crouch flying in at about 12,000 feet, still steadily climbing to reach the intended operating height of 16,000 feet over the capital. They were immediately assailed by shells, both HE and shrapnel from the mobile 13pdr 9cwt AA gun pairs of the Harwich AA Command then at Asheldham, Burnham-on-Crouch, Great Stambridge and Heybridge, and a single fixed 3-inch 20cwt on the experimental ranges at Shoeburyness. In the little over five minutes that Kagohl 3 was in range, these guns discharged 248 HE and 221 shrapnel shells – an average of about fifty rounds per gun, a most creditable achievement. Unfortunately, some British pilots were to be archied as well, the consequence of the lack of gun/aircraft areas. As soon as the formation had passed out of range, the AA commander at Shoeburyness detailed off a 13pdr 9cwt mobile pair from the experimental ranges to proceed with all speed to the airfield at Rochford, in order to engage the Gothas, at shorter range, on their return from London. The formation, meanwhile, opened out soon after the first shellbursts began mushrooming below. The left-hand and right-hand flights, behind the leader, were now at somewhat different altitudes, whilst a group of four Gothas brought up the rear, these latter machines including the photo-reconnaissance ones. The outermost Gothas of the two wings were about one mile apart by the time the air armada was flying insolently over No. 37 Squadron's airfield at Stow Maries.

At least four RFC machines flew through the AA fusillade in the area in order to mount individual attacks on the bombers.

Captain D. Clappen, piloting a DH4 from AAP Hendon, with First Air Mechanic Wills as observer, followed the raiders from the coast to London, shooting as opportunity offered. Their machine was hit about the tail by return fire, then developed engine trouble and its machine-guns were rendered inoperative by jamming. Such mishaps were to be fairly common among the defence aircraft: one fifth of those making contact with the enemy were to be damaged; one third would suffer engine problems; and incredibly more than one half were to be inhibited by gun stoppages caused by defective ammunition.

Kleine led the two wings of Kagohl 3 in a westerly direction passing close to Wickford, Billericay and Brentwood, where a sharp turn to the north-west was made, heading for the land-mark of the Epping Forest. The plan was to approach the London area from the north-east, and thence to fly south to the City and back along the Thames to the North Sea. Somewhere in the Brentwood area Captain E. Mason, in a Pup from No. 37 Squadron at Stow Maries, opened fire on a Gotha straggling somewhat from the main force. His bullets apparently had little effect, but cross-fire from other Gothas seriously damaged his machine. The top main spar was shot through as the Captain discovered on his return to Stow Maries.

At about 10.15, the guns at Epping, Lambourne End and Theydon Bois came into action, closely followed by those at Chingford, Enfield, Higham Hill, Newmans, Parndon, Temple, Warlies Park and Woodford. Braving the shell bursts, five RFC aircraft and the two Camels from RNAS Eastchurch pressed home their attacks. The naval pilots fired about 200 rounds apiece before gun jams afflicted both machines.

It was over Chingford that the first bomb in the London area was released; it fell and exploded harmlessly in a field. No fewer than four 50kg bombs then straddled the Tottenham gasworks but no damage was done to the installations. Stoke Newington-Dalston then received five bombs, the most serious incident occuring in Boleyn Road, where nine people died and nine others were injured. On their way south to the City of London, the principal target, the raiders showered sixteen bombs on the triangle Islington-Clerkenwell-Hoxton, three of them landing in Wenlock Road, seriously damaging a timber yard, zinc mills and houses nearby. One bomb, which luckily failed to explode, actually fell on a military target, the

Honourable Artillery Company's parade ground at Finsbury.

The guns at Finchley, Highbury, Kenton, Palmers Green, Parliament Hill, Ridgeway and Wanstead boomed out as the bomber formation passed overhead at about 10.30. Through this largely ineffectual and unco-ordinated AA bombardment flew several of the RFC's slow night-fighter aeroplanes, making desperate and usually unavailing attempts to overhaul the speedier Gothas. Among them was Lieutenant Watkins whose BE12 was to develop engine trouble just as he was catching up with the raiders.

A few modern fighters did open fire at this time but to little effect because of the prevalence of gun jams, engine defects and the accurate return fire from the Gotha phalanx. Lieutenant Thompson from Stow Maries was extremely lucky not to have been shot down – his Pup was hit four times. Lieutenant N. Chandler from No. 50 Squadron at Throwley fared badly also: apart from a gun jam and engine problems, he was 'all the time under heavy anti-aircraft fire' and his goggles were smothered in oil.

The bombers, directed by Kleine, then sailed over the City in a south-easterly direction, unloading about thirty bombs as they did so. The distribution covered an area bounded by King Edward Street in the west to Aldgate in the east, from the Barbican in the north and the Thames in the south. The majority of these missiles fell in the eastern part of the City, and damage to business houses was considerable, the loss subsequently being assessed at about £250,000, a vast sum for those days. Casualties in the City, on the other hand, were quite low – some thirteen dead and twenty-six injured – probably because the City was comparatively empty on a Saturday morning.

The most serious incident, from the Government's point of view, was occasioned by a 50kg bomb falling on the GPO's Central Telegraph Office in St Martin's-le-Grand. The building was set on fire, and the roof and wireless telegraphic facilities on the first floor were destroyed. A soldier was killed here and four other men injured. In the same district, a group of four bombs fell in the area of Little Britain, close to St Bartholomew's Hospital, causing fires and damage to warehouses and dwellings round about. Six people died and eight were injured but the hospital itself was untouched. (Curiously, it may have been the concussion of the bombs in Bartholomew Close that brought down eighteenth-century plaster revealing the brick and timber of a Tudor gatehouse of 1595.)

A bomb demolished waterfront buildings in Lower Thames Street, causing the death of four people and injuring seven others. The barge *Glencairn* moored in the river was sunk by a direct hit, whilst another bomb damaged a pier off Billingsgate fish market.

Three bombs fell in Fenchurch Street with consequent damage to the Ironmongers' Hall, shops and offices of various firms. One bomb dropped close to Moorgate Street railway station but luckily failed to go off. Two floors of a bank in Lothbury were damaged by a bomb probably intended for the Bank of England.

One bomb, which also failed to explode, fell on a warehouse in Aldermanbury, close to the Wren church of St Mary the Virgin. (Narrowly escaping destruction in this Great War raid, the church was to be gutted during the fire Blitzes of 1940. It now stands, rebuilt, in Fulton, Missouri, USA, as a memorial to Sir Winston Churchill.)

The 75mm guns at Acton and Hanwell and the 3-inch 20cwt ones at Hyde Park and Tower Bridge came into action and peppered the air with shell bursts rather below the Gothas, as Kleine banked to port at the Thames and set course eastwards again. About this time, also, Captain Palethorpe's DH4 arrived on the scene and immediately attacked with both guns firing. Unfortunately, the front Vickers gun soon jammed and the DH4 was hit several times by enemy fire. Captain Palethorpe was wounded in the hip and was forced to land at Rochford to seek medical attention.

Second Lieutenant R. Martin, in a Pup from No. 40 (Training) Squadron at Croydon, engaged a Gotha at very close range and fired fifty rounds into it. The bomber thereupon went into a spin but Martin was unable to follow it down because he was attacked by other Gothas.

The lessons of air defence were being demonstrated over London for all to see – particularly the top brass at the War Office and the Admiralty, and the MPs at Westminster. The AA fire, for instance, was manifestly not achieving its primary purpose, to break up the ranks of the bombers so that the fighters could pounce on stragglers. On the contrary, the artillery was so badly controlled and directed that many British fighters at lower levels were bombarded whilst the Gothas passed unscathed overhead. It is, of course, true that the conditions over the capital were somewhat hazy, and this may have contributed to poor aircraft recognition techniques.

In any event, the failure of the AA artillery to disrupt Kagohl 3 meant that those fighter pilots who succeeded in making attacks were repelled by the massive and concentrated machine-gun fire from the enemy aircraft. Once again, the piecemeal assaults by the RFC and RNAS machines, although pressed home with great gallantry, were, in the main, quite nugatory and foolhardy.

As the Tower Bridge gun fired off sixty-five rounds, one Gotha replied with a bomb on Tower Hill itself. Several houses were destroyed or damaged, and eight people died, with fifteen injured. This was to be the last serious incident in the raid, although a few more bombs were to descend on Southwark, Bermondsey, Bethnal Green, Canning Town and Plaistow as the Gothas winged their way back along the Thames.

The Gothas formation had by this time become rather ragged, although not broken, and some of the bombers swept along the south side of the Thames. A few of Lieutenant-Colonel Rawlinson's 75mm guns in South London now came into action, at rather long range. These batteries were stationed at Beckenham, Dulwich, Grove Park, Norbiton and Richmond, and it may be that using shrapnel and firing at low angles they could have been responsible for several of the casualties caused by AA fire on this day, ten dead and fifty-five injured. Rawlinson, later, was to state that the enemy machines 'though clearly in sight from the West Sub-Command at Putney did not come within range of our stations',[11] whereas in fact ten of his guns actually opened fire during the raid.

Clearing the Isle of Dogs, the raiders began to swing in a north-easterly direction, making for the Crouch and Foulness. On their way they were bombarded first by the Blackwall gun and then by those grouped around the Woolwich area at Abbey Wood, Beckton, Bostall Heath, Erith, Outfall, Shooter's Hill and Tunnel Farm.

All along the return route from London, the Gothas were harried or tailed by multifarious types of British aircraft. Among these was the Pup piloted by Captain James McCudden, who had arrived over Southend at 16,000 feet and then flown westwards along the north bank of the Thames in search of the enemy. His own very vivid account of what followed is given below:

Very soon I saw the welcome cloud of British Archie bursting over Tilbury and I could now discern a lot of big machines in good formation flying east. I had plenty of time to determine what to do, and also a lot of height to spare. As soon as all the formation had passed by, I dived on the rearmost machine and fired a whole drum at close range. In diving I came rather too near the top-plane of the Gotha and had to level out so violently to avoid running into him that the downward pressure of my weight as I pulled the joy-stick back was so great that my seat-bearers broke, and I was glad it wasn't my wings.

I remained above again and now thought of a different way to attack the rearmost Gotha. I put on a new drum and dived from the Hun's right rear to within 300 feet, when I suddenly swerved, and changing over to his left rear, closed to fifty yards and finished my drum before the enemy gunner could swing his gun from the side at which I first dived. I zoomed away but the Hun still appeared to be OK. Then I put on my third and last drum and made up my mind that I should have a good go at getting him. I repeated the manoeuvre of changing from one side to the other and had the satisfaction of seeing my tracer bullets strike all about his fuselage and wings, but beyond causing the Gotha to push his nose down a little, it had not the desired effect. I was very disappointed, as I had used up all of my ammunition and the Huns were only just over Southend.* It was very silly of me only to carry three single drums of ammunition when I could easily have carried a dozen without affecting the climb and speed of my machine, for I now had nothing else to do except to fly alongside the Huns and make faces at them. The rearmost Hun had the letters KA on the side of his fuselage and another one had S on his. I flew abreast of the last Gotha at about 200 yards range, in such a position that the rear gunner could not fire at me, owing to his wings and struts being in the way. My idea in flying alongside was to try to monopolise the Huns gunner's attention so that some of our other machines, of which there were a lot in attendance, could fly up behind the Hun unperceived and shoot at him whilst he was looking at me.

* Presumably the most southerly Gothas.

However, my comrades had their own attractions, and I escorted this rear Gotha for twenty-five minutes at 200 yards range and had not a shot to fire at him.

My feelings can be much better imagined than described, and owing to my carelessness the Hun finally put a good burst of bullets through my machine, one of which went bang through my wind-screen, much to my consternation. I now got rather fed up with acting as ground-bait for other people, who apparently had no idea of appreciating my generous intentions, so I flew a little farther away from the KA Gothas, whose gunner I decided was a very nasty man. Meanwhile, many other British machines were engaging the Gothas with varying luck. Two of them, who were at least half a mile from the nearest Hun, were firing away for all they were worth, and whether they thought I was a Hun scout just because I was painted blue I do not know, but I could hear their bullets quite distinctly.[12]

As they flew across Essex, the by now lightly loaded, and thus speedier, bombers were shelled by the 3-inch 20cwt guns on the eastern AA ring at Chadwell Heath, Ockendon, Rainham and Romford. Somewhere in this area, Second Lieutenant W. Salmon, in a Pup from No. 63 (Training) Squadron at Joyce Green, made a brave attack on a Gotha but was injured in the eye by a bullet. He attempted to return to his airfield but lost control when only 100 feet above the grass, crashed and was killed.

The Thames and Medway Garrison's 12pdr 12cwt AA guns at Bowers Gifford and Hawkesbury Bush banged away at the Gothas, followed by the Harwich Command's 13pdr 9cwt gun pairs at Asheldham, Burnham-on-Crouch, Great Stambridge and Heybridge, these pairs having thus opened fire twice within the hour. The 13pdr 9cwt pair sent to Rochford from Shoeburyness also joined in, together with the 3-inch 20cwt at Shoeburyness itself.

Four of the No. 37 Squadron's 1½-Strutters were patrolling their Joyce Green-Goldhanger line awaiting the return of the Gothas from London. The pilots concerned were Captains C. Cooke and Holman and Second Lieutenants E. Edwardes and J. Young. Two of these, Captain Cooke and Second Lieutenant Young, had engaged the Gothas on 13 June and were presumably well aware that the 1½-Strutter was too slow to be able to keep up with the lightened bombers. However, using their height to full advantage, they made resolute attacks, in company with Major B. Moore in his Vickers FB12c fighter from No. 198 (Depot) Squadron and Captain H. Tizard in a Camel from Martlesham.

The concentrated crossfire from the Gothas was devastating: Second Lieutenant Young's aircraft was hit and was seen by Major Moore going down in a nosedive at 12,000 feet. Captain Cooke's machine received three bursts but he managed to land at Rochford quite safely. None of the Gothas was brought down at this time although some most certainly were damaged.

Young's machine came down in the sea, and a naval vessel hurried to the spot. The pilot was entangled in the wreckage and was drowned, but his gunner, Air Mechanic C. Taylor, was rescued, although wounded.

Off the Essex coast, just after 11.00, the bombers were attacked by a prototype British Fighter BF2a from Orfordness, flown by Lieutenant F. Holden, and a Pup from No. 37 Squadron at Stow Maries, with Captain C. Ridley at the controls. The latter's Vickers gun jammed during the engagement, and his machine was peppered with holes from a Gotha ventral gun position. His report is interesting: 'I am doubtful if attacking underneath is the best position, as they can shoot vertically downwards.' This observation clearly indicates that the pilots of No. 37 Squadron, at least, had received no effective instruction, since 13 June, concerning the Gothas' 'sting in the tail'. The Captain also stated that the raiders had regained their usual tight formation by that time but a few were certainly straggling, probably due to gun-fire damage.

An Armstrong-Whitworth FK8 from No. 50 Squadron, piloted by Second Lieutenant F. Grace and with Second Lieutenant G. Murray as observer, patrolling near the North Foreland, pounced on a detached bomber limping along at a fairly low altitude. This Gotha, from *Staffel* No. 14 at Melle-Gontrode, lacking the usual crossfire support, was fairly easy meat for the AW. Black smoke issued from the bomber's engines, and its pilot had no option but to put the machine down on the sea. Two of the crew clambered out onto the wings as the stricken Gotha wallowed in the swell, whilst the British aviators endeavoured to assist by firing off all their Very lights in an attempt to bring naval vessels to the scene. It was, however, all in vain: the bomber soon sank and the crew members were lost.[13]

The six RNAS Sopwith fighters that had been sent up from Manston earlier that morning were airborne again at about 11.00, in company with three additional Bristol Scouts. Four of the Sopwith pilots, Squadron Commander Butler, Flight Lieutenants J. Scott and R. Daly, and Flight Sub-Lieutenant A. Lofft, launched harassing attacks on the retiring Gothas all the way across the North Sea to the Dutch coast. Butler claimed a bomber downed near the Kentish Knock lightship, whilst Scott claimed one some thirty miles east-north-east of the North Foreland. In addition, Daly reported that he had shot down a third Gotha and attacked another near the estuary of the Scheldt river. However, his gun jammed during the latter fight and he was unable to continue the engagement. Lofft, in a Camel, said that he had driven down an enemy machine off the coast of Walcheren island. Unfortunately, his engine failed on returning to Essex, and his Camel crashed, although he was unhurt. Regrettably, however, none of the home-based RNAS' claims was supported by German accounts of the day's operations. Although all twenty-one Gothas managed to reach their airfields at about 13.00, no fewer than four were written off in landing crashes brought about by a combination of damage in action, cross-winds on the airfields, lack of petrol and the notorious instability of the Gotha G.IV when lightly loaded. It seems quite likely that Kleine had led his force close to or over the Scheldt river area in an attempt to avoid the RNAS at Dunkirk. In this he was probably successful but the increase in flight time proved disastrous for some of his bombers, even with the auxiliary petrol tanks provided.

On receipt of a warning (about 11.00) from Dover that the Gothas were clearing the Essex coast, No. 4 (Naval) Squadron at Bray Dunes sent up a patrol of nine Camels, led, once again, by Flight Commander Shook. No sign of the Gothas or their flight escorts was discovered but other hostile aircraft were certainly encountered. Flight Sub-Lieutenant Enstone claimed to have shot down an Aviatik and a seaplane, whilst Flight Sub-Lieutenant Ellis reported similar success against another seaplane. At about one o'clock the patrol returned to Bray Dunes for refuelling, but five of the Camels resumed the patrol shortly afterwards. A further three seaplanes were driven down during this subsequent sally.

No. 3 (Naval) Squadron from Furnes also scrambled a patrol

to carry out an anti-bomber sweep. Ten Camels and Pups were sent up but, oddly enough, not until 13.20 – far too late to catch any of the Gothas. However, the sortie was not in vain; the squadron attacked nine seaplanes off Ostend. Flight Lieutenant J. Fall reported downing three of these, and Flight Sub-Lieutenant Glen brought down another. One Pup was lost because of engine trouble but the pilot was rescued.

Although Kagohl 3 had effectively lost five of the twenty-two Gothas that had crossed the English coast, Kleine could not have been too despondent: only one bomber had fallen in the enemy's territorial area. Some seventy-six bombs, weighing a little over three tons, had been delivered, most of them descending on the London area. Fifty-seven people had been killed and 193 had been wounded, but these figures were far fewer than those of 13 June – the main reason being, of course, the reduced bombload carried by the Gothas. No doubt the casualty list would have been longer had Kleine's bombs been more reliable. The Metropolitan Police records show that seventeen per cent of all known bombs failed to explode, but the overall percentage must have been well above that. Strangely, perhaps, the damage in monetary terms was over twice that of 13 June, presumably because of the large number of warehouses gutted on this occasion.

Of the ninety-one aeroplanes scrambled by home defence establishments (both RFC and RNAS) only thirty-six had been able to open fire on the bombers, but half of these, as we have seen, were plagued by gun jams whilst a third suffered from engine troubles. In point of fact, the number of engagements on this day was to be the highest the defences would ever achieve during the day raids. Unfortunately, however, the RFC home defence pilots had yet to be organized to attack in group or squadron formation. Once again their lone assaults had invariably been beaten off by the Gothas' multiple fire-power.

The AA artillery had fired a prodigious quantity of shells at the raiders – and, in a number of cases, at friendly aircraft as well. The London batteries had expended some 2,000 rounds, nearly all of them being the common explosive type of which Rawlinson had been so contemptuous. The guns outside London had discharged about 1,000 rounds between them, but neither they nor the London ones had achieved very much, although the Gothas had been forced to open out their formation to present less of a target to the gunners. Once again it had been clearly demonstrated that defending aircraft and AA guns would have to be under a single overall command and that operating zones for each must be delineated.

If the London public had been angered by the raid of 13 June, it was absolutely infuriated by that of 7 July. For the second time within a month, a German air fleet had sailed across England in broad daylight apparently little affected by the efforts of the defence forces. Again there had been no warning at all and, perhaps inevitably, a rebellious mood was setting in. In the East End mobs began assembling after the raid, eager for vengeance, and soon began rioting. After dark they turned their fury against the premises of any trader unfortunate enough to possess a German-sounding name, and there were many such, or who had even the remotest German connection. The very name of the royal family (Saxe-Coburg-Gotha) was now reviled because it included, by an extraordinary coincidence, the name of the bombers that had visited death and destruction on the city that the founder of the House, Albert, the Prince Consort, had done so much to promote and improve. King George V moved rapidly, however, and on 17 July a proclamation was issued stating that from thenceforth the royal name would be Windsor.

The Gothas had certainly terrorized the people of London, but there was no public demand for peace, as Ludendorf had hoped. Quite the contrary, in fact: the cry that went up after the raid was for protection, first and foremost, but also for retaliation against German cities, just as the mobs in the East End had indicated.

A meeting of the War Cabinet was convened at 10 Downing Street within hours of the end of the raid.[14] When the meeting opened at 15.30, the Prime Minister had four permanent members in attendance, Mr G. Barnes, Mr Bonar Law, Lord Milner and Lieutenant-General Smuts, whilst co-opted members included the CIGS, Lord French, Lieutenant-General Henderson, Admiral Jellicoe, Commodore Paine and Major-General Shaw.

Lord French began the proceedings with a review of damage and casualties in the metropolis, together with details of Gothas reportedly shot down in combat. The FM wasted little time, however, and launched into a rather acerbic harangue concerning his insufficient air forces – 'a patchwork concern'. He pointed out, in no uncertain terms, that no raid on London had occurred whilst Nos. 56 and 66 Squadrons had been under his command, but an attack on the city had followed within twenty-four hours of their return to Estrée Blanche. At this point Henderson interposed to point out that, 'Except on the day of the Harwich raid, there had been no flying day suitable for a long-distance raid while they (the squadrons) were there.'[15] The War Cabinet was, however, of the opinion that the setting up of a raid immediately after the withdrawal of the two squadrons pointed to an effective system of enemy espionage.

The CIGS, in a letter written to FM Haig on Sunday the 9th, stated that there was so much excitement at the meeting that, 'One would have thought the whole world was coming to an end.' He claimed that he 'could not get a word in edge-ways' whilst the Field Marshal was in full spate, but Robertson agreed that French did not have a very good force: 'It is made up of oddments, and, of course, oddments will not do.'[16]

There can be little doubt that French also referred to his letter of 2 July to the War Office and the lack of a reply thereto. However, as the Secretary to the War Office was not present at this meeting, the matter was presumably held over until the next one.

The War Cabinet came, finally, to the conclusion that two methods of dealing with the raiders were possible: first, to maintain an efficient force of machines in England, and second, to make counter-strikes against German towns, 'such as Mannheim'. Henderson, in an attempt to improve the defence capability, proposed the diversion to Home Service of a squadron then 'forming and mobilizing to proceed to France'. What squadron Henderson was referring to is not clear from the records, and certainly nothing further was heard of this proposal during the day raids, i.e. up to the end of August. In any event, the development of day-fighting detachments from Nos. 37, 39 and 50 (HD) Squadrons was already under way, No. 39's SE5 group of experienced pilots at Sutton's Farm being but one example.

The War Cabinet decided to make the following orders: first, that the squadron mentioned by Henderson should be allotted to home defence; second, that the War Office should recall two fighting squadrons from the Western Front immediately; and third, that the War Office should inform FM Haig 'that they would be glad if he could spare enough machines to carry out an attack on Mannheim'. However, the War Cabinet left the latter point open by stating that the matter should not be pressed if Haig replied that such a bombing raid would dislocate his plans. And with that the War Cabinet adjourned for the weekend, leaving General Robertson to contact the C.-in-C. by telegram.

The CIGS (who had, in fact, attempted to dissuade the Cabinet from asking for two squadrons from the Western Front at such a critical time) telegraphed FM Haig, immediately after the meeting, in the following terms:

In view of today's raid and prospect of its early repetition, Cabinet have decided at a special meeting this afternoon that Home Defence Forces must be strengthened at once by two first-class fighting squadrons and have accordingly ordered me to direct you to dispatch two squadrons tomorrow to England, aeroplanes by air, personnel by boat, as in previous cases. Exact period for which the squadrons will be needed cannot be given, but it is hoped it may be possible to reinforce Home Defence from other sources so as to allow one squadron to return in about a fortnight. Cabinet are further desirous of your making an air raid on Mannheim, but before deciding they wish you to report to what extent this will interfere with your operations.[17]

The Commander-in-Chief penned an immediate reply telegram in which he stated that arrangements would certainly be made to send 'two good fighting squadrons' on the following day (the 8th), but he hastened to point out that the fight for air supremacy in preparation for the opening of the third Battle of Ypres had already begun. That air struggle was going to be the hardest yet, and 'The withdrawal of two fighting squadrons would delay a favourable decision in the air, and make victory more difficult and more costly in aeroplanes and pilots. If, in addition, the raid on Mannheim had to be undertaken, the plans for the whole offensive would require to be reconsidered, and the operations, dependent as they were on the gaining of air supremacy, might have to be stopped.'[18]

Haig firmly believed that one result of a successful compaign in Flanders would be the re-occupation of the Gotha bases around Ghent, thus removing the threat to London and south-east England at a stroke. From the Commander-in-Chief's point of view, then, his fighting squadrons would be making a greater contribution to home defence by carrying out their normal duties in France than they would by moving to England!

The War Cabinet would not be meeting in full session until the Monday morning but Haig's arguments were obviously considered during that Sunday. The CIGS, in his letter to Haig of 9 July commented: 'When we received your wire yesterday the Cabinet were inclined to go back on their decision, and agree to ask you for less than two squadrons and perhaps for none.'[19]

And there this rather indecisive matter rested until the following morning.

Other noteworthy events were, however, taking place over the weekend. The first occurred very early on the Sunday morning, when RNAS aircraft from Dunkirk bombed the airfield at Ghistelles, following up their attack on Melle-Gontrode and St-Denis Westrem the previous night. Then, later in the day, No. 39 Squadron's flight at Sutton's Farm, including the day-fighter detachment, received orders to pack up and move to Hainault Farm, to provide room at Sutton's for any squadron that might be detached from France. In any event, it was intended that No. 39's staff from Sutton's Farm should amalgamate with the squadron's C Flight already at Hainault Farm to become the nucleus of a new day-fighter squadron (No. 44) to be formed later in the month. Initially this new unit was to be equipped with the obsolescent $1\frac{1}{2}$-Strutter, for training purposes (particularly formation flying), and be supplied with Camels as soon as such machines became available.

In accordance with an emergency order given by FM Haig, the personnel of No. 66 Squadron at Estrée Blanche were sent over to England during Sunday and took up the vacated quarters at Sutton's Farm.[20] Curiously enough, however, the squadron's Pups were left in France, possibly to delude enemy agents into thinking that the squadron was still at Estrée Blanche when in fact it was at Hornchurch. It is a matter of conjecture as to what aircraft No. 66 was to use whilst at Sutton's Farm, but presumably sufficient Pups were by then available to the Southern Home Defence Wing.

At 11.30 on the Monday morning, the War Cabinet re-assembled at No. 10 in order to continue its discussion of the London raid and matters appertaining thereto. The PM again took the chair, whilst five permanent members, this time including Lord Curzon, shuffled their papers for what promised to be a fairly stormy session.

All co-opted members who had been present on the previous Friday, were again called in, together with the War Minister (Lord Derby), the Secretary of the War Office (Sir Reginald Brade), Sir William Weir from the Air Board, and several others.

Lord French read to the assembly his two letters of 2 and 6 July, addressed to the Secretary of the War Office and the CIGS respectively. The Minutes of this meeting echo the astonishment of the War Cabinet concerning the treatment of the letter of 2 July: 'The War Cabinet commented severely and adversely on the fact that the letter of the 2nd July had not been brought to their attention, particularly as the Cabinet Committee on War Policy had discussed the matter very fully with Field-Marshal Sir Douglas Haig and General Trenchard, the latter of whom had been specially brought to this country for the purpose. On enquiry it became clear that Lord French's letter of the 2nd instant had not been seen by the Secretary of State for War.'[21]

The Secretary of the War Office then had the somewhat unenviable task of explaining why he had sent the original letter to Henderson, and not directly to the War Minister. In mitigation, we may perhaps wonder why Lord French had not addressed his letter to Derby in the first place.

The meeting then heard the full story of the raid, including the numbers of home-based RFC and RNAS aircraft involved and the known results obtained. Lieutenant-General Henderson spoke up for the defenders, as the Minutes recall: 'General Henderson pointed out in this connection that one reason why the losses inflicted were not greater was that our machines arrived, to a large extent, singly or in small groups, and it was difficult for these to attack a number of enemy machines in formation.'

Lord Derby then read out the telegram from Sir Douglas Haig, thus provoking much discussion that recalled the cogent remarks written by the retired Admiral in Folkestone a few weeks before. The Minutes summed it all up as follows: 'The War Cabinet recognized that the protection of the public against hostile aircraft attack is a matter of increasing importance, particularly in the present state of the war, when the issue depends almost as much on the endurance of the people as on that of the armies. Nevertheless, in view of the immediate and critical importance of Field Marshal Sir Douglas Haig's demands and in conformity with the advice of the CIGS, the War Cabinet decided that only one fighting squadron instead of two ... should be recalled' and further, 'that the proposal to raid Mannheim should be abandoned for the present'.

The all too obvious fact that the country did not yet have sufficient aircraft for both offence and defence was offset, largely, by a statement from Sir William Weir, who reported on the progress achieved by the Air Board in stepping up the vital aero-engine production. His figures showed that twice as many engines were then being produced as in the same period the previous year, and soon production would rise to be three times as many. Lloyd George discussed the matter in his Memoirs: 'The figures which Sir William Weir was able to give us as to the rate of production of aero-engines showed that we should soon possess an air fleet much in excess of the necessary demands of the Army and Navy. But it would be some weeks before these would begin to take shape as additional trained squadrons.[22]

The Prime Minister then drew the War Cabinet's attention to the large number of questions put down for answer in the House of Commons in regard to the latest raid on London. The War Cabinet appreciated the 'impossibility of giving complete and frank replies without revealing matters which, in the public interest, must be kept secret'. The Premier intended, therefore, to ask Parliament to meet in secret session later that night for a full discussion of the Government's policy with regard to home defence.

The concluding part of General Robertson's letter of the 9th to FM Haig dealt with the War Cabinet's decision to ask for just one fighting squadron, and the CIGS's views concerning future air defence policy:

Today they [the War Cabinet] had another meeting, at which French was again present, and the old ground was re-traversed. The result was that you have now to send back one squadron in place of two. I am afraid I cannot say when the squadron will be returned. Of course it is necessary that these raids should be put an end to, or at any rate be severely punished. We saw Saturday's raid from the War Office windows. Our anti-aircraft artillery was apparently of no use, and our airmen arrived in driblets and were powerless, but succeeded in getting one machine down. The fact is we have not got enough machines to meet our requirements. I find that I have brought the question before the Cabinet no fewer than six times during the present year. I doubt if any real progress will be made until a different organization is established. The Army and Navy now say what they want, the Air Board consider their wants, and then Addison (Minister of Munitions) makes the machines. I am inclined to think that we need a separate air service, but that would be a big business. There is a special debate on the subject to-night, and it will probably be followed by a secret session.[23]

At the secret session Lloyd George gave the House an unequivocal statement of the air defence situation. He produced figures that showed how aircraft construction was being expanded through the Air Board's sterling efforts, and that the time would soon come when there would be adequate supplies of aeroplanes for all requirements – military operations, independent air bombing attacks and home defence. Until that time arrived, however, military operations must have priority:

The first consideration before the Government is to see that the Army in France is sufficiently supplied with aeroplanes. A sufficiency of aeroplanes means everything to that Army. They are the eyes of the Army, which cannot advance without them. By their means the Army discovers the enemy's trenches, guns and machine-gun emplacements. To photograph these requires air supremacy, and without that air supremacy it is sheer murder to allow troops to advance ... The slightest deficiency in the work of observation from the air, a single machine-gun emplacement overlooked, might in a few minutes mean the loss of thousands of gallant lives. The first duty of the country is to protect these men. The Germans realise the importance of this question quite as much as we do. The second means by which they are attempting to diminish our superiority is by trying to force us to withdraw our machines from France in order to protect our own towns. If the Germans know that by bombing English towns they can force us to withdraw fighting squadrons from France, there could be nothing which would encourage them more ... If the aeroplanes can be provided for the Front and for our defence against raids, that will, of course, be done. If not, the Army must come first, and it is vitally important that the Germans should know it.[24]

Although this statement satisfied the House for the time being, public disapprobation following the latest raid was now bringing substantial pressure to bear upon the Government to look at service aeronautics in greater depth, in order to ensure 'the best possible use of the air weapon, alike for attack or defence'.[25]

Trenchard's choice of a fighter squadron to be detached to Sutton's Farm actually fell on Major P. Babington's No. 46 (Pups), then stationed at Bruay. No. 66 Squadron's personnel, who had filled the breach, as it were, between 8 and 10 July, were returned to France. Later on the 10th, No. 46 Squadron made an impressive arrival at Sutton's Farm, its well-drilled formation flying being described as 'splendid' by observers in the area. The squadron soon demonstrated, furthermore, that it was capable of responding to an alert without delay: eighteen of its Pups could be airborne within five minutes of the raid hooter sounding.[26] There can be no doubt that espionage agents, in both France and the UK, wasted little time in reporting No. 46's movements to the German intelligence service, who would, in turn, have informed Kleine at Melle-Gontrode.

At Hainault Farm, formation flying was also the order of the day, as the embryo fighter squadron later to be No. 44 began to take shape. The new unit was rapidly dubbed 'the Circus' by the thousands of people who came to watch the stunting and formating during the summer evenings.

The vociferous demands for air-raid warnings, following the raid of the 7th, forced the War Cabinet to reconsider its absurd decision of 26 June. On 10 July that decision was reversed: a five-minute warning was to be given 'at the circumference of a circle with a radius of ten miles from Charing Cross, that is to say, a circle which would cover the main populated districts of London'.[27]

It was, however, one thing to permit warnings to be given but it was quite another to devise a system capable of being heard over such a wide area. Whilst many ideas were put forward, only those advocating the use of sirens or signal rockets (maroons) were seriously considered. Few sirens of the necessary power existed, however, and tests soon showed that large numbers of them would be required. After much deliberation, the proposal to use sirens was dropped, and the decision was taken to establish a sound system based on the type of naval maroons normally employed to alert lifeboatmen. Such a system could not, of course, be set up overnight, and in the interim period the Commissioner of the Metropolitan Police proposed to send his men, both regular and special, through the London streets, exhibiting a placard with the inscription 'POLICE NOTICE – TAKE COVER', whenever intelligence was received that enemy aircraft were flying towards the city.

Across the Channel, meanwhile, the preparations for the third Battle of Ypres, due to open at the end of the month, included the movement of four fighter squadrons from the Western Front to the Dunkirk area. These squadrons, part of the RFC's 14th Wing (4th Brigade) were No. 6 (Naval) equipped with Camels, No. 48 (Bristol Fighter), No. 9 (Naval), now using a mixture of Camels and Triplanes, and No. 54 (Pups). No. 6 (Naval) and No. 48 flew into the Frontier aerodrome whilst No. 9 (Naval) and No. 54 went to Leffrinckhoucke.[28] The redeployment of these squadrons, completed by 10 July, was to have some effect upon the succeeding air raids on England, because the 14th Wing was able to order some of its squadrons to take part in anti-Gotha sweeps, when they were available to do so.

On Wednesday 11 July the War Cabinet, at its 181st meeting, again discussed the vexatious problems of air defence and the conduct of air operations generally. As Jones later wrote: 'Apart altogether from the question of allaying the general disquiet, it was obvious to the Government that the problem of home defence against air attack could not be isolated, [and] that it must take its place in a survey of the whole air policy and organisation.'[29]

Lloyd George decided that a committee should immediately be set up to conduct such a survey. Although this committee was to be headed by the Prime Minister himself, the affairs of state precluded anything but a nominal chairmanship. The actual burden of the work to be done was, sensibly, to be left to a 'fresh and able mind, free from departmental prejudices'. Lloyd George already had such a person pencilled in for the task: the Minister without Portfolio sitting in the War Cabinet itself, Lieutenant-General Jan Smuts.

The former Boer War leader, then aged forty-seven, who only fifteen years before had fought against the British, had been of great service to the War Cabinet since he had come to London as the South African delegate to the Imperial War Cabinet the previous May. He had a luxurious suite at the Savoy Hotel but spent little time there because he was continually working on War Cabinet assignments. He wrote later that he had never worked so hard in his life before – 'My hair became white at fifty.' Described at the time as the most intellectual member of the War Cabinet, Smuts possessed an analytical brain capable of making a rapid assessment of the essentials of any particular problem. On this occasion, although quite unbiased, he was somewhat reluctant to become involved in such a contentious and onerous duty but, assured of a free hand, eventually agreed to do so.

The Committee on Air Organization and Home Defence against Air Raids came into being that day, as Minute 3 of that War Cabinet meeting stated:

> That the Prime Minister and General Smuts, in consultation with representatives of the Admiralty, General Staff and Field Marshal, Commanding-in-Chief Home Forces, with such other experts as they may desire should examine:
> 1 The defence arrangements for home defence against air-raids.
> 2 The air organization generally and the direction of aerial operations.[30]

The first part of this brief was the more pressing, the second part by far the more important and significant. Two reports would therefore be required: the first to be produced as rapidly as possible in order to make urgent recommendations concerning the improvement of the air defence of the Metropolitan area; and the second at the end of a more detailed and searching examination of the entire field of service aeronautics.

Smuts wasted no time in beginning his investigation of the problem of air defence, interviewing a succession of Army and Navy experts who were connected with it, including Lieutenant-General Henderson, Lieutenant-Colonel Higgins, Commodore Paine, Major-General Shaw, Lieutenant-Colonel Simon and many others. The Chairman spent long hours listening patiently to everyone, tirelessly ploughing through masses of sometimes irrelevant detail in order to extract the vital key facts required for his first report to the War Cabinet. Lloyd George obviously expected the report on the air defences to be drafted quickly but even he could hardly have expected that Smuts would have it ready by 19 July, just eight days later.

This quite remarkable achievement would owe a great deal to one man, Lieutenant-General Henderson, who, in contrast to Trenchard, believed passionately in a separate and independent air service. In the Smuts brief, he saw the opening he had wished for during weary months of inter-service acrimony over air matters. Sir David, who had had the misfortune to be saddled with two full-time jobs for years, was now able to leave that of DGMA to Brancker, his deputy, in order to spend as much time as possible advising Smuts. Brancker would, in fact, take over as DGMA later in the month.

Whilst Smuts was beginning his deliberations in London, the RNAS bombers from Nos. 5 and 7 (Naval) Squadrons at Coudekerque, Dunkirk, continued their determined attacks on German airfields in Flanders. On the night of 11/12 July they struck at St-Denis Westrem and Ghistelles, and during the following night they returned to Ghistelles yet again.

On the 13th Trenchard was astonished to receive a letter from the War Office informing him that twenty-four Camels and four DH4s intended to re-equip Nos. 43 and 45 Squadrons on the Western Front would be diverted to home defence squadrons. The Camels were to be re-directed from the factory to Hainault Farm for the new day-fighter squadron being formed from No. 39 Squadron. This re-arrangement had been made without any consultation with Trenchard whatsoever, and he was, quite naturally, infuriated. He reported the facts to Haig who wrote a testy note to the CIGS on the following day (the 14th):

A serious reduction has been made at the last moment in the supply of aircraft on which I was counting for my operations. I have no information as to the authority on which such an important decision has been arrived at, and I have only learnt of it through these communications addressed by a Directorate to a General Officer under my command, who has brought them to my notice. You will appreciate, without explanation from me, the unsatisfactory nature of such method of procedure, and still more the seriousness of my being deprived suddenly and unexpectedly, at the present juncture, of forces on which I was counting to carry through an offensive of such great importance, the preparations for which have reached such an advanced stage that no alteration or modification can now be made without grave disadvantage.[31]

On this occasion the War Cabinet virtually turned a deaf ear to the Field Marshal's protestations – evidently it was determined to establish No. 44 Squadron as a top-line day-fighter squadron in UK as quickly as possible. This attitude contrasted somewhat sharply with Lloyd George's statement to the House during the secret session of Parliament on the 9th, only a few days previously. Kleine would have been delighted to learn that Kagohl 3's actions were being of direct benefit to the German Air Force on the Western Front in that Nos. 43 and 45 Squadrons would, perforce, have to continue operating with their outdated 1½-Strutters for several weeks longer than had been planned.

The number of fighter aircraft intended for the defence of London was thus rising quite rapidly. Twelve more Pups were delivered to Nos. 37 and 50 Squadrons on or about 15 July, as Lord French had stated in his letter of the 6th. These aircraft were intended eventually to equip two other new day-fighter squadrons to be formed from flights of the two parent squadrons.

Lieutenant-General Smuts, busy marshalling facts and figures for his report on air defence, received, on Monday the 16th, an official memorandum from Sir David Henderson in confirmation of the latter's verbal statements to the Committee.

Although more concerned with the second part of Smut's brief, Henderson made no bones about the need for unity of command for the air defence forces: 'I would suggest that the whole of our defences against air attack – observation, communication, aeroplanes and guns – should be organised under a single command. As the aeroplane is by far the most important means of defence, the commander should be an officer of the Royal Flying Corps. It is desirable that he should still be under the general command of the C.-in-C., Home Forces.'[32]

At this time, also, Lieutenant-Colonels Simon and Higgins were engaged in preparing written proposals for improving the effectiveness of their particular branches of air defence; and both men would have discussed their individual schemes with Smuts prior to the presentation of their official proposals to

Lord French. Simon's proposal, presented to GHQHF on 16 July, involved 'the construction of a ring of gun stations round London to meet the bombing formations with heavy bursts of gun-fire about twenty-five miles from the capital with the idea of breaking up the formations to enable the home defence pilots to engage the raiders in detachments or individually.'[33] This plan for a London barrage was a development of that previously proposed by the AADC on 21 June, which, as we have seen, had been rejected at that time by the War Cabinet on the grounds of insufficient guns and artillerymen.

Higgins' paper, which would not be presented until 19 July, propounded that '... five additional home defence squadrons should be formed for day fighting. The existing squadrons are responsible for day and night fighting, for wireless co-operation with coastal batteries, for wireless tracking, and for certain specified duties in the event of an attempted invasion. It seems evident that one squadron commander cannot sufficiently supervise the administration, training and operations entailed by these various duties which involve totally different classes of pilots and machines.'[34]

Higgins was, of course, most anxious that his men should not be expected to operate both by day and night, as some of them undoubtedly had had to do in June. His demand for five new day-fighting squadrons obviously reflected his opinion that the development of such units was not proceeding rapidly enough to meet the apparent daytime threat to the capital. Three new day squadrons were certainly projected at this time – No. 44 at Hainault Farm (an offshoot of No. 39 Squadron), No. 61 at Rochford (from No. 37 Squadron) and No. 112 at Throwley (from No. 50 Squadron) – but of these only No. 44 was by then nearing its formation date.

These three proposals, and others, were exhaustively studied by the industrious Smuts before he began the drafting chore for his first report. The document, ran to five closely typewritten pages and was delivered to Lloyd George, as mentioned, on Thursday 19 July. This paper, although hurriedly produced, was in fact to have a profound effect on the structuring of the air defence of Great Britain not only for the remainder of the Great War but for many years thereafter.

The text of the first report, is given, in full, in Appendix IV, from which it will be seen that three of the report's four

recommendations sprang directly from the respective sug-
gestions of Henderson, Simon and Higgins.[35] The first, for
example, recognized the imperative need for unity of command,
just as Henderson, the spokesman for many, had pointed out in
his memorandum. It is, of course, possible to argue that Smuts
himself, the victor of German East Africa, would also have
considered a supremo for air defence essential to success.

The second recommendation echoed the submission put
forward by Simon with regard to an AA gun barrage around
London. The statement that 'special endeavours should
therefore be made to provide an adequate number of guns for
this purpose' is interesting because it clearly indicated a change
in Smuts' thinking on the subject of AA artillery since his
participation in the War Cabinet's decision of 21 June that
rejected Simon's earlier proposal.

The third recommendation, whilst urging a speed-up in the
formation of the day-fighting squadron Nos. 44, 61 and 112, did
not support the proposal by Higgins that another two day
squadrons should also be formed. In fact, five months would
pass before two more squadrons for home defence would be
authorized (Nos. 141 and 143), and they, paradoxically, would
be night-fighter units.

The fourth recommendation, calling for a reserve force, 'in
accordance with the general and elementary principles of
warfare', could well have been prompted by the two feints
attempted by Kleine at Margate on 13 June and 7 July. (Lord
French had indicated the need for a reserve force in his letter to
the Secretary of the War Office on 2 July.)

On the day after the Smuts paper was submitted to the War
Cabinet for consideration, the Home Secretary was able to
report that sufficient quantities of the signal maroons required
for the new air-raid system for London had been delivered to
eighty selected fire stations in the prescribed area around
Charing Cross. On the receipt of an air-raid warning from
County Hall, each of these fire stations was to set off three of the
rockets at fifteen-second intervals. An announcement concerning the inception of the new system was issued by the Home
Office on Saturday the 21st, but too late for it to be publicized
that day. Whilst apparently of little consequence, this delay in
notification was to cause some distress to the citizens of London
the following Sunday morning.

For two weeks after the raid of the 7th, there had been a welcome respite from Gotha attacks on the English mainland. This break was not of the restless Kleine's choosing but due entirely to a spell of appalling weather conditions that set in immediately after the 7th. Depressions, usually with gale-force winds, had been common in the North Sea, either grounding the Gothas or confining them to sorties in France or Belgium. On the 21st, however, barometric pressure began to rise again, and *Leutnant* Georgii was able to report to Kleine that Sunday the 22nd might well prove to be a reasonable day for the next incursion against England, although he could not, of course, be certain about the conditions on the other side of the Channel.

After much thought, Kleine authorized an operation for the 22nd but chose to make another coastal raid rather than to go inland to London. Apart from the problems of the weather, he was presumably well aware of the presence of No. 46 Squadron at Sutton's Farm, astride the usual route to the capital. In any event, tip-and-run coastal raids would still serve to keep the defences on their toes, as Ludendorf had demanded, even if the propagandistic effect was that much less.

Kleine decided that this raid should have the same target areas as that of the 4th – Harwich and Felixstowe – with a quick assault early in the morning so that Kagohl 3 would be gone before the defences could be brought properly to action.

At about 06.30 on the 22nd, a clear, sunny morning, twenty-two Gothas began thundering off from St-Denis Westrem and Melle-Gontrode, the squadron finally setting course over the sea well to the north, just as it had on the 4th. The North Sea (or German Sea as it was originally called) was for once very calm, and the wind, such as it was, a gentle zephyr from the north-west. Even the Gothas' aero-engines seemed less fractious today – only one bomber was forced to give up and return to base.

At Harwich and Felixstowe a thick sea fog had blanketed the towns since dawn but by 07.30 it had rolled away, the sun shining brilliantly from a cloudless if somewhat hazy sky. Towards eight o'clock a distant humming became audible at Hollesley Bay as the Gothas approached the coastline in their usual V-formation and at an altitude of 14,000 feet. The bombers were fortunate to be flying in out of the sun, and this fact, coupled with the hazy conditions, was to make observation from the ground extremely difficult.

On receipt of a telephone call from Felixstowe, a green warning was issued to the five Warning Districts involved in the day warning system, resulting in a response of ninety-six aircraft from the RFC and twenty-five from the RNAS air stations. No fewer than sixteen different types of aeroplanes took part but the majority were now modern fighters such as the Camel and Pup. No. 46 Squadron scrambled eighteen of its Pups within a very short time after the receipt of the warning, and they began climbing up to 16,000 feet in order to patrol between Joyce Green and Hainault Farm. No. 37 Squadron had eleven of its new Pups aloft, and they flew in formation in two flights between Rochford and the Blackwater river. No. 39 Squadron's day-fighters put up ten Camels to patrol, in formation, from Hainault Farm northwards to North Weald Bassett. All this activity was to be, in the main, quite nugatory: the defending fighters protecting London were taking off or climbing whilst the Gothas were already on their way back to Belgium. As Ashmore was to state later: 'It must be accepted as an axiom that no practical scale of aeroplane defence in England can be effective against surprise air attacks on the coastline.'[36]

Once across the coast, Kleine turned his squadron south-west and headed directly down towards Felixstowe. Over the River Deben the bombers were greeted by introductory shell bursts from the same seven 3-inch 20cwt AA batteries of the Harwich Command that had been in action on the 4th. On that occasion the gun crews had been surprised, but they certainly were not so on this Sunday morning. Between them, the guns fired off 273 rounds in approximately twelve minutes, the time the Gothas were actually within range. This was a very fine performance indeed, particularly so when one considers the difficulty of observation against the glaring sun. The battery commander at Rose Farm, Shotley, was to sum it up in his report: 'Observation both from the gun and flank observer posts was very difficult owing to the strong sun behind the targets. Upper atmosphere was hazy while target was approaching.'[37] Although the guns did not succeed in shooting down any of the raiders, they did manage to disrupt the formation, which opened out into two separate groups, one slightly higher than the other.

Fifty-five bombs were then showered by the Gothas on Harwich and Felixstowe, the usual proportion of which failed to explode, whilst at least thirteen plumped in mudflats or on the seashore. At Felixstowe, bathers took exception to this but prudently sought shelter out of the water. Harwich suffered some slight damage to houses but had no casualties at all. Felixstowe, however, and the air station in particular, was again the focus of the attack. A recently completed Engineer's Workshop on the station was almost demolished by a 50kg bomb, one naval rating being killed and three others injured. An Army barracks nearby was also hit, leaving eleven soldiers of the Suffolk Regiment dead and twenty wounded. Civilian property damaged or destroyed included the Ordnance Hotel, where a barman died, six houses and two churches. Total casualties in the raid were thirteen killed and twenty-six injured – figures comparable with those of 4 July.

It was now about 08.15 and, skirting the Naze, the raiders turned south-east and, as far as the ground observers were concerned, soon disappeared in the hazy conditions out to sea. However, Kagohl 3 had not seen the last of the home defenders: a solitary two-seater from Orfordness which had gone up at about 08.05 arrived over Harwich just as the bombers were re-crossing the coastline. This machine, a Vickers FB14d piloted by Captain Vernon Brown and with Captain Melville Jones as observer, was unusual in that it was fitted with a new periscopic gunsight designed by Captain Jones, who was most anxious to try it out. This device enabled the pilot to lay the sight onto a target for the observer to fire the guns, allowance being made for the relative speeds of the two aircraft concerned.

Accordingly, the FB14d set off in pursuit of the raiders but, not being a particularly speedy machine, had to chase the enemy formation some fifty miles before getting close enough to open fire on two Gothas lagging at the rear of the squadron. About one hundred rounds were fired by Jones, but other Gothas then turned to assist their comrades and the Vickers was forced to break off the fight and return to Orfordness. This engagement was to be the only one the home-based RFC and RNAS would be able to mount on this occasion, another rather curious parallel to the events of the 4th July.

Both the military and naval authorities in the Dunkirk area were informed by telephone or signal when the Gothas were leaving Harwich, and the RFC's 14th Wing at once ordered No. 48 Squadron to send up a patrol of its Bristol Fighter F2b machines from the Frontier aerodrome. This patrol took off at about 08.30 and climbed away eastwards to lie in wait at 16,000 feet for the returning bombers. Seven miles north of Ostend, the patrol pounced down, out of the sun, on five Gothas flying along at about 10,000 feet. One of the bombers was shot down into the sea by a machine piloted by Captain B. Baker with Lieutenant G. Spencer as observer. The other Gothas fled back to Belgium with the Bristols harassing them on the way.

The available records show that the RNAS at Dunkirk responded to the alert by sending up ten Sopwith fighters to hunt for the Gothas.[38] Five of these were Camels from No. 4 (Naval) Squadron, but which naval squadron sent up the other five fighters is not clear.

No. 4 (Naval) Squadron's patrol, led, as usual, by Flight Commander Shook, patrolled the offshore area between 10.00 and 12.00 but was unable to locate any of the raiders. It seems quite likely that most of the bombers had made the safety of Belgium before No. 4 (Naval) appeared on the scene.

Back across the Channel, meanwhile, extraordinary events were occurring, on this Sunday morning, that were the outcome of an almost incredible breakdown in air-raid warning procedures. These events were to highlight, in no uncertain manner, the crying need for an effectively co-ordinated control and communication system for the defence network, just as Lieutenant-General Henderson had postulated in his memo to Smuts on the 16th.

As had been seen, the Gothas departed from Harwich at approximately 08.15, and one could be forgiven for supposing that the cancellation of the green warning and the institution of the yellow (*All Clear*) would have followed shortly afterwards. What actually happened, in the London and Essex areas, was very different. It seems likely that the *All Clear* message was misunderstood, possibly by Headquarters, Eastern Command, and a red (*Take Air Raid Action*) was in fact transmitted. At about 08.30, therefore, London's County Hall passed this message on to all the eighty-five stations equipped with the naval maroons, and seventy-nine of them began firing off their rockets soon after. The slumbering, and largely unsuspecting, citizens of London were thus rudely awakened by a cacophony of some 237 firework explosions high overhead. Naturally enough, many people assumed, whilst the noise lasted, that the city was under attack but when silence returned, about thirty seconds later, it was quite evident, from what followed, that most of the Londoners realized that the fusillade was indeed merely a warning, and a highly effective one at that.

There was no panic or commotion, and whole families in the poorer districts emerged from their houses and tenements and made their way quietly to their nearest railway or underground station, for greater protection. Buses and trains were halted and passengers alighted and sought shelter nearby. All this contrasted somewhat sharply with the events of the previous daylight raids when the lack of any warning at all had put hundreds of people needlessly at risk on the open streets.

The actual warning lasted until about ten o'clock, by which time the London Warning Controller had managed to issue an *All Clear,* promulgated by means of placards carried by bicycle-riding policemen.

Whilst this false alarm had been very upsetting for Londoners, it did have one saving grace: it had provided a useful test of the effectiveness of the new warning system. In Essex, however, the pseudo-warning triggered off a series of serious mistakes on the part of six AA batteries, i.e. five of the mobile 13pdrs 9cwt located at Barling, Goldsands Bridges, Leigh-on-Sea, Southminster and Tillingham, and the 3-inch 20cwt fixed gun at Canvey Island. These six batteries fired, and continued to fire, upon RFC aeroplanes between 08.45 and 09.45, which meant that British aircraft were still being bombarded, by their comrades-in-arms on the ground, $1\frac{1}{2}$ hours after the German bombers had flown out to sea! Up to 09.45 these six AA batteries fired a total of 297 rounds, of which Canvey Island fired fourteen, Goldsands Bridges eighteen, Barling thirty-seven, Tillingham forty-four, Leigh-on-Sea seventy-three and Southminster an almost unbelieveable 111.

Aircrew from Orfordness and Stow Maries (No. 37 Squadron) were the unfortunate targets of most of these rounds, four two-seaters from the former being shelled, and a formation of seven Pups from the latter. The pilots concerned reported that the gunfire was heaviest over Maldon and Southend, but no one was injured in the brushes, although two aircraft were damaged. Captain Ridley, from Stow Maries, leading a formation of Pups on a patrol between the Blackwater river and the Thames estuary, came under heavy shellfire in the area of Southend. His machine was hit by shrapnel and actually lost its engine cowling, whereupon he was forced to land. Lieutenant Holden, from Orfordness, piloting his prototype Bristol F2a again, with Sergeant Ashby as gunner, was fired on over Maldon and later over Southend. He complained somewhat bitterly, on his return to Orfordness, that the roundels on his machine 'were perfectly distinct'.

However, in fairness to the AA Mobile Brigade, it must be stated that the brilliant sunshine and haziness made recognition extremely difficult, as the gunlayers at Harwich and Felixstowe had already discovered. The whole sorry business underlined, yet again, the imperative need for aircraft patrol areas to be well clear of AA gun sites, unless and until operational necessity demanded otherwise.

On the day after this near-disaster for the AA artillery, Lord French – with good timing, perhaps – presented Lieutenant-Colonel Simon's gunfire scheme of 16 July to the Army Council. The main feature of this plan, echoed in the Smuts Report, entailed a ring of gun stations around London some twenty-five miles out from the city centre. It was envisaged that these guns would be able to put up a heavy barrage in order, hopefully, to disrupt the advancing bomber formations and thus enable the fighters, waiting clear of the shellbursts, to engage the scattering Gothas.

In his covering letter, Lord French wrote bluntly about the futility of isolated attacks by fighters on unbroken enemy formations, describing them as 'a useless sacrifice'. He regarded co-ordinated tactical operations by AA guns and fighters, with separate zones for each, as 'not only possible, but essential to success'.[39]

To implement this plan, the FM asked, initially, for sufficient 3-inch 20cwt guns 'to provide a barrage arc covering London from attack from any direction from the north, by way of east, to the south'.[40]

Later, when more guns should become available, Lord French hoped to be able to complete the gun circle around the capital and thus provide protection from every direction. He estimated that 110 guns would be required for the initial semi-circle to the east, plus another eighty to close the ring completely.

The War Office replied that the scheme would be laid before the War Cabinet 'but that, meanwhile, he should consider taking guns from places less likely to be attacked'.[41]

By Tuesday the 24th, the weather had entered another dismal period characterized by frequent low-pressure systems with heavy rain and high winds – conditions that would effectively inhibit Gotha sorties across the North Sea. Kleine was not to know that this period of adverse conditions would continue for about a month and would thus provide few opportunities for further attacks on England.

On that Tuesday, the 24th, No. 44 (Home Defence) Squadron was officially formed at Hainault Farm, under Major T. Hubbard, with Camels and, presumably, a few 1½-Strutters. No. 39 Squadron, which had produced this day-fighter offspring, reverted to a mainly night-fighting role, as a safeguard against any further Zeppelin raids, although these were unlikely. No. 39 Squadron's long and chequered association with Sutton's Farm and Hainault Farm, throughout the Zeppelin campaign, was thus concluded; in future the squadron would be stationed at North Weald Bassett only.

In the very early morning of the 29th, No. 7 (Naval) Squadron at Coudekerque, Dunkirk, despatched a raiding force of Handley Page 0/100 and DH4 aeroplanes to drop bombs on the airfield at Ghistelles. Such raids were probably intended, in the main, to discourage the use of this forward airfield in the period immediately prior to the imminent offensive at Ypres. However, Kleine was by no means discouraged; he was anxious to set out across the North Sea again as soon as possible. In fact, he arranged another raid on England for that very day, the 29th, despite head-shaking from Georgii. The Gothas took off and began the North Sea crossing, but increasing cloud to the west and a freshening wind indicated the presence of a depression over the Channel. The enterprise was thus far too risky, and Kleine reluctantly signalled a return to Belgium.[42]

During the following day, the 30th, the second of the new day-fighting home defence squadrons was formed at Throwley, Kent, developed from the old B Flight of No. 50 Squadron. This new unit was No. 112 (Home Defence) Squadron, commanded by Captain G. Allen, and it took over the Pups that had been supplied to the parent squadron for daytime use. No. 50, like No. 39 a few days earlier, now became a predominantly night-fighting squadron once again, operating out of Bekesbourne and Detling, although its Armstrong-Whitworth FK8 and wireless-equipped BE12 aircraft, the latter acting as trackers, would still take part in subsequent day operations.

In the meantime, the War Cabinet had approved the proposals set out in Smuts' first report on air defence and instructed the War Office to implement them without delay. Accordingly, therefore, on 31 July the Army Council issued an order establishing the combined command to be known as the London Air Defence Area (LADA). The command was actually to be far larger than its title implied, being, in fact, the whole area considered to be liable to aeroplane attack, the triangle Southwold-London-Rottingdean. The military units to be included, as Smuts had recommended, were:

a.   The fixed and mobile gun batteries in the AA Commands of Dover/Thanet, Harwich, London and Thames/Medway, including the Mobile AA Brigade.

b.   The RFC's Southern Home Defence Wing, comprising Nos. 37, 39, 44, 50, 51 (Hingham), 61 (then forming at Rochford), 75 (Goldington), 78 and 112.

c.   The observation posts manned by the Royal Defence Corps in the warning districts east of the line Grantham-Portsmouth.[43]

Such, then, were the Command's constituent parts, but who was to be placed at its head, to provide the very necessary unity of command? Suitable candidates to fill the post cannot have been numerous; apart from having the right background, i.e. in ordnance and aeronautics, the GOC LADA would need foresight and imagination to weld the diverse military formations into a co-ordinated and co-operative force – and within a very short time, too. Furthermore, he would require much tact and patience in dealing with his service superiors and the high-ranking civil servants with whom inevitably he would come into contact.

Brigadier-General Edward B. Ashmore, a forty-five-year-old career artilleryman who was also a qualified pilot, was chosen to take on this onerous task. When the summons reached him, he was commanding the artillery of the 29th Division north of Ypres, but previously he had had wide air experience in France, culminating in the command of the RFC's 4th Brigade.

As the artillery in the Salient had been bombarding German positions almost continuously since about the beginning of July, in preparation for the forthcoming third Battle of Ypres, and, furthermore, the British lines were 'drenched in gas on most nights', the prospect of an early return to the UK must have been quite welcome to Ashmore. He wrote later: 'The bombing on the Army fronts had not up to that time amounted to very much, and I am afraid we of the Expeditionary Force were inclined to look on the troubles of London somewhat light-heartedly. The fact that I was exchanging the comparative safety of the Front for the probability of being hanged in the streets of London did not worry me.'[44]

The last day of July 1917 was made famous by a far more momentous event than the establishment of LADA: Haig's long-awaited offensive in Flanders began. Nine divisions of the British 5th Army, supported by the British 2nd Army on the right and the French 1st Army on the left, stormed out of the Ypres Salient and advanced nearly two miles in one day. Six thousand German soldiers were captured, and British hopes ran high that a breakthrough to the Belgium coast would follow, with the elimination of the Gotha bases around Ghent as an important if minor bonus. But it was not to be: by the evening of the first day the weather had intervened in the conflict, and heavy and continuous rain fell on the Flanders plain, turning the shell-torn ground into a morass. The appalling weather was to continue for at least another three weeks, bogging down troops, transport and tanks. The great offensive, on which such high hopes had been pinned, was to end in the bloody stalemate of Passchendaele, only seven miles from Ypres, ultimate British casualties being commensurate with those of the Somme.

7

August

If July's weather had been patchy, from Kleine's viewpoint, August's was to prove almost cataclysmic by comparison. Two vast anticyclonic systems had become established by the end of July – one over Greenland, the other over the Azores. Between them a broad belt of low-pressure fronts moved successively in a north-easterly direction, usually across the British Isles towards the Continent. Whilst Allied meteorologists had some warning of the approach of these fronts, the Germans, lacking reliable data from the west, had none and thus were unaware that the weather during August was to be quite exceptionally bad – even by British standards, a period so inclement that it would be described subsequently as the worst August for fifty years.

The first three weeks of the month were to provide a spell of almost incessant and sometimes torrential rainfall, with high winds frequently up to severe gale force. Whilst spelling disaster for Haig's forces in Flanders, this extraordinarily wet period was, curiously enough, also to signal the end of Kagohl 3's daytime activities against England: it is perhaps difficult not to feel some sympathy with Kleine.

Ashmore, on the other hand, looking out at the downpour from his new office in the Horse Guards, was quite content: the rain and high winds were godsends to the infant LADA, the Gothas were grounded in Belgium, and his organization was thus granted an unexpected but vital breathing-space in which to become fully established and operational.

Although Ashmore was not formally appointed as GOC LADA, in the rank of Major-General, until the 5th, he spent the first few days of the month choosing and assembling 'a small staff', his principal staff officer being Lieutenant-Colonel C.

Hankey, 'an old friend from my Horse Artillery days'.[1] That four AA Commands, Dover/Thanet, Harwich, London and Thames/Medway, now came under the GOC LADA's direction was a situation not wholly to the liking of some AA officers, as Ashmore was later to relate:

> In the first days of my new command, I was confronted with a fundamental difficulty in organization. I was responsible to Lord French for the whole of the air defences in the South of England. The anti-aircraft branch of his staff had controlled the ground part of the organization before I came on the scene. Anti-aircraft work was at that time considered a highly specialist business, and consequently this control by a section of the staff had amounted, in practice, to actual command. And this command they were very loath to relinquish. For instance, I had ideas of my own as to the best place for the mobile anti-aircraft guns outside London and I settled to move them accordingly. The anti-aircraft branch of the staff considered that they could not prevent me moving the guns as I wished, but they proposed to checkmate me by refusing to provide the necessary telephone communications for the new positions ... Lord French, who was always kindness itself to me, at once put an end to all difficulties of this sort. The anti-aircraft staff had done good work in the Zeppelin times, and he was grateful to them, but he decided that from now on I was to be considered as his principal adviser in air defence matters. This arrangement was loyally adhered to, and so thoroughly that Sir Frederick Shaw, Chief of the Staff to the Field Marshal, would not give advice against my wishes, even if he disagreed with me. My plans, in future, went on without interference.[2]

His plans had to take account of three separate contingencies: the rather remote possibility of renewed Zeppelin attacks on London, the continuance of the aeroplane raids by day and the probability that the Gothas would be switched to night attacks if their losses by day should become too heavy.

However, the day raiding by Gotha formations was the primary concern at that time, and Ashmore's first task was to organize the establishment of an AA gun barrage on the eastern perimeter of the city, as proposed by Lord French in his statement to the War Office of 23 July. The War Cabinet approved the eastern barrage scheme on 9 August but, as

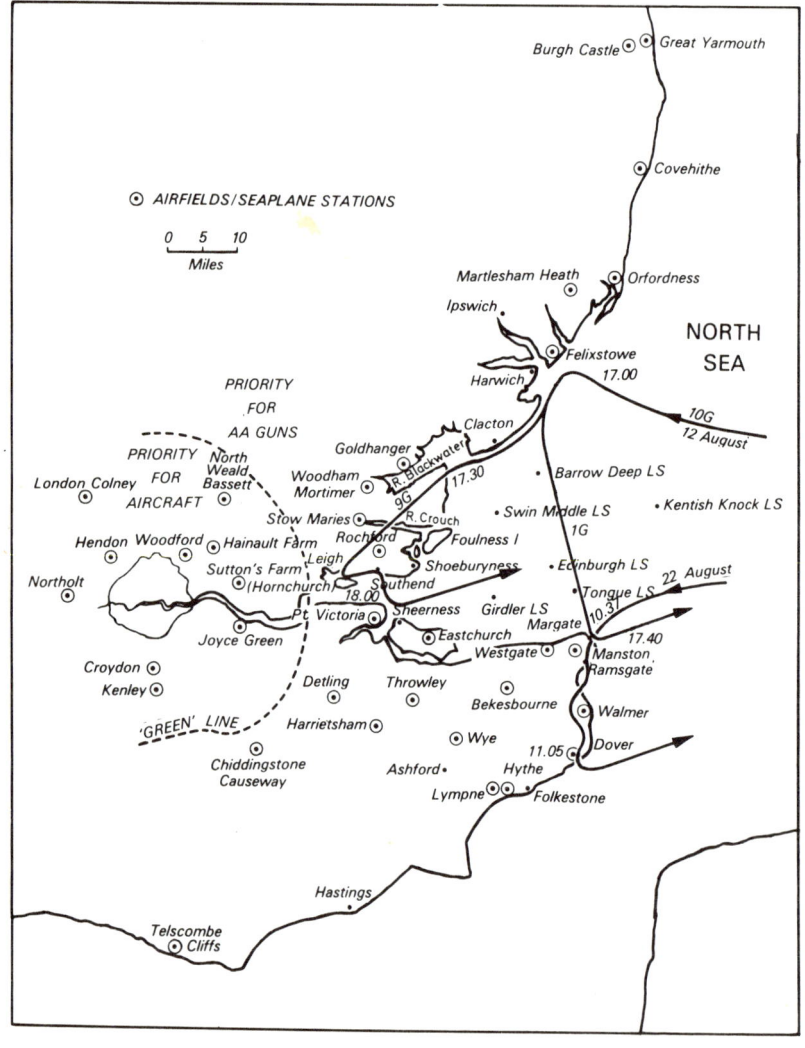

Great Yarmouth

Burgh Castle

Covehithe

○ AIRFIELDS/SEAPLANE STATIONS

0　5　10
Miles

NORTH
SEA

Martlesham Heath

Orfordness

Ipswich

Felixstowe
17.00

Harwich

10G
12 August

PRIORITY
FOR
AA GUNS

Goldhanger

Clacton

PRIORITY　North
FOR　　 Weald
AIRCRAFT　Bassett

London Colney

Barrow Deep LS

Woodham
Mortimer

9G

17.30

Kentish Knock LS

Stow Maries

R. Crouch

Swin Middle LS

Hendon Woodford

Hainault Farm

Rochford

Foulness I

1G

Northolt

Sutton's Farm
(Hornchurch)

Leigh

Shoeburyness

Edinburgh LS

22 August

Pt Victoria

Southend
18.00

Sheerness

Girdler LS

Tongue LS

Joyce Green

Margate

10.3

Croydon

Eastchurch

Westgate

Manston
Ramsgate

17.40

Kenley

Detling

Throwley

Bekesbourne

Walmer

'GREEN' LINE

Harrietsham

Wye

Dover

Chiddingstone
Causeway

Ashford

Hythe

11.05

Lympne

Folkestone

Hastings

Telscombe
Cliffs

9. Operations in August

expected, refused to allow 110 3-inch 20cwt guns to be set aside for it; the mercantile marine still had first priority. However, permission was given to resite thirty-four guns to new positions along the proposed barrage line, ten of them from the London Sub-Commands and twenty-four from the provinces. The gun ring was to be a semi-circle whose radius would be between twenty and twenty-five miles from Hyde Park, the most northerly point being Ware, thence via Harlow, Ongar, Shenfield, Billericay, Benfleet, Gravesend, Rochester, Wrotham and Sevenoaks to the most southerly battery at Oxted.

Whilst these barrage guns would not be too concerned with accurate height observation and control, such matters were vital to the success of those that would be directly engaging the raiders. The AA crews were by now more experienced and better trained than they had been at the outset of the day campaign, but new methods of sighting and reporting were now being devised and practised – that by Colonel Thompson, the officer commanding the Dover/Thanet AA Command, being a most important and effective example.[3]

The next and most important step in the development of LADA involved the urgent delineation of priority zones for fighter aircraft and AA guns in the London area – the embarrassing idiocies of the 22nd July could no longer be countenanced. The plan for co-ordination between the two services was quite simple and was based, essentially, on an inner semi-circle (to be known as the Green Line) a few miles nearer London than the gun barrage (Map 9). The details of the combined action required between the guns and aircraft were laid down in a LADA operational order that was, according to Ashmore, not easy to draft but which finally ran as follows:

During such time as any hostile formation is approaching London, all guns outside the Green Line will normally have priority of action; that is to say, while crossing all gun areas, any formation of our machines will fly to a flank, to give unrestricted action to anti-aircraft guns. If, however, at any time, while the hostile formation is crossing these gun areas, the patrol leader considers he has a really favourable opportunity to attack, he will do so, and the anti-aircraft guns will stop firing.

Inside the Green Line our machines will always have priority of action, that is to say, all anti-aircraft guns will give preference to our machines, and will fire only up to that time when it becomes plain that our pilots have seen the enemy, and are in a position to attack him.[4]

Much thought was also given to the problems associated with ground-to-air communications by day – the existing Ingram signals took a considerable time to set out and were sometimes difficult to read from the air. Ashmore finally arranged that large white arrows should be manufactured and supplied to service units in the metropolitan districts. Whenever the Gothas were in sight, the arrows would be exposed and kept pointing in the appropriate direction until the bombers had disappeared and their engine noise had died away. In clear conditions the arrows could be seen at heights up to 17,000 feet, the fighter pilots then knowing the direction of the enemy aircraft and the approximate distance to be flown to engage them.

In the meantime, necessary modifications to the air defence operations control were in hand at the Horse Guards. An operations room was being set up, with plotting arrangements on a large squared map. Delays on the telephone network were to be progressively eliminated by the installation of direct through lines to airfields, gun sites, observer posts etc., the lines to be held open during operational periods. By this means it was hoped to speed up the scrambling of fighter aircraft and the alerting of AA batteries. Radio-fitted BE aircraft from the original home defence squadrons were now properly organized to track the bomber formations and report, by wireless telegraphy, the enemy's speed and heading. By the end of August four BE aeroplanes would be available for this duty in the London area – two patrolling the north side of the Thames and two on the south. A wave-length of 1,250 metres was allocated for the former pair and 1,100 metres for the latter, the necessary wireless receiving facilities being installed at Wormwood Scrubs and the Hotel Cecil.[5]

Although the Southern Home Defence Wing was now part of Ashmore's command and thus subject to his operational control, the same could not be said for the fighters that the Admiralty might wish to scramble during raids on London or the south-east. Negotiations between the War Office and the Admiralty therefore began in the early part of the month and, incredibly, were quite successful, an agreement concerning

RNAS/RFC co-operation being finalized by the 11th.[6] This agreement presumably recognized that RNAS fighters from Eastchurch, Manston and Walmer should patrol the coastal areas during a raid but should not penetrate inland towards the capital.

The proposed expansion of the Southern Wing, as underlined by Smuts, was completed on 2 August, when the last of the three day-fighter squadrons (No. 61) was formed at Rochford from the parent squadron, No. 37. Pups that had operated under the latter's insignia throughout July were then taken on charge by the new squadron. No. 37's connection with Rochford also came to an end, but the squadron would continue to operate from Goldhanger and Stow Maries as a night-fighter unit.

By 10 August, Ashmore's new arrangements were in fairly good working order: the barrage guns were in position, despite the adverse weather conditions; the RFC's home defence day-fighter squadrons were at operational readiness; the air defence control system had been established, and communication links either improved or initiated, as required.

Rudolf Kleine, effectively grounded at Melle-Gontrode since 22 July, had grown more and more impatient as the rain teemed down day after day. His temper was not improved when the RNAS bombers from Dunkirk attacked Ghistelles, yet again, on Friday the 10th, but the raid actually presaged a temporary improvement in the weather situation over Belgium. During Sunday the 12th the sky cleared and Kleine made an extraordinarily impulsive decision to make a sortie against London that very afternoon. It is doubtful if Georgii supported this proposal – he probably had misgivings as to the wisdom of venturing out over the North Sea whilst conditions were so unsettled. His meteorological apprehension would have been well founded: a shallow depression was lying over the British Isles at that very moment, although the fitful sunshine in Belgium belied it. This depression would be responsible for a gusty south-westerly wind across the western part of the North Sea, with speed at times reaching 30 m.p.h.

It seems likely that Kleine's hasty order took the bomber crews by surprise, and not all were readily available at that time. This is evident from the fact that only thirteen Gothas were prepared for the intended take-off time at 14.30, i.e. the smallest number of bombers ever to be sent on a day raid against the UK. A departure time as late as 14.30 was also somewhat foolhardy because sunset would occur at about 20.30 and thus there would be very little margin of daylight available for delays or detours. The prime objective, on this occasion, was to be London, but secondary targets selected included naval facilities in the Medway, if for any reason London could not be attained. Kleine himself would not be going on this foray – possibly because his pilot could not be found in time – and *Oberleutnant* Richard Walter, the CO of Staffel 15 at St-Denis Westrem, was deputed as leader.

In fair conditions, then, the Gothas crossed the Belgian coast and set course for Essex. They were seen by British observers in Belgium, and two Camels were sent up from No. 4 (Naval) Squadron at Bray Dunes.[7] However, the Gothas had disappeared long before the Camels could climb to the required height, and no interception took place.

The bombers had not gone very far before the usual technical problems arose; three of them suffered engine troubles and had to return. The remaining ten machines closed up the formation, and Walter fervently hoped that there would be no further disturbance until the English shores should be in view. Kagohl 3 was, however, out of luck that day because Flight Lieutenant H. Beamish, leading a flight of four Camels from No. 3 (Naval) Squadron on a routine oversea patrol, had sighted the bombers about half-way across the North Sea. The British machines pursued the Gothas for some distance but were able to make only limited harassing attacks because their petrol supplies were running low. Finally the four had to break off the engagement and fly direct to England to refuel – Beamish to Rochford and the others to Manston and Eastchurch.

Before the naval pilots had landed, however, the raiders were approaching the mainland in the vicinity of Felixstowe (Map 9), from whence, at approximately 17.00, a warning was flashed to the LADA control at the Horse Guards. Walter, recognizing the naval base, realized that the freshening wind had blown his force some twenty miles off course, and he immediately signalled to the formation to swing in a south-westerly direction down the shoreline towards the intended landfall of the Blackwater.

A few minutes later, a single Gotha detached itself from the main formation and flew south to make the usual feint upon

Margate. Some authorities have stated that this machine could have been affected by engine trouble, but this seems unlikely; a good turn of speed was essential for a bomber operating alone, especially one required to attack targets in a predominantly naval area such as the Isle of Thanet.

Ashmore's updated telephone communication network rose to the occasion on receipt of the general alarm, and the air defences came to full readiness in a very short time, the RFC sending up a total of 110 aircraft. Nos. 44, 46 and 112 Squadrons were scrambled, the first away being the more experienced No. 46 at Sutton's Farm, whose Pups were airborne by 17.15. No. 112's Pups and No. 44's Camels swept off from Throwley and Hainault Farm respectively at about 17.30. Nos. 44 and 46 Squadrons flew along their designated strips inside the Green Line, whilst No. 112 patrolled its Kentish territory south of the Thames. No. 61 Squadron, on the other hand, was not immediately sent up from Rochford because it would have had little chance of ascending to the Gothas' height of 14,000 feet on the inward run. Ashmore therefore decided to hold No. 61 on the ground, in reserve, until the bomber's return route could be predicted with some certainty.

The senior home defence squadrons, Nos. 37, 39, 50 and 78, were also involved and put up a total of twenty-one two-seater machines, of which fifteen were BE12s including the wireless-equipped trackers. In addition, thirty aircraft, mostly modern fighters, took off from the RFC's training, experimental and depot establishments, in contrast to the motley collections scrambled during the earlier day raids. Ashmore, however, had this to say about the support given by such establishments: 'These, although not under my command, were supposed to help in the defence. The difference between co-operation and command showed clearly in their case. In spite of most careful arrangements made for these machines to rendezvous for combined action, I could never get them to work except as individuals; they were, in consequence, of little real use.'[8]

One of the pilots from No. 63 (Training) Squadron at Joyce Green was Captain James McCudden, who had returned from France a few days earlier. He was on leave in Rochester when the alarm was given and immediately sped back to Joyce Green on his motorcycle. On arrival, he at once took off in his blue Pup, narrowly missing a BE2, and flew eastwards towards Herne Bay.[9]

In response to the Felixstowe warning, the Admiralty sent up twenty-four RNAS machines from Eastchurch, Manston and Walmer. Nineteen of these aircraft were up-to-date fighters, Manston, for instance, providing eight Camels in two separate flights.

The commandant of the lone Gotha heading towards Margate had, as yet, no notion of the size of the RNAS force buzzing about Thanet but he would, no doubt, be happy to divert as many fighters as possible away from Kagohl 3's return route.

By 17.30 the main bomber force, flying in a triangular box formation of one, three and five, had turned inland near the mouth of the Blackwater and was heading south-west against the wind in the general direction of Gravesend. The leader took care to skirt the AA Mobile Brigade's 13pdr 9cwt batteries extending from Tillingham to Barling, and by about 17.40 the bombers were within the earshot and view of the astonished pilots of No. 61 Squadron sitting around waiting at Rochford. Most of the Gothas probably passed to the east of the airfield on the run down to the Thames but one actually flew over the field and dropped three bombs, damaging a hangar and some tents nearby and wounding two mechanics, one seriously. This daring incident was sufficient to cause No. 61's squadron commander to take matters into his own hands and order his squadron to scramble off in pursuit of the raiders, without waiting for a direct order from the Horse Guards. This entirely unauthorized action must have displeased Ashmore for two reasons: first, the squadron commander could have been falling for a diversionary attack such as that being carried out at Margate at that very time; and second, the squadron's Pups would take at least twenty minutes to climb up to the Gothas' height of 14,000 feet, by which time the bombers would be some twenty-five miles away, and overhauling them would not be easy.

The nine Gothas were now approaching the area of Canvey Island[10] and were about to turn westwards up river to the city. At this point they were coming within range of the AA batteries concentrated on the eastern side of the Green Line, the gunlayers already preparing to open fire. On the western side of the Line, meanwhile, the fighter formations of Nos. 44 and 46 Squadrons patrolled watchfully, warned by Ashmore's arrows of the direction of the enemy formation. Kagohl 3, perhaps unwittingly, avoided disaster on this occasion because the weather over the London area was steadily deteriorating; dark rain clouds had formed ahead of the bombers,[11] and Walter wisely decided to give up the attack on London, go about and seek secondary targets elsewhere, as planned. He did not turn south towards the Medway, immediately, however; he led the *Geschwader* due east towards the 'soft target' areas of Leigh-on-Sea, Westcliff-on-Sea and Southend, all at that time crowded with summer visitors. Everyone in the district must have been startled when five guns of the Shoeburyness range and school AA batteries suddenly opened up at 17.50, presumably firing over Southend at the advancing raiders. For the moment, these were the only AA guns in action – even the 3-inch 20cwt one at Canvey Island remained silent, although it must earlier have had an excellent opening. The crackling gunfire should have sent the populace scurrying for shelter but, lacking a warning system of any kind, they probably assumed that an exercise was in progress. No warning hooters or sirens had yet been installed in Southend, the only large town in Essex not so equipped. The Chief Constable of Southend received the official alert at 17.22 but apart from informing the ambulance and fire services he could do little more than send out his whistle-blowing men on their placarded bicycles.

Apparently quite untroubled by the Shoeburyness bombardment, Kagohl 3, calmly maintaining its formation, began dropping bombs as it traversed the four miles from Leigh-on-Sea to Southend. About thirty-four bombs fell in the next five minutes, possibly half of which failed to detonate. The bombs were scattered fairly evenly over the three districts, more than thirty houses being damaged or destroyed. The casualty list, when finalized, named thirty-two dead and forty-three injured.

The majority of the fatalities and injuries resulted from a stick of six bombs, possibly aimed at the Great Eastern Railway, that crashed down on the centre of Southend. One of these, a 50kg, exploded on the pavement in Victoria Avenue, close to the railway station, causing the most horrific incident of all. At that hour on a Sunday evening, the street was crowded with holiday-makers and churchgoers, fifteen of whom were killed in the blast whilst a similar number were wounded. Other 50kg bombs of the stick dropped in nearby Milton Street and Guildford Road, inflicting a similar number of casualties to those of Victoria Avenue.

By about 18.00 the Gothas had finished their run over

Southend and were heading out over the estuary towards Sheerness and the Medway. The public services in stricken Southend were left to ferry the injured to hospital, extinguish the fires, search for people trapped in demolished houses and dig for the unexploded bombs.

As the bombers approached the Kentish side of the estuary, the 3-inch 20cwt guns of the Thames and Medway Garrison at Canvey Island, All Hallows and Whitehouse Farm on Grain, and Barton's Point and Neat's Court on Sheppey, somewhat belatedly opened fire, the height of the target being subsequently reported by the artillery observers and height-finders as about 13,000 feet. It seems probably that the AA gunfire hereabouts proved, once again, very accurate – Gotha 660 had been lost in this area on 5 June, almost certainly due to the Barton's Point battery. Seeing No. 61 Squadron's Pups rapidly ascending, Walter must have been in something of a dilemma: if he opened out the formation to reduce the AA target area, the scattering Gothas could be easy meat for the approaching Pups. Mindful, also, of the strong wind, the leader took the most realistic decision: to give up the raid, turn east and make all speed for home. Accordingly, a flare arced up from the command Gotha, whereupon the formation obediently banked round to port and sped with the wind down the estuary, pursued by numerous shellbursts and with No. 61 Squadron still climbing doggedly below. Aircraft recognition procedures must have been much improved on this day: the AA guns fired only when the Pups and other friendly aircraft were clear of the line of sight.

As the Gothas passed, they were fired on by the 3-inch 20cwt gun on the RNAS airfield at Eastchurch, but it managed only three rounds, possibly because of the rather long range. In all, the eight gun stations in the Thames estuary area had discharged about 300 rounds between them, the majority fired by the Shoeburyness batteries.

It will be convenient, at this point, to leave the Gotha main force for the moment and return to approximately 17.40 when the lone diversionary bomber made a brief appearance over Margate at about 14,000 feet.

The Dover Command's 3-inch 20cwt AA guns stationed at St Peter's and Hengrove immediately began rapid fire as four bombs whistled down, one of which destroyed an empty house in Surrey Road and wounded one woman passer-by. The Gotha, then being harassed by at least five of the RNAS fighters, flew directly out to the sea over the Ramsgate area, the mobile 13pdr 9cwt guns at Broadstairs and the 3-inch 20cwt at Cliffsend (Pegwell Bay) peppering the air around it. Colonel Thompson's four Thanet guns had fired 132 rounds in the few minutes the Gotha had been in range, a very creditable performance.

Then began one of the most remarkable feats of the entire daylight campaign: a solitary bomber was to do battle with at least eleven British fighters – ten RNAS and one RFC, admittedly not all at the same time – over a distance of about eighty miles. The tables were now turned and the German crew was to be at the receiving end of the sort of concentrated machine-gun fire that Captain Palethorpe/Air Mechanic Jessop, and many others, had faced in the earlier raids.

Under normal circumstances, the odds against the Gothas' survival would have been very heavy, but when one of its Mercedes engines was put out of action by a bullet, no one could have expected the crippled machine to return to dry land. However, the pilot was experienced enough to throttle back the other engine and prevent the heavy aeroplane going into a fatal spin, as had happened to Gotha 660 on 5 June. The bomber then commenced a long powered glide across the North Sea, its large wing area and reduced load enabling it to do so, aided by the strong wind. The loss of height was probably about 200 feet per mile and, whilst steadily descending, the machine was under attack by the British machines.

Although the fighters scored many hits on the Gotha, they did not have it all their own way by any means, the two German gunners continuing to fire their Parabellums all the way across the North Sea. At least three of the attacking aircraft were hit, and one of them, a Camel from Eastchurch, was forced to return home with a bullet in the engine.[12] Six of the fighters were plagued by gun jams whilst another had to break off because of engine trouble.

The gusty wind pushed the Gotha much further north than the pilot would have liked, but in the end he managed to come down on the beach at Zeebrugge. The bullet-riddled machine was wrecked but the heroic crew survived. By their magnificent performance in the face of great adversity they had decoyed a large number of fighters away at a crucial time for Kagohl 3.

Flight-Lieutenant H. Kerby, in a Pup from RNAS Walmer, in

company with three other naval Pups, had followed the limping Gotha across the North Sea but lost sight of it about fifteen miles from Zeebrugge. On returning to the mouth of the Thames, however, he spotted the main enemy formation on its homeward flight. The Gothas had, by this time, collected an impressive tail of British aircraft, each of which was trying to catch up with the bombers whilst at the same time endeavouring to rise above them. The German commanders countered these attempts by jettisoning their remaining bombloads in the sea, and consequently most of the Gothas were able to reach an altitude of 18,000 feet – an action that effectively threw off some of the heavier and slower fighters, though the bomber crews had to endure a period of icy conditions coupled with a much thinner atmosphere. The pursuing machines included ten of the sixteen Pups from No. 61 Squadron, a Vickers FB12c from No. 198 (Depot) Squadron at Rochford, a Martinsyde G.102 and a Vickers FB19 from Martlesham, a Pup from No. 112 Squadron at Throwley, and a Triplane from Manston.

For some forty miles out from the Thames estuary, the British pilots continued their harassing attacks but Flight-Lieutenant Kerby was the only one to score a success. A 'lame duck' bomber was discovered flying some 4,000 feet below the rest of the formation, possibly because of engine trouble. After a burst of fire from Kerby's Vickers, the Gotha went down and turned turtle in the sea. One member of the crew survived the crash and was seen clinging to the tailplane, and Kerby dropped a lifebelt in the hope that the man could stay afloat until help arrived. On his way back to Walmer, Kerby tried to direct four naval destroyers to the scene but unfortunately his Very signals were not understood. Despite his efforts, therefore, the entire crew of that particular Gotha were lost.

No. 61 Squadron had no luck at all, although all ten of its Pups were in action at one time or another, but the increasing range and height, coupled with the prospect of returning against the boisterous south-west wind, inevitably reduced the period in which attacks could be mounted.

Of the sixteen tailing fighters, no fewer than nine reported gun jams due to defective ammunition, and thus, of the twenty-seven engagements on this day, as many as fifteen had been negated by such malfunctioning. Whilst Ashmore was no doubt pleased by the increased number of interceptions, he was infuriated that gun stoppages had been responsible for a fifty per cent reduction in his air-fighting effectiveness: 'The damage to the enemy formation would have been greater had it not been for an exasperating number of gun jams in our machines. These were mostly caused by faulty ammunition, a trouble that was soon afterwards eliminated by careful inspection in the squadrons before loading up.'[13]

The Gothas' return speed was considerably higher than it had been on the inward journey, the wind now being largely in their favour. The wind was, however, still partly southerly and would again drive the ungainly and somewhat lighter Gothas to the north of their desired track. Whilst Kagohl 3 had, in the past, returned home along the Dutch coast in order to avoid the RNAS at Dunkirk (7 July was an example of this), it seems unlikely that Walter would have chosen to go so far north on this mission – petrol reserves were running pretty low by then.

At 20.00, after a two-hour flight from the Thames, the bombers were still about twenty-five miles north of Blankenbergh, with the prospect of another hour's flight to the airfields around Ghent. Furthermore, the sun would be setting in about half an hour, and landing the tricky Gothas in twilight conditions would be much more hazardous than usual.

All might still have been well if the eight raiders could have made an uninterrupted beeline for their bases, but this was not to be. After receiving a warning from Dover, No. 2 Wing at Dunkirk had sent up four Camels from No. 3 (Naval) Squadron at Furnes, led by Flight-Commanders Armstrong and Breadner. Conjecturing that the Gothas might return near the Scheldt, the RNAS fighters began patrolling near the mouths of the estuary. No escorting German fighters were present to protect the bombers, and the Camels swept into the attack without interference. The dogfight did not last long, because the guns of all four Camels jammed – a seemingly impossible mischance but a very fortunate one for the German air crews.

The further delay occasioned by this action meant that the bombers, after cutting across Dutch territory, were almost out of petrol when they arrived at their bases, and hasty landings had to be made. What with the failing light, the boisterous cross-wind and the instability of the empty Gothas, to say nothing of the possible damage sustained during air combat, it is not surprising that there were four serious crashes on landing, the machines being wrecked – another curious parallel with 7 July. Thus, of the ten raiders that had crossed the English coastline that afternoon, six had been either shot down or seriously damaged. Such a rate of loss, sixty per cent, must have been of great concern to von Hoeppner and OHL.

There can be little doubt that Kagohl 3 had been extremely fortunate not to have been completely annihilated during this raid. It had been saved from almost certain destruction by two factors: the threatening clouds over London and the high incidence of machine-gun failures in British aircraft, both RFC and RNAS. Kleine had lost only two of his bombers in actual aerial fighting, and this fact may well have masked an unpalatable truth from Kogenluft: the RFC's build-up of day fighter squadrons around London was now so formidable that further daytime assaults on the capital would be fraught with the gravest danger for the G-bomber force.

Two days later, on Tuesday the 14th, and again on Thursday the 16th, the RNAS at Dunkirk replied and sent its DH4 and Handley Page 0/100 bombers in day raids against the airfield at Ghistelles. There are no reports of attacks on the main bases near Ghent – probably they were under good fighter cover during daylight hours.

On 17 August, Lieutenant-Generel Smuts presented his second report concerning 'the air organization generally and the direction of aerial operations'. Since his first report on air defence, tabled on 19 July, Smuts had beavered away on this second and more important Cabinet task, consulting all naval, military and civil authorities concerned with air matters. In this work he was ably assisted, once again, by the indefatigable Lieutenant-General Henderson, the only senior officer of the RFC who fully accepted that a separate air force under its own Minister was the only real answer to the Army/Navy squabbles that had bedevilled service aeronautics for years. In the introductory passages of his report, Smuts prophetically looked forward to the time, not so far distant, when strategic air warfare would be waged on a fearful scale:

> Air Service ... can be used as independent means of war operations. Nobody that witnessed the attack on London on the 11th [*sic*] July could have any doubt on that point. Unlike artillery, an air fleet can conduct extensive operations far from, and

independently of, both Army and Navy. As far as can at present be foreseen, there is absolutely no limit to the scale of its future independent war use. And the day may not be far off when aerial operations, with their devastation of enemy lands and destruction of industrial and populous centres on a vast scale, may become the principal operations of war, to which the older forms of military and naval operations may become secondary and subordinate ...

In our opinion there is no reason why the Air Board should any longer continue in its present form as practically no more than a conference room between the older Services, and there is every reason why it should be raised to the status of an independent Ministry in control of its own War Service.

The report summed up its conclusions in eight recommendations:

1 That an Air Ministry should be instituted forthwith, to administer all matters connected with aerial warfare.
2 That it should have an Air Staff to make plans, direct operations, collect intelligence and train personnel.
3 That the Ministry and Staff should arrange for the amalgamation of the RNAS and the RFC.
4 That the personnel of these services should only be transferred to the new force with their own consent.
5 That close liaison should be established and maintained between the Army, Navy and Air Staffs.
6 That the Air Staff should provide air units for service with the Army and Navy, to act during such attachment under naval or military control, and with such types of machines as those services desired.
7 That regular officers of the Navy and Army should be seconded to the Air Force for fixed periods for employment with the naval and military air contingents.
8 That officers and other ranks should be able to transfer permanently to the Air Force if they wished.[14]

And so the die was finally cast. The War Cabinet would approve the report on the 24th and set the administrative wheels in motion, an action that would culminate, in eight months' time, in the inauguration of the Royal Air Force, a body born out of the fusion of the RFC and the RNAS. In just three months, then, Kagohl 3 had, quite unintentionally, brought about a reform that had been mooted since 1914. There were many dissenters, of course. The Admiralty, for instance, whilst grudgingly accepting that the new force would be able to conduct the air war divorced from Army/Navy rivalries, nevertheless felt that Smuts' logic was faulty in suggesting that, because an independent air force was necessary, the other two services would no longer require their own air arms.

On the day Smuts was presenting his report to the War Cabinet, the weather over Belgium began to improve as a large anticyclone developed over Germany. Kleine, anxious as always to continue the attacks on London, was hopeful that the following day might provide the right conditions for another expedition across the North Sea. Initial preparations were put in hand but the take-off time was to await the early morning forecast on the next day, the 18th.

After *Leutnant* Georgii had studied the incoming weather reports, particularly that from Hamburg, he strongly advised the Commanding Officer to call off the raid. High south-west winds across the North Sea were predicted with a strong possibility of unsettled weather over England. In this the forecast was quite correct: a deep depression was then lying over north-west Scotland which, with the associated high-pressure system over Germany, would shortly freshen up the wind to near gale force. Kleine, however, noting the rising barometer, was not impressed; he virtually pooh-poohed the ominous forecast and rashly gave orders for the take-off at about 06.30. In so doing, the scene was set for the worst day in Kagohl 3's history, a near catastrophe that would highlight the inadequacy of the Gotha G.IV for long-distance missions in other than reasonably calm conditions.

Making some concessions to the gloomy meteorological prognostications, the commander decided to lead the squadron directly to the nearest point on the English mainland, i.e. the North Foreland. On arrival there he proposed to select a target objective within a range determined by the petrol supplies remaining after a possibly difficult crossing of the North Sea.

In bright sunshine twenty-eight bombers set out, fifteen from St-Denis Westrem and thirteen from Melle-Gontrode, the largest number ever achieved for a daylight raid. Considering the losses sustained on the 12th, only six days previously, it is surprising that Kleine should have been able to muster such a large force, although his numbers on that day had been low because of the haste with which that operation had been initiated.

The Gothas droned away towards the coastline, probably intending to cross somewhere near the Blankenbergh area, but they were very soon in trouble, as the wind from the south-west began steadily to rise. Instead of passing to the west of Bruges, as usual, the large and somewhat under-powered Gothas were blown to the east of the town and, shortly thereafter, they passed over the Dutch frontier close to St-Laureins. Immediately, Dutch AA batteries at Aardenburg, Sluis and Oostburg came into action, first with warning shots and then with a bombardment in earnest, but none of the Gothas was hit, and the squadron thankfully scuttled away out to sea over the Cadzand region.

It would seem almost unbelievable that Kleine should have continued the mission after such a clear demonstration of the wind's force, but obstinately he resolved to press on, although the aircrews must have had serious misgivings, particularly the pilots as they endeavoured to hold their formation in such blustery conditions.

As the bombers flew westwards against the wind, their air speed fell progressively to about 50 mph and a dense cloud layer was encountered. The Gothas climbed slowly above the clouds, for safety reasons, but were then denied any visual sighting of lightships to correct navigation.

After almost three hours of the planes labouring against the wind, the clouds thinned sufficiently for the commander to see the English coast through the rain ahead. He was appalled, although he really should not have been, to identify an approaching port below him as Harwich – almost forty miles north of his intended landfall of Thanet.

It was now obvious to Kleine that Kagohl 3's snail-like progress plus the large northerly drift had used up precious petrol supplies at a prodigious rate. There was, therefore, nothing for it but to abandon the attack, turn about and make for home as quickly as possible, if many of the Gothas were not to be lost at sea because of fuel exhaustion. Accordingly a signal flare arced up from the 'pulpit' of the command Gotha, cancelling the operation and ordering an immediate return to base. As soon as the bombers turned eastwards again, they began flying before the wind, and their speed rose to more than 90 mph and probably even higher, as the heavier bombs were quickly dumped into the sea.

The strong to gale-force wind, coupled with squally showers, now drove the Gothas before it in complete disarray. The flight across the North Sea took approximately half the time the inward journey had exacted but it was still too long for two of the bombers. Their fuel ran out and they desperately tried to glide back to land. One may have succeeded in landing on the beach near Zeebrugge but the other certainly descended into the sea.

Although the remaining Gothas strove to make landfall on the Belgian coast, they were driven north to Holland, just as had occurred on the 12th. The majority of the bombers crossed the Dutch coastline between and over the islands of Walcheren and Schouwen but two machines were later seen crossing near the Hook of Holland, about sixty miles north of their usual track. It appears that once they had established their positions, these two wanderers headed for the Zuider Zee in the hope of making it to Germany. On the way they dropped a few bombs, presumably to lighten the aircraft, but no casualties or damage resulted. The saga ended when one Gotha landed in a field because of lack of fuel, whilst the other received a rifle bullet through one engine and was forced to come down. The crews of both Gothas were uninjured and were captured by Dutch army patrols.

AA guns at Westkapelle and Domburg on Walcheren boomed out as Gothas crossed the island, but to little effect. On the island of Schouwen three bombs were released, probably to reduce weight, as before. There were no casualties, and little damage was reported.

Kleine managed, finally, to regain some control of his straggling flock and lead the depleted squadron in a south-westerly direction towards the Belgian coast. To do this successfully, he had to bring the Gothas down below the scudding clouds, in order to avoid collisions, and they were thus at fairly low altitude when they came inland near Cadzand, over which they had passed about five hours before. The Dutch gunners opened up again and subsequently claimed to have shot down one bomber on the Belgian side of the border.

The worst part of this ill-fated expedition was yet to come. The fuel of all the bombers was now very low, and it appears that five of them failed to reach their bases and crashed when their engines stopped. Those that did succeed in attaining the aerodromes fared little better because of the strong wind blowing across the fields. Possibly four of the Gothas came to grief in landing, with severe damage and casualties to the crews.

Of the twenty-eight raiders that had set out in the early morning, no fewer than thirteen had been either lost or seriously damaged, a loss rate of close on fifty per cent. On top of this disaster for OHL came an acid protest note from the Dutch Government, to which Berlin could only apologize and offer compensation for the damage caused.

What Kogenluft had to say to Kleine concerning this calamity is not recorded but the squadron commander must have received a severe reprimand for his foolhardiness in setting out across the North Sea against an adverse wind, particularly as he had been warned that bad weather was likely. From OHL's point of view, the severe losses and international repercussions could not even be balanced against any effective activation of the British defence system; if any warning had been given from Harwich at all, it must assuredly have been cancelled soon afterwards. After such a deplorable set-back, Kleine would in future make no attempt to force the operational pace but would be content to await a favourable forecast from Georgii before initiating new raids against England.

The dismal wet and windy weather conditions over the British Isles continued into the following week as a deep depression, with attendant thunderstorms, struck the west coast of Ireland on the 21st and moved slowly north-eastwards towards the North Sea. At that time, however, the weather over the Continent had moderated, and anticyclonic conditions had again become established, with clearing skies and sunny periods. Looking out from his office at the pleasant prospect, Kleine was most anxious to continue the bombing campaign despite the mounting casualties and the extraordinary weather conditions of the past few weeks. He still believed that day-bombing could make an effective contribution to the overall war effort – as indeed it had already done. But summer was by now well advanced and little time remained for daylight expeditions. Whilst he was keen, therefore, to be off as soon as possible, he was none the less not prepared to override his 'tree frog' again.

In the event, he did not have to wait very long: Georgii

reported to him that Wednesday the 22nd should be quite clement and thus probably suitable for another overseas sortie. The meteorological officer might well have revised his forecast if he had known about that depression moving across Ireland but, luckily for Kagohl 3, the events of the 18th were not to be repeated on the 22nd, although the wind would certainly freshen up from the south-west later in the day.

Preparations were put in hand for a take-off at about 09.00 but only fifteen Gothas could be mustered for this raid, a consequence of the severe losses of the previous Saturday. London was the main target but secondary alternatives selected were Southend, the Medway and Dover. The operational plan involved, as before, a direct flight to the North Foreland and thence westwards up the Thames to London. If the capital should be unattainable as a result of adverse weather or fighter cover, the squadron would divide, one party proceeding to Southend or the Medway, the other turning south to Dover. Such a division, over enemy territory, would, naturally, mean a major reduction in the squadron's defensive capability. The very fact that Kleine should authorize such an extraordinary manoeuvre suggests that he was, even then, unaware of the full strength of the forces ranged against him.

On this clear and relatively calm morning, the Gothas set off from St-Denis Westrem and Melle-Gontrode and, when assembled, steered directly for the coast. Today there was no danger of being blown across the frontier into Dutch air space, the wind being no more than a moderate breeze compared to the south-west gale that had caused the embarrassing fiasco of the 18th.

Kagohl 3's flight to the Isle of Thanet on this occasion was not disturbed by chance encounters with RNAS fighters from Dunkirk, as had happened several times before, but other disturbances there certainly were. No fewer than five of the bombers, i.e. one third of the force, were disabled by the inevitable engine disorders and had to break from the formation and swing round for home. The squadron was actually within sight of the Kentish coast when the last of these engine-plagued machines faltered and fell away. This one, however, was different from the other four: it was Kleine's own Gotha that was in difficulties. Kleine hastened to fire off a red flare from his 'pulpit' to indicate not only that he must turn back but that

Oberleutnant Walter must assume command once again. The CO was, however, unlucky even in this parting duty – his flare failed to ignite and a trail of smoke was all that was produced. Confusion reigned temporarily as the bomber crews saw the red-painted Gotha banking round to the east, but Walter quickly moved up the front position, and the formation was soon re-established.[15]

There seems little doubt that the bombers must have been sighted some distance out to sea – possibly as much as forty miles from the North Foreland – because a warning was issued by GHQ, Home Forces, as early as 10.05. The whereabouts of the observers who were responsible for this early warning is obscure, but the signal could have emanated from a lightship, an RNAS flying-boat on patrol or a naval vessel. The establishment of look-out posts at sea, together with the necessary communication links, had been the subject of much discussion after the inception of the daylight attacks, and the stationing of trained observers on lightships had been a step in the right direction, although such vessels were not always necessarily useful vantage points. It is, however, doubtful if this day's prompt alert had sprung from any extension of the seaward surveillance arrangements as 'The difficulties in the way of the establishment of such a system would have been great, perhaps insuperable ...'[16]

However, it may have come about, the early warning, fortuitous or not, was to enable some of the defending aircraft to climb up to, or above, the raiders' height before the battle was joined, a circumstance that was to have very serious consequences for the bombers. Furthermore, the AA guns in the Dover and Thanet Command, under Colonel Thompson, would have plenty of time in which to set up the new system of height-finding and ranging that the CO had recently introduced.

At 10.10, eighteen of No. 46 Squadron's Pups began their usual rapid take-off from Sutton's Farm, followed at 10.15 by five Camels from Manston (led by Squadron-Commander Butler) and three Pups from Walmer. Nos. 44 and 112 Squadrons were only a few minutes later, the former putting up fifteen Camels and the latter eleven Pups. A procession of other aircraft followed until about 11.00, by which time the RFC had 120 machines in the air, whilst the RNAS at home had sixteen. For the very first time, therefore, the British machines were able to begin patrolling their allotted beats before the Gothas had crossed the coastline. At 10.37, or thereabouts, the bombers approached Margate and were immediately greeted by a fusillade from the Army's 3-inch 20cwt guns at Cliffsend, Hengrove, Old Haven, Richborough Castle, Sandwich Bay and St Peter's, and the 13pdr 9cwt mobile pair at Broadstairs. These guns were to fire off about 1,000 rounds in the next ten minutes, ably supported by a variety of naval ordnance from vessels inshore. Using Colonel Thompson's techniques, the sky around the Gothas was soon full of mushrooming Archie bursts from the military guns and, to protect themselves, the bombers hastily fanned out to present a much more diffuse target for the AA gunners. In the midst of this vigorous bombardment flew the intrepid naval pilots from Dover, Manston and Walmer, launching their attacks as and when they were able to do so. Although the Isle of Thanet had no designated zones for gun and aircraft, some AA gun commanders were careful to open fire only when fighters were clear of artillery's intended targets.

One Gotha was soon in dire straits – it spun steeply down from about 14,000 feet and finally crashed into the sea at Walpole Bay, Margate, about one mile offshore. Miraculously one member of the crew survived the crash and was rescued from the wreckage. It is impossible to pinpoint who shot down this raider because Flight Lieutenant Kerby from Walmer, Flight Commander G. Hervey from Dover and other RNAS pilots opened fire on it, whilst the AA guns at Hengrove and St Peter's also laid claim to the success. Flight Lieutenant Kerby, the victor of the 12th, was less fortunate on this day: his Pup developed engine trouble during the engagement and he was forced to land on the beach at Margate.

In the face of the well-prepared and successful defences, and the strengthening wind, Walter had little alternative but to abandon not only the raid on London but the proposed secondary one on Southend/Medway as well. It would have been suicidal to proceed any further inland with such a small formation. All that could now be done was to keep the squadron together and concentrate on Dover as the only target. Walter wrote later in his report: 'I therefore tried, by firing three star flares in quick succession, several times, to instruct the crews to raid Objective No. 3 (Dover). A raid on Dover, in view of the importance of this town to the battle proceeding in Flanders, would have been of the utmost importance.'[17] Unfortunately for Walter, however, the white star signals were not properly understood by all the Gotha commanders, and the squadron was thrown into some confusion yet again. In the heat of the battle such bewilderment was hardly surprising – the unreliable firework flares in use were a feeble substitute for radio communications.

The *Geschwader,* in somewhat ragged array, now turned south, on a follow-my-leader basis but with some commanders quite uncertain when and where to release their bombs. At least one Gotha dropped five bombs on Margate before departing from the town, the missiles falling in a stick astride Approach Road, close to Dane Park in the centre of the town. No one was injured in these incidents, but an empty house, in Windsor Avenue, was destroyed by a 50kg bomb.

Shortly afterwards a Gotha, possibly the Margate one, was hit by accurate AA fire and was seen gliding down at low altitude, trailing smoke. No doubt the pilot hoped to land before the fire became too intense but the machine soon broke up and fell burning in three pieces on or adjacent to the Hengrove Golf course. All three members of the crew were lost.

The remaining eight bombers flew on over Ramsgate, harried all the while by AA guns and RNAS aircraft. Some of the bemused bomber commanders proceeded to dump their bombs on this town, thankful, perhaps, for the opportunity to lighten their machines as quickly as possible. Records show a total of twenty-eight bombs descending in an area of about one square mile, possible aimed at the bisecting High Street. The usual proportion of the missiles were duds, but many houses, schools and churches were hit, although casualties were quite light compared to those sustained at Southend, for example. Nine people died, and twenty-one were injured, some of whom, two dead and nine wounded, were Canadian soldiers.

The worst incident occurred when a 50kg bomb wrecked a store on the Military Road, a thoroughfare running alongside the Inner Harbour. Six men and a child sheltering in the store were killed and several others injured. Two schools (Chatham House and Townley Castle) used as a Canadian Army Hospital were struck but casualties were very few because at least 200 of the patients were in the grounds watching the Gotha falling in flames over Margate. One bomb exploded on a platform at the railway station destroying a canteen used by servicemen, but there were no casualties there.

Walter, probably incensed with his commanders who had bombed Ramsgate, now led the squadron out to sea, dodging shellbursts and the RNAS, before recrossing the coastline near Deal. The 12pdr 12cwt gun at Deal came into action and fired sixty-one rounds as the Gothas made a wide sweep around the Walmer area before finally heading down to Dover.

At approximately 11.00 the Gothas were within range of Colonel Thompson's artillery in the Dover area – the 3-inch 20cwt guns at Cauldham, Citadel, Frith Farm, Langdon Bay, River Bottom Wood and West Hougham, i.e. the AA batteries that had seen action during the first daylight raid on 25 May. Naval vessels in the harbour also joined the fray to create a daunting barrage for the approaching bombers.

Eight RNAS machines had followed the raiders from Ramsgate, all the while continuing their resolute assaults. Flight Commander Hervey, after his attacks at Margate, had had to land at Manston with a jammed gun but he took off again as soon as the stoppage was cleared. Over Dover he fired about 300 rounds into a Gotha and reported that, 'Both gunners were apparently killed, as there was no reply even at twenty yards range.'

Flight Lieutenant A. Brandon, from Manston, had swopped Camels when the first ran out of ammunition after the desperate fighting near Ramsgate. In his second machine he repeatedly attacked the enemy formation and was to follow it home across the North Sea. For their determined efforts on this day both he and Hervey would later receive Distinguished Service Crosses.

The few Gothas that still had bombs aboard now began dropping them as they flew across the Dover naval base from north to south. A total of nine bombs fell on the town whilst five others landed either on the foreshore or in the sea. Casualties were comparatively light: three dead and five injured, all but one being military personnel.

Two bombs exploded near Dover Castle, wounding an army cook, and three more fell near Dover College, close to the ancient priory, where two soldiers on the green were killed. One 50kg missile shattered the Admiral Harvey public house in St Paul's Place, mortally wounding a young barmaid standing at the door. Blast from this particular bomb caused extensive damage to properties nearby.

The eight bombers, on leaving the town, then banked round to the east, still harassed by the accurate AA cannonade and the attentions of fighters, the RNAS ones then being joined by a variety of RFC machines from No. 62 (Training) Squadron at Dover, No. 50 (HD) Squadron at Detling and the AAP at Lympne.

Redoubling their efforts in the final moments of the raid, the home defenders were rewarded when another Gotha was hit and came spinning down to crash in the sea, no crew member surviving. Whilst some AA artillery commanders claimed this success, it is generally accepted that the victor was Flight Sub-Lieutenant J. Drake from Manston.

It was now about 11.10, and Walter led his very depleted force back across the North Sea, anxious to make the earliest contact with his fighter escort off the Belgian coast. At least four RNAS home-based machines were to continue their attacks on the bombers throughout the return journey, in company with seven RFC two-seaters.

Nos. 3 and 4 (Naval) Squadrons were alerted, as usual, the former sending up two Camels piloted by Flight Commander Breadner and Flight Lieutenant Fall. They fell in with the seven Gothas off Zeebrugge, and each fired about 600 rounds but to no great effect, although smoke was seen coming from one bomber. No. 4 Squadron sent up ten Camels in two flights but they were, evidently, too early for the Gothas' return. However, they did succeed in locating twenty-five waiting escort fighters, and a spirited dogfight ensued, 'five enemy machines being driven down completely out of control'.

Possibly the oddest occurrence of the day was reported by one of the RNAS pilots from Walmer, who said he had last seen the Gothas being attacked by five DH4s off Ostend. This engagement is not recorded elsewhere but No. 5 (Naval) Squadron certainly had sent up DH4s to attack Ghistelles during this day. It would appear probable, therefore, that the five reported machines contacted the Gothas after the raid at Ghistelles, the latter airfield being only about five miles inland from Ostend.

Kagohl 3 could count itself lucky that no other Gotha was lost during the hazardous flight back to Flanders, where the seven bullet-holed survivors landed at about 12.30. Of the original fifteen, five had turned back because of engine troubles, three had been shot down, and the rest had been severely mauled with precious little of propagandistic or military value to show for the day's tribulations. Kleine, when reviewing the losses sustained by Kagohl 3 during August, (twenty-two bombers with probably some forty fatalities among the crews), must have had serious misgivings about the wisdom of continuing the mass raids by day. OHL could have been in no doubt that the air defences before London, both guns and aircraft, had become very efficient indeed and quite capable of breaking up the Gothas' defensive formation at 14,000 feet. The wheel had, therefore, turned full circle. The German Army's day-bombers were now facing the same difficulties as had confronted the Zeppelins by night at the end of 1916: the defences, under unified control, had become too strong, and further day attacks would inevitably lead to a steadily escalating rate of loss.

A few days later, therefore, OHL reviewed the situation and came to the conclusion that the improved competence of the British defence forces indicated that the loaded G.IV bomber, in daylight, would have to fly as high as 19,000 feet to have any hope of avoiding the defending guns and aircraft.[18] As there was little likelihood of the Gotha G.IV reaching such an altitude, the alternative was to abandon the day raids and make future forays on clear, moonlit nights, thus enabling the bombers to operate at lower heights under cover of relative darkness, in calm weather conditions.

It is interesting to note that *Oberleutnant* Weese, the commander of No. 14 Staffel at Melle-Gontrode, had in the previous February presented a treatise on air raids on Great Britain, in which he prophesied that attacks in daylight 'would be limited to at most three months, as by that time the effect of the AA defence would be felt, and it would be necessary to carry out raids at night instead.'[19]

With this remarkably percipient prediction on file, it was little wonder that OHL should decide against the continuation of the day raids and authorize the change-over to night-time operations. However, the prospect of an early resumption of the day attacks still remained because it was hoped that the next Gotha variant, the G.V, then just coming into service, would possess improved characteristics that would make diurnal raids a possibility again. The hoped-for tactical plan for the future envisaged attacks by day (using the G.V) and by night (using the Giant Staaken R.VI) in order to force the British Army Council to maintain large defence forces in UK on round-the-clock readiness. Luckily for the citizens of London, however, the G.V could not meet the new requirements, and thus raids on the capital by day never again became a reality during the remainder of the Great War.

Whatever the future might hold for the Home Forces Command, it was felt that No. 46 Squadron could then safely be returned to France. On the morning of 30 August, therefore, its Pups took off from Hainault Farm for the last time, assembled in the usual impeccable formation and saluted the base before flying back across the Channel to Bruay. Although No. 46 had never engaged the Gothas whilst stationed in the UK, its very presence on the eastern side of the city had been a most effective deterrent.

8

Retrospect

Kagohl 3's campaign against London and south-east England, in daylight, had lasted three months, almost to the day, just as *Oberleutnant* Weese had predicted. During the campaign, which had opened and closed, with raids on or near the Cinque Port of Dover, some 648 bombs (approximately 21 tonnes) had fallen on land, killing 400 people and injuring nearly 1,000 others, one fifth of the combined total being military and naval personnel. Damage to property was of the order of £400,000, a vast sum for those days. On the other side of the balance sheet, however, Kagohl 3 lost probaby thirty-two Gothas, the majority because of inclement weather, a loss rate approaching twenty per cent.

As we saw in Chapter 2, the Ludendorf plan for propagandistic air raids on London and south-east England, by day, had had two distinct but not necessarily compatible aims, i.e. a primary terroristic one directed at the civilian population of London, and a secondary tactical one against selected military targets within the triangle Harwich-London-Folkestone.

Rather naïvely perhaps, the German High Command had hoped that terroristic bombing would intimidate the citizens of London to such an extent that the British Government would be overthrown and the war brought to a speedy conclusion before the Americans could make an effective contribution to the Allied cause. More realistically, however, OHL expected that secondary bombing would greatly assist the German forces on the Western Front – directly, by attacks on supply ports and transit camps etc., and indirectly, by forcing the British War Office, under pressure from an indignant public, to withdraw fighting aeroplanes and AA guns from the Continental battlegrounds to bolster the feeble air defences of the UK.

In reviewing Kagohl 3's success or failure in implementing this somewhat grandiose scheme, it will be recalled that the squadron faced many difficult problems in attempting the first-ever strategic bombing raids by aeroplanes.

Firstly, and most importantly, shortcomings in aircraft production were such that the number of bombers actually supplied for *Türkencreuz* was far less than the figure originally estimated. The official forecasts had shown that at least a hundred bombers would have been needed to make a really effective strike against England, but in fact twenty-eight was the largest number of Gothas ever mustered by Kagohl 3 for a daylight sortie. Such a minute force precluded the attacks from being little more than nuisance affairs, albeit quite serious enough.

Secondly, the chosen vehicle itself, the Gotha G.IV, was technically less than adequate for long-distance overseas flights. The bomber was basically underpowered and, encumbered with a 150kg overload to boot, could be operated safely only in relatively calm weather conditions. Unfortunately for Kagohl 3, the atrocious summer of 1917 was noticeably lacking in such halcyon days: gales and rainstorms were commonplace, especially in August.

Thirdly, the bombers' Mercedes engines were notoriously unreliable even though they had been redesigned at least once prior to acceptance of the aeroplane by *Hauptmann* Brandenburg. An incredible twelve per cent of all Gothas setting out for England were afflicted by engine trouble and were forced to return to Belgium without completing their missions.

Fourthly, the 50kg penetration bombs carried over long distances at such expense were of rather uncertain quality. No less than one third of them failed to explode whilst others detonated before reaching the ground. No doubt the latter defect must have been viewed with some concern by the German aircrews.

Fifthly, the pyrotechnic flares used for signalling between the command Gotha and the rest of the squadron, in flight, left much to be desired. On several occasions the flares failed to ignite, and the commanders of the other Gothas were left wondering what instructions were actually intended.

Such logistical deficiencies were cogent factors in reducing the effectiveness of the Ludendorf brief – a rather ironic commentary on the supposed Teutonic thoroughness. However, equipment failures were not all the squadron had to contend with during that summer. The weather was subsequently to be described as the worst for fifty years, and it is not too much to say that the remarkably unsettled conditions contributed, in no small measure, to the protection of London, although they spelt disaster for the British Army in Flanders. Kagohl 3 was always hampered by incomplete or unreliable data concerning the weather situation in the Western Approaches. *Hauptmann* Kleine, mistrustful of meteorological forecasting, made some appalling operational decisions, that of 18 August being the crassest, which were partly responsible for the ultimate cancellation of the daylight campaign.

Despite all the setbacks, however, OHL must have been very well pleased with the results of its limited air offensive against England. A few sporadic and relatively cheap raids with a small group of bombers served to keep the British air defences on their toes day after day. The Gothas, in the intervals between the occasional expeditions against England, were able to busy themselves bombing the back areas of the Western Front, and thus were fully occupied in an offensive role at all times, weather permitting. The defenders, on the other hand, spent most of their time waiting – an entirely passive activity that tied down valuable resources in men and machines.

In the circumstances, then, Kagohl 3 made the very best possible use of the scant technical means available to it. If the pocket *Geschwader* did not have sufficient strength to achieve the main terroristic purpose, notable successes were scored in the secondary one. Considerable damage was inflicted on army camps, naval air stations, factories, port installations, railway facilities and warehouses etc. War production in munition and other plants was frequently interrupted by air-raid alarms, although bombs did not necessarily fall anywhere near such establishments. However, there can be little doubt that Kagohl 3's major achievement was to compel the Lloyd George Government to order a substantial reinforcement and restructuring of the London air defence organization, at the expense, essentially, of British forces overseas. The London Air Defence Area, under Major-General Ashmore, had to be established in order to achieve the essential unity of command that Jan Smuts had demanded after the heavy raid of 7 July.

The number of guns in and around the city was greatly

increased and many were deployed to form the Green Line barrage system on the eastern perimeter. Three first-line fighter squadrons (Nos. 46, 56 and 66) were detached from France to GHQ, Home Forces, at a time when the RFC on the Western Front was engaged in desperate battles to retain air superiority against the fighter wings led by Richthofen and others. In addition, three entirely new day-fighter squadrons had to be formed for service at home (Nos. 44, 61 and 112) built up from the replacements, in both pilots and aircraft, that would otherwise have gone to support the RFC overseas. By late August the RFC in London and the south-east had been reinforced to such an extent that it was able to deploy up to 150 first-class single-seater fighter aircraft compared with the few obsolete two-seaters it had possessed the previous May.

Although compelled to give up daytime attacks after three months because of the improved efficiency of the British defences, Kagohl 3 was fortunate not to have suffered much heavier losses than it did. The RNAS bombers from Dunkirk, for instance, frequently attacked German airfields in Flanders, but for some reason they were not concentrated, at that time, on the main Gotha bases at Mariakerke, Melle-Gontrode and St-Denis Westrem. A sustained assault on these aerodromes would surely have paid higher dividends than the reinforcement of defence units at home. Again, many of the Gothas returned unscathed to Belgium because of two very serious failings in the home defence organization, i.e. the numerous gun jams suffered by RFC and RNAS pilots, prior to the institution of ammunition inspection routines, and the bombardment, by some badly directed AA guns, of British pilots attempting to intercept the bomber formations. Furthermore, the AA artillery of the period was less effective than it might otherwise have been because the crews lacked reliable height-finding and prediction equipment and were also denied the use of brisant high-explosive shells with time fuzes.

From the German point of view, one of the most important results of the daytime campaign came, paradoxically, after its conclusion. In deciding to begin night raiding, OHL played a masterstroke, probably unwittingly, because in so doing it stultified the RFC's day-fighter formation tactics so laboriously rehearsed since Smuts. The three HD squadrons concerned then had to begin retraining for night-fighting duties, an assignment much more difficult than hitherto because single-seater fighters such as the Camel had not, till then, been flown at night.

And yet Kagohl 3's few bombers were, in the end, responsible for far-reaching effects that were actually beneficial to the British people in the long term, although they could not have been foreseen in Ludendorf's plan. The War Cabinet agreed, after the raid of 13 June, to a radical expansion of both the RFC and the RNAS – the number of squadrons to be doubled as soon as possible thereafter. The other raid on London, that of 7 July, led to the most sweeping change of all – the amalgamation of the RFC and the RNAS in the Royal Air Force so that the war in the air could be successfully prosecuted free from inter-service wrangling and wastefulness. Finally, the unified system of air defence evolved against the Gothas was to be a sound basis for the much larger organization that would be required in the Second World War.

In conclusion, tribute must be paid to the courage of the aircrews of both sides: the British who, in under-gunned and under-powered aircraft, unhesitatingly attacked the heavily defended Gotha formations, and their German adversaries who, in broad daylight, ventured so far over a hostile sea 'in ramshackle old Gothas', as McCudden was to call them, to bomb the capital of the British Empire, in the vain hope of bringing nearer a victory for the Kaiser's Germany.

Keyed Sources, by Chapter

Key

Ashmore, Major-General E. B., *Air Defence* (Longmans, Green, 1929).

Billing, Noel Pemberton, *Speech in the House of Commons, March 1917* (Hansard).

Bülow, Major Freiherr H. von, *Die Angriffe des Bombengeschwader 3 auf England,* Articles in *Die Luftwache,* May–August 1927 (PRO AIR 1/2126).

Churchill (1), Winston S., *The World Crisis 1911–1918,* Volume I (Odhams Press, 1938).

Churchill (2), Winston S., Speech in the House of Commons, 17 May 1916 (Hansard).

Dallas Brett, R., *The History of British Aviation, 1908–1914* (John Hamilton, 1933).

Gamble, C. F. Snowden, *The Story of a North Sea Air Station* (Neville Spearman, 1918).

GHQHF (GHQ, Home Forces), *Air Raids 1917–18,* Volume IA, prepared under the direction of Lieutenant-Colonel H. G. de Watteville (PRO AIR 1/2123).

Jones, H. A., *The War in the Air,* Volumes III, IV and V (Clarendon Press, 1935).

Lewis (1), C., *Sagittarius Rising* (Peter Davies, 1936).

Lewis (2), C., *Farewell to Wings* (Temple Press, 1964).

Lloyd George, David, *War Memoirs,* Volume IV (Ivor Nicholson & Watson, 1934).

McCudden, Captain James T. B., VC, *Five Years in the Royal Flying Corps* (*The Aeroplane* and General Publishing, 1918).

Morris, Captain J., *The German Air Raids on Great Britain 1914–1918* (Sampson, Low, Marston & Co., 1925).

PRO, Public Record Office, Kew.

Rawlinson, Lieutenant-Colonel A., *The Defence of London, 1915–18* (Andrew Melrose, 1924).

Robertson, General Sir William, *Soldiers and Statesmen,* Volume II (Cassell, 1926).

Sources

1. 'The Almost Hopeless Task'

1. Dallas Brett, pp. 129 and 130.
2. Churchill (1), p. 265.
3. Ibid.
4. Ibid.
5. Ibid.
6. Churchill (2), op. cit.
7. Lloyd George, p. 1848.
8. Churchill (1), p. 266.
9. Rawlinson, p. 55.
10. PRO, AIR1/2319.
11. PRO, AIR1/2312.
12. Ibid.
13. Ibid.
14. Gamble, p. 207.
15. Morris, p. 111.
16. PRO, CAB 37/147.
17. Churchill (2), op. cit.
18. PRO, ADM1/8464.
19. Ibid.
20. (PRO, AIR1/2126) Bülow, p. 5.

2. *Operation* Türkencreuz

1. (PRO, AIR1/2126) Bülow, p. 15.
2. Ibid., pp. 7 and 8.
3. GHQHF (PRO, AIR1/2123), p. 32.
4. (PRO, AIR1/2126) Bülow, p. 19.
5. Ibid., p. 27.
6. Ibid., p. 32.
7. Ibid., p. 11.

3. 'The Diminished Risk'

1. Billing.
2. Lewis (2), p. 23.
3. Ashmore, p. 30.
4. Ashmore, p. 39.
5. Jones, V, p. 7.
6. Jones, V, pp. 4 and 5.
7. Jones, V, p. 8.
8. Ibid.
9. Rawlinson, pp. 137 and 138.
10. Jones, V, pp. 11 and 12.
11. Rawlinson, pp. 200 and 201.

4. May

1. PRO, AIR1/258.
2. (PRO, AIR1/2126) Bülow, p. 19.
3. Ashmore, p. 37.
4. Jones, V, p. 477 (Appendix IV).
5. Morris, pp. 108 and 109.
6. (PRO, AIR1/2126) Bülow, op. cit.
7. GHQHF (PRO, AIR1/2123), op. cit.
8. PRO, War Cabinet, GT937 (CAB 24/15).

5. June

1. Jones, V, p. 24.
2. Jones, IV, p. 122.
3. Jones, V, pp. 24 and 25.
4. GHQHF (PRO, AIR1/2123), op. cit.
5. Jones, V, p. 26.
6. McCudden, pp. 187 and 189.
7. (PRO, AIR1/2126) Bülow, p. 29.
8. Ashmore, p. 38.
9. PRO, War Cabinet 163 (CAB 23/3).
10. Lewis (1), p. 184.
11. Jones, III, p. 178.
12. Jones, V, pp. 30 and 31.
13. Jones, V, p. 153.
14. Jones, V, p. 135.
15. Lewis (1), p. 187.
16. McCudden, p. 191.
17. Jones, V, p. 44.
18. PRO, War Cabinet 101 (CAB 23/2).
19. PRO, War Cabinet, GT 1198 (CAB 24/17).

6. July

1. PRO, War Cabinet 179 (CAB 23/3).
2. Ibid.
3. PRO, War Cabinet 176 (CAB 23/3).
4. Morris, p. 225.
5. PRO, AIR1/2314.
6. Morris, p. 225.
7. PRO, War Cabinet 179 (CAB 23/3).
8. PRO, AIR1/691.
9. PRO, War Cabinet 178 (CAB 23/3).
10. McCudden, p. 191.
11. Rawlinson, p. 178.
12. McCudden, pp. 192 and 194.
13. (PRO, AIR1/2126) Bülow, p. 31.
14. PRO, War Cabinet 178 (CAB 23/3).
15. Ibid.
16. Robertson, p. 17.
17. Jones, IV, pp. 152 and 153.
18. Jones, IV, p. 153.
19. Robertson, p. 17.
20. PRO, AIR1/1561 and 1779.
21. PRO, War Cabinet 179 (CAB 23/3).
22. Lloyd George, p. 1861.
23. Robertson, p. 17.
24. Lloyd George, pp. 1862 and 1863.
25. Ibid.
26. PRO, AIR1/692.
27. Jones, V, p. 46.
28. Jones, IV, p. 141.
29. Jones, V, p. 41.
30. PRO, War Cabinet 181 (CAB 23/3).
31. Jones, IV, p. 154.
32. Jones, V, p. 43 (Note 2).
33. Jones, V, p. 44.
34. Jones, V, pp. 138 and 139.
35. PRO, War Cabinet, GT 1451 (CAB 24/20).
36. Ashmore, pp. 37 and 38.
37. GHQHF (PRO, AIR1/2123), op. cit.
38. Ibid.

39. Jones, V, p. 45.
40. Ibid.
41. Ibid.

42. (PRO, AIR1/2126) Bülow, p. 13.
43. Jones, V, pp. 43 and 44.
44. Ashmore, p. 40.

7. *August*

1. Ashmore, p. 40.
2. Ibid., pp. 46 and 47.
3. Ibid., p. 45.
4. Ibid., p. 41 and 42.
5. PRO, AIR1/668.
6. Ashmore, p. 41.
7. PRO, AIR1/177.
8. Ashmore, p. 43.
9. McCudden, pp. 213 and 214.
10. Ashmore, p. 44.

11. PRO, AIR1/691.
12. (PRO, AIR1/2126) Bülow, p. 21.
13. Ashmore, p. 44.
14. Lloyd George, pp. 1866 and 1868.
15. (PRO, AIR1/2126) Bülow, p. 26.
16. Jones, V, p. 158.
17. (PRO, AIR1/2126) Bülow, p. 27.
18. Ibid., p. 33.
19. Ibid., p. 17.

Additional Bibliography

Air Ministry, *Handbook of German Military and Naval Aviation, 1914–1918* (1918).

Baring, M., *Flying Corps Headquarters, 1914–1918* (G. Bell & Sons, 1920).

Bruce, J. M., *British Aeroplanes, 1914–1918* (Putnam, 1957).

Fredette, R. H., *The First Battle of Britain, 1917–1918* (Cassell, 1966).

French, Major G., *Some War Diaries, Addresses and Correspondence of the Earl of Ypres* (Herbert Jenkins, 1937).

Gran, T., *Under British Flag, Krigen 1914–1918* (Gyldendalske Boghandel, 1919).

Hoeppner, General E. von, *Deutschlands Krieg in der Luft* (Von Hase & Kohler, 1921).

Hogg, I. V. and Thurston, L. F., *British Artillery Weapons and Ammunition, 1914–1918* (Ian Allan, 1972).

Jane, F., *All the World's Aircraft, 1919* (Sampson, Low, Marston & Co., 1919).

Joubert de la Ferté, ACM, Sir P., *The Third Service* (Thomas & Hudson, 1955).

Leigh, H., *Planes of the Great War, 1914–1918* (John Hamilton, 1936).

Neumann, G. D., *et al.*, *Die Deutschen Luftstreitkräfte im Welt Kriege* (Hodder & Stoughton, 1921).

Poolman, K., *Zeppelins over England* (Evans Brothers, 1960).

Popham, H., *Into Wind* (Hamish Hamilton, 1969).

Rawlings, J., *Fighter Squadrons of the RAF and their Aircraft* (MacDonald & Janes, 1969).

Slessor, MRAF, Sir J., *The Central Blue* (Cassell, 1956).

Thetford, O., *British Naval Aircraft since 1912* (Putnam, 1958).

The Times, History of the War, Volume XIX (1919).

Appendix I.

| Date and Gothas' approx. flight times (BST) | Number of Gothas that: | | Raid Areas | Number and weight of bombs dropped on land | | Casualties | | |
	Set out	Crossed coast		Number	Weight	Killed Civ.	Killed Mil.	Inj Civ.
Friday 25 May (15.00–20.00)	23	21	Folkestone, Lympne, Hythe, Ashford, Sandgate, etc.	163	4,550	77	18	91
Tuesday 5 June (16.00–21.00)	22	22	Sheerness, Shoeburyness	74	3,100	3	10	9
Wednesday 13 June (09.00–14.00)	22	20	Margate, Shoeburyness, London (Docks, East and City)	128	4,083	158 (2 by AA)	4	425 (18 by AA)
Wednesday 4 July (05.30–09.00)	25	18	Harwich, Felixstowe	65	1,152	3	14	1
Saturday 7 July (08.00–13.00)	24	22	Margate, London (North-East and City)	76	3,149	55 (10 by AA)	2	190 (55 by AA)
Sunday 22 July (06.30–10.00)	23	22	Harwich, Felixstowe	55	1,419	1	12	3
Sunday 12 August (14.30–19.30)	13 (min)	10	Rochford, Leigh, Southend, Margate	37	1,740	32	0	4
Saturday 18 August (06.30–11.30)	28 (max)	0	Nil – attack aborted before Harwich	–	–	–	–	–
Wednesday 22 August (09.00–12.30)	15	10	Margate, Ramsgate, Dover	50	2.049	8	4	12 (1 by AA)
Totals:				648	21,242	337 (12 by AA)	64	774 (74 by AA)

Statistics of the Day Raids

tary ss	Home-based defence aircraft				Gun stations in action		Remarks (G = Gotha)
	Total airborne	RFC	RNAS	Total engage-ments	London	Country	
05	73	36	37	2	–	7	1 G crashed in Belgium and 1 shot down by No. 4 (N) Squadron, Dunkirk.
03	66	44	22	5	–	9	1 G shot down by AA (Barton's Point).
98	94	57	37	12	11	9	1 British observer killed. Worst air raid of the war.
65	83	66	17	1	–	7	1 British observer killed. 1 G badly damaged.
22	91	80	11	36	41	12	1 G destroyed in combat. 2 defence aircraft destroyed, 2 British pilots killed. 4 Gs crashed on landing.
80	121	96	25	1	–	13	1 G shot down in sea off Ostend. 2 defence aircraft damaged by AA fire.
00	134	110	24	27	–	13	1 G crash-landed at Zeebrugge. 1 G destroyed in combat. 4 Gs crashed on landing.
	–	–	–	–	–	–	2 Gs lost over Holland. 2 Gs lost at sea. Possibly 9 Gs wrecked or damaged in landing crashes.
145	136	120	16	12	–	14	3 Gs shot down by AA and aircraft.
118		Military casualties about 20% of total					Possibly 32 Gothas destroyed or badly damaged.

Appendix II

RFC/RNAS Squadrons and Establishments involved in Daytime Operations

Royal Flying Corps

No. 35 (Training) Sqdn.	Northolt	Original HD (night-fighter) squadron.
No. 37 (Home Defence) Sqdn.	Goldhanger, Rochford and Stow Maries (Goldhanger only after July 1917)	
No. 39 (Home Defence) Sqdn.	Hainault Farm, North Weald Bassett and Sutton's Farm (North Weald Bassett only after July 1917)	Original HD (night-fighter squadron.
No. 40 (Training) Sqdn.	Croydon	
No. 44 (Home Defence) Sqdn.	Hainault Farm	Day-fighter squadron formed 24.7.17 from C Flight of No. 39 (HD) Squadron.
No. 46 Squadron	Sutton's Farm	Detached from Bruay 10.7.17 to 30.8.17.
No. 48 Squadron	Frontier Aerodrome (Dunkirk)	Stationed at Frontier from 10.7.17, for third Battle of Ypres.
No. 50 (Home Defence) Sqdn.	Bekesbourne, Detling and Throwley. (Not Throwley after July 1917)	Original HD (night-fighter squadron.
No. 56 Squadron	Bekesbourne and Rochford	Detached from Liettres (Estrée Blanche) 21.6.17 to 5.7.17. (A Flight only at Rochford).
No. 56 (Training(Sqdn.	London Colney	
No. 61 (Home Defence) Sqdn.	Rochford	Day-fighter squadron formed 2.8.17 from No. 37 (HD) Squadron.
No. 62 (Training) Sqdn.	Swingate Downs, Dover	
No. 63 (Training) Sqdn.	Joyce Green	
No. 65 Squadron	Wye	Probably one flight detached from Wyton, Cambs., early June to August 1917.

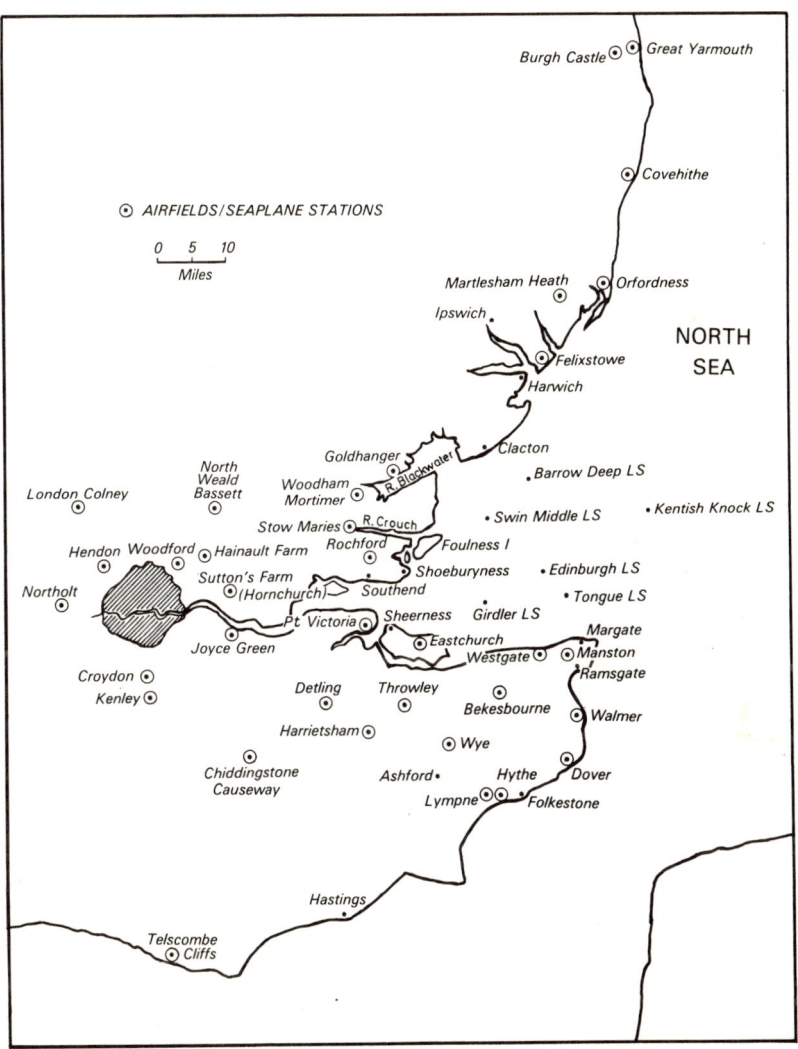

10. Airfields and seaplane stations in south-eastern England
May to August 1917

No. 66 Squadron	Calais, then Sutton's Farm	Detached to Calais (under C.-in-C., Home Forces) from Liettres (Estrée Blanche) 21.6.17 to 6.7.17. At Sutton's Farm (without machines) 8.7.17 to 10.7.17.
No. 78 (Home Defence) Sqdn.	Chiddingstone Causeway (Penshurst), Telscombe Cliffs and Gosport	Original HD (night-fighter) squadron.
No. 112 (Home Defence) Sqdn.	Throwley	Day-fighter squadron formed 30.7.17 from B Flight of No. 50 (HD) Squadron.
No. 198 (Depot) Sqdn.	Rochford	Night-fighter training squadron for home defence pilots.
Aircraft Park (AAP)	Hendon	
Aircraft Park (AAP)	Kenley	
Aircraft Park (AEP)	Lympne	
Experimental Squadron	Orfordness	
Testing Squadron	Martlesham Heath	

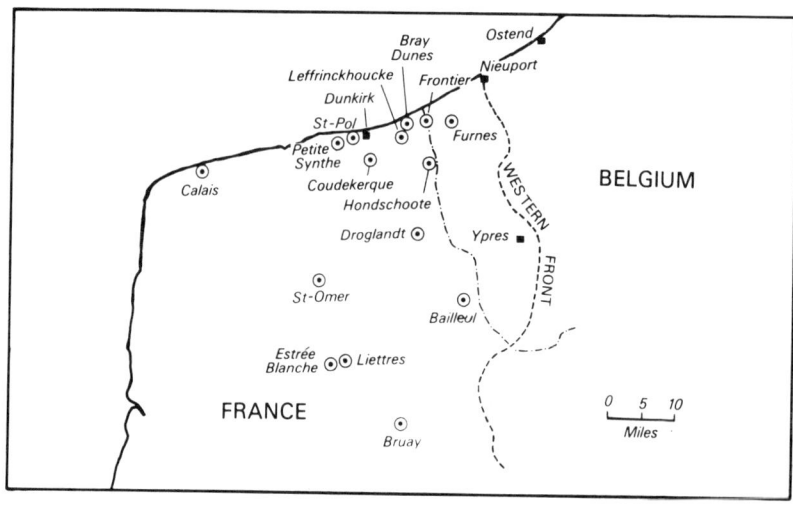

11. British airfields in northern France and Belgium,
May to August 1917

Royal Naval Air Service

Night Landing Ground	Burgh Castle (outstation of Great Yarmouth)	
Night Landing Ground	Covehithe (outstation of Great Yarmouth)	
Coastal Air Station	Dover (near Castle)	
Flying Training and Aerial Gunnery Schools	Eastchurch	
Coastal Air Station	Felixstowe	
Air War School	Manston	
Aircraft Experimental/ Repair Depot	Port Victoria, Grain	
Coastal Air Station	Walmer	
Coastal Air Station	Westgate	
Coastal Air Station	Great Yarmouth	
No. 3 (Naval) Sqdn.	Furnes	From 15.6.17*
No. 4 (Naval) Sqdn.	Bray Dunes	From April 1917*
No. 6 (Naval) Sqdn.	Bray Dunes	From 15.6.17 to 10.7.17**
	Frontier	From 10.7.17 to 27.8.17 (disbandment)**
No. 9 (Naval) Sqdn.	Furnes	From 15.5.17 to 15.6.17*
	Leffrinckhoucke	From 10.7.17**

* Part of No. 4 (Naval) Wing (HQ La Panne)
** Part of the 4th Brigade, RFC (for third Battle of Ypres)

Appendix III

Aircraft sent up from Nos. 37, 39, 50 and 78 (Home Defence) Squadrons

No. 37 Squadron (including No. 198 (Depot) Squadron, Rochford)

Aircraft Types	25 May	5 June	13 June	4 July	7 July	22 July	12 Aug	22 Aug
BE2 Series	*	*	*		1			
BE12 Series	*	*	*	4	4	4	3	3
FE2 Series	*	*	*					
RE7			1		1			
Sopwith Pup				4	6	11		
Sopwith 1½-Strutter			*	4	6			
Vickers FB12c			1*		1		1	
Totals	8	10	13	12	19	15	4	3

Sopwith Pups were not listed after 22 July; they had been transferred to No. 61 (HD) Squadron then forming at Rochford, a new unit derived from No. 37 Squadron.

No. 39 Squadron

Aircraft Types	25 May	5 June	13 June	4 July	7 July	22 July	12 Aug	22 Aug
Armstrong Whitworth FK8			*	1	1	1		
BE2 Series	*	*	*					
BE12 Series	*	*	*	5	6	3	4	5
SE5				2	2			
Sopwith Camel						10		
Totals	11	6	10	8	9	14	4	5

Sopwith Camels do not appear in the record after 22 July; they were transferred to No. 44 (HD) Squadron at Hainault Farm, a unit stemming directly from No. 39 Squadron (C Flight).

*Indicates aircraft types probably in use on these particular days. The existing records (GHQHF) are incomplete prior to 4 July 1917.

224

No. 50 Squadron

Aircraft Types	25 May	5 June	13 June	4 July	7 July	22 July	12 Aug	22 Aug
Armstrong Whitworth FK8				3	4	5	5	4
BE2 Series	*	*	*					
BE12 Series	*	*	*		3	5	5	6
Sopwith Pup				4	5	5		
Vickers ES1 Bullet				1	1			
Totals	13	8	12	8	13	15	10	10

Sopwith Pups disappeared after 22 July; they went to equip No. 112 (HD) Squadron then forming at Throwley, i.e. a direct offshoot of No. 50 Squadron (B Flight).

No. 78 Squadron

Aircraft Types	25 May	5 June	13 June	4 July	7 July	22 July	12 Aug	22 Aug
Be2 Series	*	*	*					
BE12 Series	*	*	*		5	7	3	5
SE5						2		
Sopwith 1½-Strutter							1	2
Totals	3	6	1	0	5	9	4	7

* Indicates aircraft types probably in use on these particular days. The existing records (GHQHF) are incomplete prior to 4 July 1917.

Appendix IV

War Cabinet Committee on Air Organization and Home Defence against Air Raids

First Report

1 The War Cabinet, at their 181st meeting held on 11th July 1917, decided (Minute 3):
   That the Prime Minister and General Smuts, in consultation with representatives of the Admiralty, General Staff and Field Marshal, Commanding-in-Chief Home Forces, with such other experts as they may desire, should examine:
   i The defence arrangements for home defence against air raids.
   ii The air organization generally and the direction of aerial operations.

2 We regard the first subject for our examination as the more pressing and we deal with it accordingly in this first report, so far as the defence of the Metropolitan area is concerned. The second subject of our enquiry is the more important and will consequently require more extensive and deliberate examination. We propose to deal with it in a subsequent report.

3 London occupies a peculiar position in the Empire of which it is the nerve centre, and we consider, in the circumstances, that its defence demands exceptional measures. It is probable that the air raids on London will increase to such an extent in the next twelve months that London might through aerial warfare become part of the battle front. We think, therefore, that it is necessary to take special precautions, so far as the defence of London is concerned, and so far as this may be done without undue prejudice to

operations in the field and on the high seas, as the fighting forces must, as a matter of general principle, have the first call upon our output of aircraft and anti-aircraft guns.

4 The arrangements for home defence, including that of the London area, against hostile air raids, have been undergoing a continual and rapid transformation, which, together with other causes, has militated against efficiency. In the first instance, attacks were made by Zeppelins at night and our defences were so organized as to deal with this form of attack. Anti-aircraft guns, singly or in pairs, or in larger numbers, were placed at convenient points, and aeroplanes of no great power or speed were disposed at suitable centres.

After some modification, the original dispositions were found to be adequate to meet night attacks by Zeppelins. We have, however, now to meet attacks of an entirely different character, which take the form of invasions by squadrons of aeroplanes in formation and our arrangements for defence are accordingly being adapted to meet this development.

One cannot, however, entirely preclude the possibility of a repetition of Zeppelin attacks, and it would consequently be unwise to abandon the earlier defence arrangements. Additions to these arrangements are, however, necessitated by the new 'formation attack' by day. The defence against Zeppelins was effectually carried out, not only by individual anti-aircraft guns, but also by single aeroplanes fitted with special armament.

As operations were conducted by night, there was no question of formation either for attack or defence. Now, however, that the attack is made by day by large enemy units in formation, one or two anti-aircraft guns firing from any particular point cannot hope to cause serious damage, and generally have no other effect than that of frightening the enemy pilots, while the defending aircraft, unless they can also operate in formation, are liable to very serious risk and cannot do much than hover round the outskirts of the enemy formation. An attack in formation could, we think, only be properly met by a barrage fire from guns concentrated in batteries at suitable points in front of the area to be defended, or by flights or squadrons whose object is, by concentrated attack, to break up the hostile formation and destroy individual machines after they have been scattered out of their formation

5 The relevance of these remarks is well illustrated by what happened in the air raid over London on Saturday, 7th July. The enemy machines attacked in definite formation which they maintained throughout the raid. In our view they should have been met and repelled by a heavy barrage of gunfire before they reached London. Instead of this they were only subjected to a sporadic gunfire in the London area which did them no observable damage. As regards aeroplanes on that occasion, we actually disposed of a larger number of first-class machines than the enemy, but our machines were distributed among a number of stations and some of them came in in driblets from various training centres.

Our machines were not in formation when in the air, and even when they attempted to concentrate they did not come under a unified command in the air, nor have they been trained so to fight. The result was that their very spasmodic or guerilla attacks failed to make an impression on the solid formation of the enemy, and the damage that was done by our superior numbers of first-class RFC machines was comparatively negligible. We have investigated the circumstances in some detail and are informed that the reasons why greater results were not achieved were that some of our pilots were not accustomed to the new machines they were flying, that certain machines were not used because of missing spare parts, and a certain amount of shells that were fired were useless on account of defective fuzes. These defects should, and can be remedied with all possible speed, but it is to the general arrangements and organization that we wish to refer more fully.

6 Four separate agencies contribute to the defence of the London area against air raid:

  a Royal Naval Air Service, which is not under the Home Command, but works under the direction of the senior naval officers in the naval districts, but in co-operation, as far as possible, with the Home Defences.

    There seems to be a general agreement among those whom we have consulted that for the limited purpose of the defence of London, the present division of command in this respect should not be disturbed.

The principal function of the Royal Navy Air Service Squadrons is to deal with enemy raiders on their return journey, as they recross the Channel. They did so very effectively on the occasion of the last raid, and after consideration of all the circumstances, we are disposed to think that the above squadrons should continue to operate under separate Naval Commands, but in close co-operation with the Home Defence.

b The Observation Corps (distinct from the Royal Flying Corps or Royal Naval Air Service), which consists of a number of observers round London, mostly infantry soldiers, often elderly and not specially qualified for the duties they have to perform. This Corps is directly under orders of the Field Marshal Commanding Home Defences.

c Various incomplete units or single machines of the Royal Flying Corps allocated to Home Defence, under the command of Colonel Higgins.

d The anti-aircraft guns of the London area under the command of Colonel Simon.

7 The last three agencies operate separately under orders of the Home Defence headquarters which is the only connecting link between them. This system appears to us to involve too great a dispersal of Command when dealing with a problem like the air defence of the London area, which is not only of very far-reaching military and political importance, but also constitutes a well-marked, distinct task, separable from other problems of Home Defence, which accordingly calls for a corresponding concentration of executive command. Our first recommendation, therefore, is that:

Subject to the control of the Field Marshal Commander-in-Chief of the Home Forces, a senior officer of first-rate ability and practical air experience should be placed in executive command of the air defence of the London area including the above services (b)(c)(d) of Paragraph 6 above, and that this officer should be assisted by a small but competent staff, who should be specially charged with the duty of working out all plans for London Air Defences.

This officer would take his instructions from the Field

Marshal and would in turn issue his orders to the Observation Corps, the Officer Commanding the anti-aircraft guns, and the various Air Units. The unity of command which is essential to any warlike operation, whether of an offensive or defensive character, would be thus achieved. We think that this officer should be appointed without delay so that he may at once set to work to deal with the various pressing problems connected with London air defence, some of which are referred to below.

In view of the possibility of the recurrence of Zeppelin attack, as well as for other reasons, we think it would be inadvisable to remove the anti-aircraft guns from their present stations in the London area. In our view, the best defensive use of anti-aircraft guns against hostile aeroplanes attacking by day, would be for them to put up a barrage in front of and covering London, and our second recommendation accordingly is that:

Immediate attention should be given to the question of the numbers and disposition of anti-aircraft guns to put up such a defensive barrage.

It is true that there is at present said to be an insufficiency of guns for this purpose but, as stated in Paragraph 3 above, we regard the defence of London as so important as to call for exceptional measures, and special endeavours should therefore be made to provide an adequate number of guns for this purpose.

8 A more pressing problem, in our opinion, is the provision and organization of a sufficient number of air units, trained to fight in formation and their proper disposition to dispel any air attack on London. At present the only reliable unit formed for this purpose is the squadron specially detailed a week ago from the Western Front. Three other units are in process of formation, but they neither have the necessary number of machines nor have the pilots the required training for fighting in formation. We understand that an additional squadron, complete in point of numbers, will be furnished almost immediately, and posted to the North-East of London. Another squadron to be disposed to the South-East should be complete in numbers in three or four weeks. Both of these will, however, require to be properly trained to manoeuvre in formation in suitable units. Our third

recommendation therefore is that:

> *The completion and training of these three additional squadrons, successively, be pushed on as rapidly as possible and that, in the meantime, the return of the first unit to France should not be sanctioned until the air defence of London is reasonably secure.*

9 In the course of our investigation, we considered the point whether our present type of fighting machine is the best to cope with the slower but more powerful Gotha raiders. In regard to this we make no recommendations and leave the problem for the further consideration and study of the experts of the Air Board, the Admiralty, the War Office, and the Ministry of Munitions.

10 The question of the provision of sufficient aircraft for defence purposes and for the formation of a reserve is one which, in our view, requires careful and immediate consideration. The enemy may possibly adopt the ruse of sending a small number of machines well in advance of his main attack in order to lure our squadrons into the air; the main enemy force may then appear on the scene and find himself unchecked, owing to the fact that our machines in coping with the advanced patrols had exhausted their petrol, and our pilots, their energy. We are advised that, theoretically, for our machines in the air to descend, refill with petrol, and re-ascend to the proper height, would take some forty-five minutes, but in practice, other factors would supervene and the actual time taken would be considerably longer. The result might well be that the main force would meet with practically no opposition, and after doing the maximum amount of damage, might return to its base with immunity and intact. In view of such a situation, which might well arise at any time, we submit that it might be advisable to avoid sending up more units that are necessary on the first warning of a coming raid. Such a contingency we think must be contemplated and to meet it reserves should be kept in hand. We accordingly recommend that:

> *The air defence unit for the London area should be sufficient not only to cope with feints, but to meet the real attack or a possible second attack following close on a first attack.*

The formation and retention of such a reserve is only in

accordance with the general and elementary principles of warfare.

11 We believe that if prompt effect is given to the above recommendations, subject always to the adequate and reasonable provision of aircraft for naval and military operations by land and sea, a fair measure of security for the London area from hostile raids may be obtained until, at any rate, some unforeseen development takes place.

Index